Paying the Words Extra

Harvard University
Center for the Study of World Religions

Religions of the World

Editor: Lawrence E. Sullivan

Cambridge, Massachusetts

Paying the Words Extra

Religious Discourse in the
Supreme Court of the United States

Winnifred Fallers Sullivan

Distributed by Harvard University Press
for the
Harvard University Center for the Study of World Religions

Illustration on front cover is by Sir John Tenniel, from *Through the Looking Glass* by Lewis Carroll, first published by Macmillan Children's Books, London, and reproduced here with permission.

Library of Congress Cataloging-in-Publication Data

Sullivan, Winnifred Fallers, 1950–
    Paying the words extra : religious discourse in the Supreme Court of the
United States / Winnifred Fallers Sullivan.
      p.   cm. — (Religions of the world)
    Includes bibliographical references and index.
    ISBN 0-945454-06-6 (cloth : acid-free paper) : $24.95. — ISBN
0-945454-07-4 (pbk. : acid-free paper) : $14.95
    1. Freedom of religion—United States. 2. United States. Supreme Court.
3. Religion and politics—United States. I. Title. II. Series.
KF4785.S85 1994
342.73'0852—dc20
[347.302852]   94-29503
                                              CIP

In memory of my father

Contents

Foreword   ix
Acknowledgments   xvii
Preface   xix

Chapter 1   Law and Religion   3
            Law as Cultural Discourse and Practice
            Talking about Religion
            Law and Religion

Chapter 2   Lynch v. Donnelly   47
            The Facts
            The Law
            The Appeals

Chapter 3   Discourse I: Chief Justice Burger   79
            The American Majority
            The Japanese Majority
            The Cases Compared

Chapter 4   Discourse II: Justice O'Connor   113
            Justice Black
            Justice O'Connor
            Law as Religion

Chapter 5   Discourse III: Justice Brennan   133
            A Catholic Crèche
            A Jeffersonian First Amendment
            A Jeffersonian Catholic

Chapter 6   A New Discourse and Practice   157
            Interpreting the First Amendment
            Talking and Acting about Religion
            Law and Religion

Selected Bibliography   185
Index   203

Foreword

"The First Amendment requires the Supreme Court to talk about religion. It also mandates disestablishment" (181). The solution to this contradictory pair of commandments, according to Winnifred Fallers Sullivan, is to reimagine constantly the relationship of religion and law: acknowledging the religiousness of Americans without establishing religion.

Acknowledgment is the key process that is at once so rich and so difficult to achieve. William James hoped to provoke the process of acknowledgment in himself and others. He described it as essential to reflection, analysis, and self-awareness. Acknowledgment of religion, in James's view, is particularly fundamental: "I think, therefore, that however particular questions connected with our individual destinies may be answered, it is only by *acknowledging* them as genuine questions, and living in the sphere of thought which they open up, that we become profound."[1]

In *Paying the Words Extra* Sullivan analyzes and exemplifies the process of acknowledgment. Though it is impossible to summarize her fascinating and lucid contribution to the study of law and religion here, a few points can illustrate how suitable and, at the same time, startling is the appearance of Sullivan's volume in the *Religions of the World* series. Using the decisions of the Supreme Court of the United States as the primary evidence to make her case, Sullivan argues that acknowledgment of religion is not only valuable but necessary. The United States Supreme Court plays a unique role in shaping American identity, licensed to do so by the Constitution and reconfirmed in this mission by *Marbury v. Madison*. Religion is a primary element of that self-understanding. Unlike the other branches of government, which

---

[1] William James, *The Varieties of Religious Experience*, p. 500; cited in Sullivan p. 87).

are constitutionally limited, the Supreme Court must talk about religion, for through its words the Court creates a climate and culture in which religion is both freely exercised and separated from state establishment. "How the courts talk about religion is critical, because the texture of the public discourse about religion creates a culture about religion" (163). Peoples' lives take shape in the spaces created by their powerful words. The question is: how should the Supreme Court talk about religion?

Sullivan grounds her answers on an anthropological premise, drawn from comparative and historical studies of culture and the creative human being at its heart: religion is a universal, diverse, and powerful human creation. Since no human being—not even a justice of the Supreme Court—can escape an influence so pervasive and powerful, any judicial decision about religion runs the inherent risk of merely establishing one or another unacknowledged religious viewpoint. Her analysis of the religious viewpoints that underlie the opinions of individual justices in *Lynch v. Donnelly* (the so-called Christmas crèche case) not only demonstrates her point, but also exposes, in a way both shocking and revealing, the justices' views on religion. Close readings of the opinions of Justices Burger, O'Connor, and Brennan disclose a parochialism in the justices' understanding of religion, which ultimately reveals a parochialism with regard to their use of the law as well.

Justice Burger does not view religion as different so he does not see the Pawtucket crèche as a religious symbol. It is only a "passive symbol" reminding one of the origins of a holiday in a post-Christian world. On the basis of Burger's opinion, Sullivan argues that he regards religion as a kind of sentiment engendering "a friendly community spirit of goodwill" (86). Burger wishes to "accommodate" this religion that "seems to lack all depth, danger, and particularity" (87) since it is both harmless and supportive of the state. Sullivan worries about the consequences of Burger's rendering of religion. Does it flatten and demystify the symbolic meaning attached to religious signs that have value and meaning to particular communities? Does it impeach the meaning of distinctive features of particular religions? Is it anti-Catholic? If William James's *Varieties of Religious Experience* may be said to draw "a contour map of individual religious experience, the effect of Burger's opinion is that of a steam roller" (88). Unlike historians of religion who search for the particularity of religious experiences—the powerful elements that make a difference and set religions apart as distinctive, "Burger. . .wishes to accommodate a religion with no difference, no otherness. In doing so, he attempts to collapse the sacred and secular into one category" (88–89) and views the Christmas crèche as simply a secular sign of the holiday season.

Sullivan astutely observes the similarities and differences between Burger's decision and that of the Supreme Court of Japan when, in 1988, it decided in a fourteen to one decision that the apotheosis (ritual conferral of the status of an immortal god) of Mr. Takafumi Nakaya at the Shinto shrine of Yasukuni was a celebration of national pride and was not about religion. Through the so-called MacArthur Constitution established in Japan after the close of World War II, the Japanese Constitution becomes a genetic permutation of the American Constitution. Studying the respective treatments of religion in the two constitutions and in Court interpretations is illuminating.

In examining the opinions of the Japanese Supreme Court justices with the same care as the American ones, Sullivan casts in high relief the paradoxes created by the Courts' readings in both cases and she strengthens her case for the value of comparative study of law and religion. The similarities between Burger's opinion in *Lynch* and the majority in the Nakaya case highlight how both systems seek to affirm traditional religious forms constitutive of their cultural identity even if they must do so by secularizing them. At issue for these Courts, says Sullivan, is "how to acknowledge, support, and celebrate the whole— 'the inherent sacredness of central authority,' in Geertz's words—in the context of a religiously pluralistic but highly secular society" (109). The problem is that, by defining the center—even religious elements central to a culture's self-understanding—as secular, Burger and the Japanese Court exclude religion as such from that center and, conversely, define religion by the extremes, forcing it to use only the prophetic voice in the public sphere (112).

Justice O'Connor, in Sullivan's view, does not talk about religion; hers is a discourse about law. O'Connor's avoidance of a discourse about particular religion, following in the tradition of Justice Hugo Lafayette Black, carries vast implications for the practice and understanding of religion in America. In *A Constitutional Faith*, Black announced that the "Constitution is my legal bible." This is the faith to which O'Connor adheres and into which she deposits religiosity. It is a faith in law and the political process. But, asks Sullivan, is this faith broad enough to safeguard the free exercise of religion? Sullivan questions whether the religion clauses of the First Amendment can be completely housed within protections of speech, press, and freedom of conscience without leaving important dimensions of life out in the cold.

Sullivan reminds us that "the establishment clause as a judicial doctrine was invented in the last fifty years and should therefore be understood in the light of the history and culture of the last fifty years" (119), particularly the preoccupation with issues of political equality. The jurisprudence of the religion clauses—a very contemporary creation—reflects, then, a contemporary concern to treat the believer and the non-believer equally. Justice O'Connor, unlike both the majority and the dissent in *Lynch*, "is uninterested in protecting, acknowledging, or accommodating *religion*. For her, it seems, religion *as* religion is irrelevant in the political community. . . . O'Connor, like Black, thinks that the only religion the Supreme Court should be protecting is the religion of the Constitution" (126). And the Constitution is about political equality.

Sullivan challenges the translation of religious freedom into political equality. Such a move installs law as the moral system and a faith in law, especially its liberal neutrality toward religion, as the principal location for thinking about the good life. Sullivan challenges the displacement of religion in favor of faith in law on both cultural and philosophical grounds.

Writing in dissent in *Lynch*, Justice Brennan (joined by Justices Marshall, Blackmun, and Stevens) composed a detailed opinion twice as long as that of the majority. For Brennan, the crèche has an irreducibly religious meaning that is specifically Christian. Using the language of their opinions, Sullivan traces the differences between Burger's and Brennan's theologies of Christ. Brennan is able to confirm the religiousness of the crèche, but unable to move beyond his Catholic devotional or sacramental approach toward the crèche to see its secularity—a sensibility that is more Protestant. Sullivan perceives a Brennan committed to the ideal of separation of law and religion as two different kinds of social facts, in the tradition of Jefferson. Strict separation can be maintained for Brennan because he regards religion as located within the individual person. Religion is in the private realm, "it is not about culture or society or political power" (156).

Each in their own way, the justices incline toward a view of religion that is their own. The risk of establishment must be and can be overcome, as the First Amendment requires, if the particularity of religiousness at play in the case is acknowledged and deconstructed. Acknowledgment requires not only critical self-awareness on the part of the justices. It calls for contextualized, cultural analysis and awareness of the broad history both of law and religions. Deconstruction, as outlined and exemplified by Sullivan, protects the meaning of religion from efforts to narrow it, wittingly or unwittingly, to the interpretation of any particular viewpoint, secular or religious.

Sullivan's volume is not only extraordinarily knowledgeable but unusually wise. She is at home in legal studies, anthropology, comparative religion, and history. Her close reading of *Lynch* is also a broad reading of American culture within the even wider, relevant context of the world scene. She foresees the problems being engendered by the present state of judicial discourse and proposes solutions based both on history and a view toward the future.

The justices of the Supreme Court of the United States are heading now toward the religiously volatile change of millennium at a time when immigrants bring with them their devotion to a spectrum of religious expression and legal expectation which is wider than ever before. At this moment, national legal systems around the globe are recalibrating their relations to religion; and religious legal systems (whether regarding food, marriage, banking, or the taking of life) are reevaluating their relationship to civil law, for the sake of the ongoing process that shapes the identities of their citizenry. From the states of the former Soviet Union to India, Israel, Iran, Northern Ireland, China, Japan, Indonesia, Latin America, and elsewhere, human beings are using the discourses of law and religion and their shifting relations to construct their identities. Naturally enough, then, the same process is going on in the United States, as seen in Supreme Court opinions as well as in more explosive settings, as witnessed during the clash between Branch Davidians and the federal government in Waco, Texas.[2]

---

[2] Lawrence E. Sullivan, *Recommendations to the U. S. Departments of Justice and the Treasury concerning Incidents such as the Branch Davidian Standoff in Waco, Texas*. Washington, D. C.: Department of Justice, 1993.

Paying the Words Extra helps us understand that process of constructing identity and, in its own right, is an important contribution to it.

The *Religions of the World* book series is published by the Harvard University Center for the Study of World Religions. Through its research and educational programs the Center fosters excellence in the study of religion and its book series encourages multiple disciplinary approaches to the full range of religious expressions: in art, medicine, literature, music, liturgy, economy, anthropology, and the cosmological sciences. Sullivan admirably shows how the study of law enriches the study of religion and, conversely, how the study of comparative religion furnishes an important new discourse for the study of law.

Sullivan argues forcefully on behalf of a cross-cultural understanding of both law and religion. She has been a leading figure in the comparative "Religion, Law, and the Construction of Identities" project unfolding jointly at the Harvard University Center for the Study of World Religions and the Institute for the Advanced Study of Religion at the University of Chicago Divinity School. She finds American lawyers and judges increasingly hampered by their lack of broad comparative awareness. "It is the purporting to talk about Law or Religion or Theology without acknowledging that one is talking about American law or about only one of a variety of Judaisms and Christianities, and without acknowledging the limitations those contexts imply, that concerns me" (21).

Drawing on the comparative and historical study of religions, Sullivan strongly resists the idea that secularization is all but complete or that religion can be explained away in secular terms (such as freedom of conscience or the ethics of the moral good). She proposes to use the history of religions as a practical political discourse and contends, in fact, that "humans cannot be understood completely without understanding them as religious as well as social, cultural, and economic beings. The data look different if one is open to the possibility of a religious understanding of them. One sees other things" (28). If Sullivan champions the discipline of history of religions, on the one hand, she is, on the other hand, taking the language and perspective of that discipline where it has seldom ventured before. Generally historians of religions are at work on the comparative study of symbolic expressions in Hinduism, Buddhism, Islam, and the religions of tribal societies. Sullivan invites them to focus on the language of the courts and shows them a way to do it.

In reducing lived religious life to words, as the Supreme Court must inevitably do, one must indeed pay the words extra for the additional freight they carry. If Sullivan is correct, the Court must have the courage and insight to acknowledge in so many words the meaning and function of religion.

Special thanks are due Kathryn Dodgson Taylor for her skill in editing this manuscript and her excellent management of the publication program at the Center.

Lawrence E. Sullivan, Director
Harvard University Center
for the Study of World Religions

Acknowledgments

I wish to thank my teachers, those who encouraged me at difficult points along the way, and those who read drafts of the manuscript: Anne Blackburn, Jonathan Bunge, Margaret Fallers, Laura Grillo, Stanley Katz, Beth Lamanna, Anne Luther, Martin Marty, Carolyn Osiek, Frank Reynolds, Lawrence Rosen, Helen Scharbach, Julie Seavy, Jonathan Z. Smith, Barry Sullivan, Lawrence E. Sullivan, and James Boyd White.

I also wish to thank the Charlotte Newcombe Foundation for its support of the project that resulted in this book.

Preface

"When *I* use a word," Humpty Dumpty said, in rather a scornful tone, "it means just what I choose it to mean—neither more nor less."

"The question is," said Alice, "whether you *can* make words mean so many different things."

"The question is," said Humpty Dumpty," which is to be master—that's all."

Alice was too much puzzled to say anything; so after a minute Humpty Dumpty began again. "They've a temper, some of them—particularly verbs: they're the proudest—adjectives you can do anything with, but not verbs—however, *I* can manage the whole lot of them! Impenetrability! That's what *I* say!"

"Would you tell me please," said Alice, "what that means?"

"Now you talk like a reasonable child," said Humpty Dumpty, looking very much pleased. "I meant by 'impenetrability' that we've had enough of that subject, and it would be just as well if you'd mention what you mean to do next, as I suppose you don't mean to stop here all the rest of your life."

"That's a great deal to make one word mean," Alice said in a thoughtful tone.

"When I make a word do a lot of work like that," said Humpty Dumpty, "I always pay it extra."

"Oh!" said Alice.

—Lewis Carroll, *Through the Looking-Glass*[1]

In 1984, Warren Burger, then Chief Justice of the United States, writing for the majority in the case of *Lynch v. Donnelly,*[2] declared that display of a crèche, at public expense, as a part of a public Christmas display,

---

[1] *The Complete Illustrated Lewis Carroll* (New York: Gallery Books, 1991), 196–97.

[2] 465 U.S. 668 (1983). I will follow the conventions of legal citation in the format prescribed by the Harvard Law Review Association, *A Uniform System of Citation*, 13th ed. (1981).

was not an unconstitutional establishment of religion. The decision rested, in part, on the argument that a crèche is not a religious symbol in the context of a civic Christmas display and here was being displayed in order to effect a purely secular purpose. In 1977 the Supreme Court of Japan declared that a Shinto grounds-purification ceremony, *Jichinsai*, was not a religious ceremony and, therefore, could be constitutionally sponsored by a public body.[3] In 1988 the Japanese Court held that deification of the dead is not a religious act when performed to honor military casualties.[4]

In these cases, the language that each court uses in its opinions to talk about religion seems to stretch the words close to the breaking point. They seem deliberately to use words in paradoxical and contradictory ways. One is continually being brought up short. What can be more religious than display of a representation of the incarnation of a deity, a ritual of consecration, or an apotheosis? What can religion be if these acts are not included? With Alice, in response to the pronouncements of Humpty Dumpty, the reader suspects that there is something devious and high-handed in making words "mean so many different things."

Why are these courts turning traditional categories on their heads? Are these judges simply flaunting their power by arbitrarily changing the meaning of words? Are they, as Humpty Dumpty coyly suggests, simply "masters" of the words? The two courts, the American and the Japanese—as well as Humpty Dumpty—can, in my view, more helpfully be seen as refusing to be bound rigidly by legal and cultural categories, rather than as abusing them. Declaring these events to be secular may be the only alternative the courts see to the insistent tunnel vision of the orthodox separation of church and state, on the one hand, or to a naïve "accommodation"—the restoration of a *de facto* establishment—on the other.

This refusal by the courts to use the conventional political discourse of disestablishment, examples of which could be multiplied many times over, challenges students of religion and of law to see the courts as

---

[3] Showa 52 [1977] July 13. Showa 52 refers to the fifty-second year of the reign of Emperor Hirohito. All Japanese government documents are dated by reign year. I will add the year of the Common Era in brackets.

[4] Showa 63 [1988] June 1.

creative, though often clumsy, constructors of a new cultural language, "opening space for cultural futures,"[5] in James Clifford's words, and to take a closer look at the subtle and slippery interplay between so-called religious and secular symbols and institutions.[6]

For some time before I started graduate school, I was a practicing lawyer, a corporate litigator. I am still licensed to practice law and consider myself a lawyer. I am often asked to explain the connection between my life as a lawyer and my life as a student of religion. Those asking often make their own assumptions about possible connections between religion and law. Some, involved in ministry—especially those with social justice agendas—have assumed that my purpose is to be a lawyer for the disadvantaged. Law as ministry, in effect. Others, more philosophically inclined perhaps, assume the connection to be in the study of ethics. Still others, perhaps those with real-life experience of big firm practice, assume I've thrown over the law in favor of the holy life!—a choice they often view with envy. Some assume that I intend to become a canon lawyer.

These are all worthy occupations; but each, for me, however, in some way appears to finesse the real differences in the language and practice—the culture—of the study and practice of law and the study and practice of religion. Each finds a way of merging law and religion. Many poverty lawyers redefine law as religion, or, perhaps more accurately, religion as law or justice. Ethicists often find a common ground in philosophical language, while mystics may have given up on law altogether. Canon lawyers, on the other hand, are just lawyers with a different body of laws and a different set of clients.

I am interested in staying with the tension between religion and law. If each is, in Clifford Geertz's words, "a distinctive manner of

---

[5] James Clifford, *The Predicament of Culture* (Cambridge: Harvard University Press, 1988), 15.

[6] There is a danger in seeing what appears to be dysfunctional as creative. It can preclude criticism. By attempting to see the creative aspects of these opinions, I do not wish to deny the need for and the value of criticizing them and of insisting on an accurate and sensitive understanding of religion by these courts. It cannot be denied that the majorities in these cases are on the right of the political spectrum and often, perhaps unwittingly, play into the hands of the far right.

imagining the real,"[7] what happens when these two cultures, law as law, religion as religion, interact?

Between the time that I left law practice and when I went to divinity school, I was asked to contribute to a project which included the planned publication of a two-volume collection of bibliographies and bibliographic essays on the church and state issue in the United States. I was asked to prepare an essay and bibliography surveying scholarship on church and state and law in the United States since the Civil War.[8]

Putting aside the sheer quantity of material on church and state law in the United States, which is monumental, I was surprised at the polemical nature of almost everything I read. Even books of serious academic pretension had an ax to grind. They were briefs, not academic texts. Shelves and shelves of books, not to mention endless pages of law review articles, existed on the proper relationship between church and state in the United States. In general, either religion was seen as the source of all evil and should be kept firmly in its place while it withered away like the Marxist state, or public religion of some undefined but unthreatening nature was necessary to preserve public virtue. According to these writers, either the First Amendment requires a desperate struggle to maintain a Jeffersonian wall of separation or it is intended to protect and foster the inherently and beneficial religious nature of Americans.[9] There was little middle ground and there was too little serious consideration of American religious history or of the First Amendment and its history.[10] Too often the same quotations from Madison and Jefferson and the same conclusory remarks about colonial establishments were simply props employed by both sides.

---

[7] Clifford Geertz, "Local Knowledge: Fact and Law in Comparative Perspective," in his *Local Knowledge: Further Essays in Interpretive Anthropology* (New York: Basic Books, 1983), 184.

[8] Subsequently published as Winnifred F. Sullivan, "Religion and Law in the United States: 1870 to the Present," in John F. Wilson, ed., *Church and State in America: A Bibliographical Guide.* Vol. 2: *The Civil War to the Present Day.* (New York: Greenwood Press, 1987), 339–71.

[9] The First Amendment to the United States Constitution provides, in part, that "Congress shall make no law respecting an establishment of religion or prohibiting the free exercise thereof."

[10] The situation has changed somewhat in the last ten years as the result of a renewed academic focus on the subject.

In my chapter I found myself, too, like others before and since, describing the law in this area as defined by two poles, the "separationists" and the "accommodationists." I was troubled, though, by the impoverished nature of the conversation, by the lawyers' limited understanding of religion and by the religious historians' limited knowledge of law. No wonder there was widespread dissatisfaction with the Supreme Court decisions in this area. I decided to go back to school to learn more about how religious scholars talk about religion.

What is religion? What role does religion play in American life? In any culture? Where does the Supreme Court fit in? Are Jefferson and Madison any help? How about Roger Williams? When I went to divinity school, I saw my sojourn there as sort of an experiment. What would happen if you took a practicing lawyer and put her in the midst of the academic study of religion? What kind of conversation would ensue? Could there even be one? How would you talk about religion and law in such a place?

My first course in divinity school was "The Modern Study of Religion," an introduction to history of religions, taught by Lawrence Sullivan. It was a revelation to me. I can even remember where I was sitting when it suddenly struck me. Here was a language about religion which might begin to answer the Supreme Court's needs. Here was a discipline which sought to take religion seriously without confessional commitment—without establishing religion. Might this be a solution for the Supreme Court? Could a lawyer learn to speak this language? I have spent the last six or seven years trying to answer these questions.

Centering on a close examination of the written opinions in one American case concerned with the appropriate relationship between law and religion, *Lynch v. Donnelly*, I offer here a reading of those opinions as revealing a paradox of postmodern industrial society: religious disestablishment, the separation of church and state, while it remains essential to pluralistic civil society is, as conceived in the language and culture of the writers of the Constitution, impossible.[11] Government cannot be purged of religion, though it is not through want of trying.

---

[11] This point has often been made by cultural critics of modernity. For example, in his new introduction to *Tokugawa Religion: The Cultural Roots of Modern Japan*, rev. ed. (New York: The Free Press, 1985), Robert Bellah criticizes his own earlier

While each of the opinions in *Lynch v. Donnelly* contains important perceptions about the relationship of law and religion in American society, each is also handicapped by a discourse about religion, created largely in the context of the Enlightenment and of evangelical Protestantism,[12] and profoundly influenced by the politics of equality, that is inadequate to give an account of the religiousness of Americans. The inadequacy of that discourse about religion, in turn, hobbles the development of a shared public discourse about the meaning of the First Amendment religion clauses.

Can we, by giving attention to the circumstances and variety of the lives of Americans, as religious people with a profound commitment to the rule of law, generate a richer discourse and practice about religion in American public life? Can we take Humpty Dumpty's advice, and, through this commitment, in effect, "pay the words extra?"

---

work which saw religion as a means on the road to modernity and calls for a consideration of "religion as religion." The "other" of the Enlightenment, religion has returned to the center for post-modern thinkers of many stripes.

It is interesting that the Museum of Science and Industry in Chicago, a temple, one might say, to scientific positivism, has recently shown *Ring of Fire*, a terrifying film on the volcanic activity of the Pacific rim, in which religious interpretations of volcanic activity are offered on an equal basis with scientific explanations. There is no depreciation or setting apart of the religious view. One can take little comfort or even gain little understanding, the film suggests, from the power of science, at least when confronted with volcanic activity. A full explanation must include the religious point of view.

[12] I use the term evangelical Protestantism to describe the mainstream American Protestant culture of the nineteenth and early twentieth centuries. I do not use it, as it is often used today, to refer to an aggressively proselytizing and politically activist coalition of contemporary Protestant churches.

Paying the Words Extra

Chapter 1

Law and Religion

There are more things in heaven and earth, Horatio,
Than are dreamt of in your philosophy.
— Shakespeare, *Hamlet*[1]

Symbolism is inescapable. Even the most sophisticated live by symbols.
— Justice Felix Frankfurter[2]

Thomas Reed Powell used to say that if you can think about something that is related to something else without thinking about the thing to which it is related, then you have the legal mind.
— Fuller, *The Morality of Law*[3]

A certain tension between law and religion was built into American life from its beginnings. Revulsion against the patent injustices created by established religion and a romantic faith in the power of human reason, at a time when the religion of revolution was more powerful than the religions of history and tradition, led to the establishment of an idealized public life separate from religion. Government was to be of law, not of men, not of gods. The need for this separation of law from religion runs deep in the American faith and cuts across numerous other differences, as many have observed, but that conviction and its sources have considerably distorted the public conversation about

[1] *Hamlet,* 1.5. 191–92.
[2] West Virginia State Board of Education v. Barnette, 319 U.S. 624 (1943) (Frankfurter, dissenting).
[3] Lon Fuller, *The Morality of Law*, rev. ed. (New Haven: Yale University Press, 1969), 4.

religion.[4] The resulting exalted place of law, of a certain kind of law, has also crippled law and has at times resulted in an estrangement of law from the general culture.[5]

One of the skills taught in American law schools is how to separate "The Law" from "The Facts." When one learns to "state a case" in law school, one learns to give the facts and then the rule of law which has been applied to those facts. When one learns to write a brief, one learns to give the facts first and then the law, in separate sections. Juries decide about facts. Judges decide about law. There is no admitted intermingling. They must appear to be independent of each other, of the language in which they are articulated, and of the culture in which they are embedded.

This separation is also played out in legal culture. Lawyers in our culture, particularly academic lawyers, are too often strangely disassociated from other parts of society and from other disciplines in the academy. Law schools are often physically separate from the rest of universities.[6] The world is thus, physically as well as theoretically, divided, as briefs are, into two parts: The Law and The Facts.

Lawyers in American culture, as a result, seem to regard the rest of the culture and of the academy with an Olympian detachment, as a field for explanation and manipulation through the application of their expertise. Indeed, this is one of the attractions to being a lawyer. Having been trained to "think like a lawyer" (the basic goal of the law school curriculum), one can turn that facility to any new "facts" one en-

---

[4] For other expressions of this view, see, for example, Mark DeWolfe Howe, *The Garden and the Wilderness: Religion and Government in American Constitutional History* (Chicago: University of Chicago Press, 1965); John T. Noonan, *The Believer and the Powers That Are: Cases, History, and Other Data Bearing on the Relation of Religion and Government* (New York: Macmillan, 1987); Richard Neuhaus, *The Naked Public Square: Religion and Democracy in America* (New York: W. B. Eerdmans, 1984); and Robert N. Bellah and others, *Habits of the Heart: Individualism and Commitment in American Life* (Berkeley: University of California Press, 1985).

[5] See Mary Ann Glendon, *Abortion and Divorce in Western Law* (Cambridge: Harvard University Press, 1987), and *Rights Talk: The Impoverishment of Political Discourse* (New York: Free Press, 1991).

[6] This is a fairly recent phenomenon. Law schools and law faculties used to be more integrated into the life of the university. The new separation is partly the result of increased professionalization, but one might argue that the physical separation of law schools on university campuses occurred in tandem with a progressive intellectual estrangement of academic law from the rest of the academy.

counters. And one's practice as a lawyer brings one into contact with an enormous variety of interesting, often fascinating, "facts." This contact is defined, however, by the control one exercises through one's expertise.

Lawyers presume to speak authoritatively on almost every subject: literature, women, religion, economics, sex, race relations, war and peace, theology. Not only does the rest of the culture exist simply as Facts to which The Law will be applied, but the conversation of law and of lawyers often leads an independent existence, free from questions about the conditions and possibilities of knowledge, cultural biases, and the limitations of language.

This separation of The Law from The Facts has a pernicious effect, raising troubling ethical issues as well as resulting, at times, in simple inanity. The subtlety and complexity of the negotiation between any theory and cultural data is, in general, deliberately and defensively ignored in legal writing on many issues. Lawyers, especially academic lawyers, seem indeed at times to be a parody of the excesses of academic theorizing.[7] Perhaps in American law one sees the final product of Max Weber's famous rationalization process.[8]

In this book I will address the need for lawyers and judges to recognize that in talking about religion, as about anything else, they are engaging in an act of interpretation fraught with difficulties which have been, on the whole, insufficiently identified and addressed. In the first section of this chapter, I will consider challenges within the academic community to an instrumental understanding of law, with a view to locating my argument within a larger conversation about the nature of law. In the second section I will consider how to talk about

[7] See the discussion of the fact/law dichotomy and resulting "fear of fact" in American law in Clifford Geertz, "Local Knowledge: Fact and Law in Comparative Perspective" in his *Local Knowledge*, 167–84.

While I would argue that this instrumental view of law is the dominant voice in American law, it is certainly not the only one. There have been and continue to be dissenters who struggle to see law as a more complex social and cultural phenomenon.

[8] Max Weber, *The Protestant Ethic and the Spirit of Capitalism*, trans. Talcott Parsons, 2d ed. (New York: Scribner, 1976).

I have here lumped together legal scholars and practicing lawyers. That there are significant differences in the approach to the study and practice of law by these two groups and that in the American context at the present time there is an enormous gulf between the two, does not, in my view, vitiate a basic similarity of method.

religion. Finally, in the third section, I will consider the intersection of these two conversations: what happens when a lawyer tries to talk about religion? All of this is by way of theoretical introduction to the following chapters, which consider the language and practice of the United States Supreme Court in relation to religion in the case of *Lynch v. Donnelly.*

LAW AS CULTURAL DISCOURSE AND PRACTICE

There is and has been, for millennia perhaps, an ongoing conversation about what law does and can do, about law as process, law as rules, and law as institutions. The intellectual history of this conversation, at least in the West, has been and continues to be explored by Western historians. I will focus here only on certain aspects of the last one hundred years of this conversation in the Anglo-American context.

The conversation about law ranges from the highly abstract to the intensely practical. What is law? When is it successful? How does it change? Various claims are made for law: Law is a set of rules. Law is process. Law is natural. Law is constructed. Law is a raw exercise of power. Law is love. Law is bureaucratic. Law is an arcane mystical form of sorcery. Law is a conversation. Law tells a story. Law is literature. Law creates a community. Law is a tool of patriarchal oppression. Law is a mechanism for rational allocation of resources. Law is an opportunity for the exercise of economic rationality. Law is morally neutral. Law is a political instrument.[9] The range of these claims reveals something of the power of law in Western culture, while it also destabilizes its meaning.

Each of these claims has its proponents and each does teach us something about what law is and does or what we want it to be.[10] I will here regard law as a specialized and often privileged location for a set of culturally specific discourses and practices—one location that

---

[9] The theories represented in the above statements are represented in the works of the following authors, among others: Roscoe Pound, Lon Fuller, Thomas Aquinas, Montesquieu, Thomas Hobbes, John Austin, Augustine, Robert Cover, James Boyd White, Milner Ball, Mary Becker, and Richard Posner.

[10] In the West this conversation falls into at least two parts. Legal philosophers from Aristotle to John Rawls have considered the nature of law. Anthropologists and other social scientists have also considered how law works in particular cultures.

a society has in which to think and talk and act about itself and what is important to it.[11] When legislators write laws and courts decide cases, they not only make rules and adjudicate between competing arguments, they also participate in an intensely practical and multilayered discourse about what society should be like. They create and recreate a set of languages and practices that reach toward that society's constantly changing vision of itself. I do not wish to suggest that law is, on this reading, simply one among a set of competing political and symbolic discourses with no distinctiveness as law. On the contrary, I would argue that law is a distinctive kind of discourse—a particularly privileged one in the United States—and that as law it can make a special contribution to the public struggle for meaning and identity.

In criticizing legislation, the actions of government agencies, and the decisions of courts, it is thus appropriate to consider not simply the practical utility of the result, or even the logic of the legal argument which supports that result, but also the nature and texture of the discourses and practices of which that rule or decision is a part. It makes a difference not only what rules are made and what decisions are reached but what languages and what culture those rules and decisions create.

Two academic conversations in particular have tried to think about law culturally. First, European and American anthropologists and sociologists of law have been challenged, in the last one hundred years, by the pluralism of and the clashes among legal systems. This challenge occurred first in the colonial context but now continues in the situation of a global culture. It has led to studies of a range of societies in order to understand what role law plays in society.[12] These studies have asked the following questions: What does law look like in different cultural

---

[11] This view of law owes a large debt to anthropologists of law and to the law and literature movement, both of which will be further discussed below at 10ff.

[12] These efforts have been, at times, plainly in service to imperialistic legal designs. They have, however, in spite of this ideological corruption, contributed to our understanding of law, at least of our own law. For a narration of the intellectual history of this effort, see, for example, John L. Comaroff and Simon Roberts, *Rules and Processes: The Cultural Logic of Disputes in an African Context* (Chicago: University of Chicago Press, 1981); Sally Falk Moore, *Law as Process: An Anthropological Approach* (London: Routledge & Kegan Paul, 1978); and Keebet von Benda-Beckmann and Fons Strijbosch, eds., *Anthropology of Law in the Netherlands: Essays on Legal Pluralism* (Dordrecht: Foris Publications, 1986).

contexts? Is there any sense in which law is universal? How does it work? How does it change? Is it more about rules or is it more about process? Is it the same as custom or is it something different? Is it about social control or is it about adjudicating troubles?

Second, the American law and literature movement, and associated critics of American law from the perspective of the humanities and the social sciences, have sought to explore, from within the American academic legal community, law as American cultural discourse.[13] These critics of the culture of American law are concerned about how all Americans, lawyers as well as others, can come to understand American law as an ongoing cooperative project of social construction as well as a method of social control and dispute settlement.

Henry Maine is arguably the grandfather of all modern Western efforts to study law socio-scientifically. His controversial *Ancient Law*[14] traces the evolution of European law from the Romans to nineteenth-century England. Maine sought, in the face of then current utilitarian and positivist theories of law and legal education, to persuade his Victorian readers that law was inextricably bound up with history and that legal change and social change were intimately interconnected. He believed that legal change was a dynamic process which both initiated and responded to social change. Through detailed studies of the history of particular legal doctrines, procedural and substantive, such as the law of testamentary succession, Maine shows law to be a flexible and often subtle location for the negotiation of social change.

Maine has been roundly criticized by many social scientists and historians. His evolutionary social theories—his theory concerning the universality of primitive patriarchalism and his theory that progressive societies inevitably move from status to contract—have been shown to be inadequate. His sometimes seriously faulty knowledge of

[13] See, for example, Robert M. Cover, "Foreword: *Nomos* and Narrative," *Harvard Law Review* 97 (November 1983): 4–68; and James Boyd White, *The Legal Imagination: Studies in the Nature of Legal Thought and Expression* (Boston: Little, Brown, 1973), and *Justice as Translation: An Essay in Cultural and Legal Criticism* (Chicago: University of Chicago Press, 1990).

[14] Henry Sumner Maine, *Ancient Law: Its Connection with the Early History of Society, and Its Relation to Modern Ideas* (New York: Holt, 1864; reprint, Tucson: University of Arizona Press, 1986).

historical facts, especially with respect to medieval law and Indian society, has been painstakingly detailed.[15]

Putting aside for a moment, however, both the debate over his contribution to social scientific theory generally and later historical research, the enduring appeal of his book for anyone interested in the culture of law remains. His account of the relationship between legal and social change tells an exciting and convincing story of the dynamism of the relationship of law and society. It is the fineness and humor of his observations about how legal institutions work and fit into history that is one of his lasting contributions.

One can see in Maine's work the subtle and complex adjustment over time of legal rules and institutions in their remarkable flexibility and adaptability to changing social conditions. Maine warns us that:

[n]othing in law springs entirely from a sense of convenience. There are always certain ideas existing antecedently on which the sense of convenience works, and of which it can do no more than form some new combination; and to find these ideas in the present case is exactly the problem.[16]

Maine's work reveals the project of law to be ongoing, using the past to deal with the present, and then making necessary adjustments:

[T]he human mind has never grappled with any subject of thought, unless it has been provided beforehand with a proper store of language and with an apparatus of appropriate logical method.[17]

Ancient Law might be considered a monograph exploring in a detailed way the structure and culture of legal and social change rather than a history of law. While some of the history may be outdated, he has much to teach us of historical method.

R. C. J. Cocks, a biographer of Maine, writes:

It was as if, in Maine's view, it was better for the jurist to travel than to arrive. In *Ancient Law* in particular his thought has an open-ended quality; he attacks

---

[15] See the Foreword by Lawrence Rosen and Introduction by Theodore Dwight to the 1986 University of Arizona Press edition of *Ancient Law*.

For a discussion of the importance of Maine for the development of the theories of Tonnies, Durkheim and Weber, see Edward Shils, "Henry Sumner Maine in the Tradition of the Analysis of Society," in Allen Diamond, ed., *The Victorian Achievement of Sir Henry Maine: A Centennial Reappraisal* (Cambridge: Cambridge University Press, 1991), 143–78.

[16] Maine, *Ancient Law*, 226.

[17] Maine, *Ancient Law*, 329.

well-established assumptions and suggests new lines of inquiry without seeking to impose a complete explanation upon all facts of law and legal history.[18]

And, as Lawrence Rosen says in his foreword to the 1986 Arizona Press edition of *Ancient Law*:

Contemporary readers might, therefore, be stimulated to rethink the role of law in particular historical situations, concentrating not on institutional change alone but on the systemic repercussions that ensue when a broad range of cultural issues come [sic] to be articulated in the language of the law.[19]

Law is, for Maine, a continual process of language and of culture and of their interrelationship. The practicing lawyer *and* the legal historian, both of whom Maine sought to address, are advised to proceed with this in mind.[20]

Anthropologists of law in the first half of the twentieth century, although often in response to Maine's larger theoretical proposals, focused largely on finding law in non-Western cultures.[21] Bronislaw Malinowski, Karl Llewellyn, E. Adamson Hoebel, and Max Gluckman all looked for and found, in Llewellyn's words, "law-stuff,"[22] in Melanesian, Cheyenne, and Lozi societies. In their fieldwork they explored cultural variations in social ordering, the making and enforcing of rules, and the adjudication of particular cases, challenging Western assumptions both about primitive law and about the historical uniqueness and superiority of Western law.

Malinowski displayed the economic practicality and negotiability of Trobriand Island rules about fishing and trading, which he saw as a

---

[18] R. C. J. Cocks, *Sir Henry Maine: A Study in Victorian Jurisprudence* (Cambridge: Cambridge University Press, 1988), 214.

[19] Maine, *Ancient Law*, xviii.

[20] Maine also sought to influence legal education in England, which he believed to be insufficiently historical. He believed one would be a better lawyer if one understood the nature and the culture of legal change. See, for example, Maine, *Ancient Law*, 6–8, 166, and 301.

[21] It was largely left to legal historians to give a criticism of the details of Maine's argument with respect to the Western context. See the essays in Diamond, *The Victorian Achievement*, for a summary of the current criticism of Maine.

[22] Karl N. Llewellyn and E. Adamson Hoebel, *The Cheyenne Way: Conflict and Case Law in Primitive Jurisprudence* (Norman: University of Oklahoma Press, 1941), viii.

kind of civil law.[23] While disdaining Maine's and Durkheim's ideas about primitive society, Malinowski agreed with Maine that "the true problem is not to study how human life submits to rules—it simply does not; the real problem is how the rules become adapted to life."[24]

Llewellyn and Hoebel celebrated the beauty and subtlety of Cheyenne judicial reasoning as revealed in legends of decisions by the tribal council. Examining a set of Cheyenne "cases," distilled by legend and recalled for them by a single Cheyenne "informant," they attempted a systematic summary of the Cheyenne law of homicide, rape, and property, carefully documenting what they saw as the subtlety of the distinctions made by the tribal council, depending on the facts of each case. Llewellyn and Hoebel also admired the adaptability of Cheyenne legal institutions. In the late nineteenth century the Cheyenne had instituted soldier societies as policing organizations, apparently in response to the greater integration of Cheyenne groups, and what Llewellyn and Hoebel saw to be a more complex state.

Gluckman was one of the first Western academics to record and study carefully actual cases heard in non-Western courts.[25] Other colonial field researchers had attempted to collect and codify customary law in the colonial countries they created, but Gluckman was the first to focus, through the collection of cases, on the decision-making process of a non-Western judiciary. He analyzed and evaluated the complex Lozi judicial process involving the ranked delivery of many judicial opinions in a single trial, using British and American theorists, especially Benjamin Cardozo's *The Nature of the Judicial Process.*[26]

---

[23] Bronislaw Malinowski, *Crime and Custom in Savage Society* (London: Kegan Paul, Trench, Trubner, 1926). Whether or not the rules Malinowski described are appropriately viewed as law or as economic custom has been extensively debated. James Boyd White suggested to me that law might be distinguished from other cultural rules by the legal institution of standing. If someone has standing, in other words, a right to complain to the authorities, it is law. If the differences are negotiated without the articulation of such a right, as they are in the Trobriand Islands, it is not law. This raises the question, among others, as to whether formal institutions are necessary for law.

[24] Malinowski, *Crime and Custom*, 127.

[25] Max Gluckman, *The Judicial Process Among the Barotse of Northern Rhodesia (Zambia)*, 2d ed. (Manchester: Manchester University Press, 1967).

[26] Benjamin N. Cardozo, *The Nature of the Judicial Process* (New Haven: Yale University Press, 1921).

Malinowski, Llewellyn, Hoebel, and Gluckman admired the cultures they studied for their gift for the law, but they all viewed law from the utilitarian perspective of the legal realist. Law for them was primarily concerned with the anticipation of society's troubles and the practical management of power. Western scholars were also involved in efforts to "discover" and "codify" "customary" law as a part of various attempts at colonial administration.[27] Today, a new generation of anthropologists and legal scholars, having seen both the explanatory power and the limitations of viewing law as a method of social control, is exploring the value of seeing law as a cultural product. The classics of legal anthropology are now being reread and mined for the "thickness" of their descriptions.

In a seminal article, Clifford Geertz defines law as "a distinctive manner of imagining the real."[28] Analogizing law and anthropology, Geertz offers an interpretive approach to law, parallel to his interpretive anthropology. In a long essay illustrated with extended examples from Islamic, Indic, and Malaysian legal traditions, Geertz demonstrates the culturally embedded nature of legal structures. In a very real sense, Geertz insists, *haqq, dharma,* and *adat* are only intelligible if contextually situated. In opposition to instrumental views of the law, Geertz argues that law is about "meaning . . . not machinery,"[29] and that comparative law is about cultural translation, not the distillation of universal concepts.[30] In Geertz's view, law, like all knowledge, is local and is culturally expressed. Legal pluralism or eclecticism is thus likely to persist, Geertz concludes, rather than disappear.

Lawrence Rosen and Sally Falk Moore, two anthropologists of law who respond in different ways to Geertz's anthropology, have studied what it is that makes law successful in particular cultural contexts in both Western and non-Western situations. In *The Anthropology of Justice,*[31] Rosen, a student of Geertz, shows that the success of a

---

[27] See, for example, J. F. Holleman, ed., *Van Vollenhoven on Indonesian Adat Law* (The Hague: M. Nijhoff, 1981).

[28] Geertz, "Local Knowledge," 184.

[29] Geertz, "Local Knowledge," 232.

[30] See also White, *Justice as Translation.*

[31] Lawrence Rosen, *The Anthropology of Justice: Law as Culture in Islamic Society* (Cambridge: Cambridge University Press, 1989).

Moroccan local court results from the congruence between the cultural style and expectations of the *qadi* and those of the litigants. What may look arbitrary to the non-Moroccan observer is in fact a highly nuanced, rule-bound, and culturally specific form of adjudication, the goal of which is restoration of the litigants to competence within their own cultural context—restoration of their capacity to "bargain for reality."[32] "[T]he entire process," Rosen informs us, "contributes to the reinforcement of the local in the context of the judicially cognizable":

[T]he analysis of legal systems, like the analysis of social systems, requires as its base an understanding of the categories of meaning by which participants themselves comprehend their experience and orient themselves toward one another in their everyday lives. . . .

By tacking back and forth across law and social life, by viewing both domains through a common frame of theory and practice, we can give serious consideration, in a way that may be applicable to a wide variety of societies, to the proposition that it is indeed possible to formulate a study of law as culture and culture as integral to law.[33]

Rosen's book exemplifies Geertz's thesis that understanding law requires an understanding of culture.[34]

Sally Falk Moore, in her *Social Facts and Fabrications*,[35] is, in contrast to Rosen, harshly critical of Geertz's interpretive method. Moore criticizes Geertz's interpretive anthropology for turning anthropology into a sort of art appreciation in which other cultures are viewed

---

[32] "Bargaining for reality" is a concept developed in Lawrence Rosen, *Bargaining for Reality: The Construction of Social Relations in a Muslim Community* (Chicago: University of Chicago Press, 1984).

For a description of the interaction of African customary law and British colonial law and of the cultural role of law in one Soga community, see Lloyd A. Fallers, *Law Without Precedent: Legal Ideas in Action in the Courts of Colonial Busoga* (Chicago: University of Chicago Press, 1969).

[33] Rosen, *Anthropology of Justice*, xiv–xv.

[34] For another recent anthropological study of the cultural particularity of a local legal style, see Carol Greenhouse, *Praying for Justice: Faith, Order and Community in an American Town* (Ithaca: Cornell University Press, 1986). Greenhouse's book describes the conscious and religiously motivated avoidance of litigation by a Baptist community in the southeastern United States.

[35] Sally Falk Moore, *Social Facts and Fabrications: "Customary" Law on Kilimanjaro, 1880–1980* (Cambridge: Cambridge University Press, 1986).

aesthetically.[36] She views Geertz's method as apolitical and therefore immoral.[37]

Moore's book carefully reconstructs the changes in legal culture over the course of one hundred years of Mount Kilimanjaro history. It is a story largely of legal failure, the failure of law to produce justice. Notwithstanding her criticism of Geertz, she depicts German colonial law, British colonial law, postcolonial socialist law, and their various "remodelings of chiefdoms" and reified constructions of "traditional law" as all failing largely because they no longer correspond culturally and therefore cannot adjudicate fairly.

There is a strong Marxist strain in Moore's work which suggests that law is always oppressive, whether traditional, colonial, or socialist. The women and the poor always lose. The entrepreneurs, whether precolonial, colonial, or postcolonial, can always manipulate the system. Ironically, perhaps, Moore's Marxist orientation and economic interpretation have, at times, an effect parallel to that of the regimes she condemns. In focusing on issues of power and utility she, like the colonial and socialist overlords she criticizes (and like the utilitarians in American law), sometimes risks separating law from culture.

The failure of law to produce justice on Mount Kilimanjaro which Moore describes can, I think, be fairly ascribed, in part, to a failure of cultural correspondence, in the sense of Geertz and Rosen.[38] The rules on Mount Kilimanjaro have become detached from culture. The historical sweep of her work, while devastating in its condemnation of successive efforts at legal reconstruction, reminds us, however, as does Maine's work, of the need to see symbolic systems within the dynamic context of history.[39]

---

[36] Moore, *Social Facts and Fabrications*, 325–26.

[37] But one can, in my opinion, justly ask whether, in resisting interpretation, she appears to rob the lives of the people she studies of meaning and creative agency.

[38] The failure of law on Mount Kilimanjaro, particularly in the socialist context, might also be understood as a failure of authority resulting from what Joseph Vining has pointed to in American courts as the bureaucratization of law. Joseph Vining, *The Authoritative and the Authoritarian* (Chicago: University of Chicago Press, 1986).

[39] See, also, on the need for history in anthropology, Marshall Sahlins, *Islands of History* (Chicago: University of Chicago Press, 1985), and Jean Comaroff and John Comaroff, *Ethnography and the Historical Imagination* (Boulder: Westview Press, 1992).

The anthropology of law is an extremely varied and often contentious discipline. I have mentioned a few of the many anthropologists and sociologists working to understand the social context of law and legal change. For scholars of American law these efforts can provide a much needed corrective. They subvert tendencies to see Western legal categories and processes as universal. They challenge American legal scholars to look again at how law works and to see American law as a part of American culture and history.

Within the American academic legal community, a loose association of legal scholars, sometimes known as the law and literature movement, influenced by the techniques of literary criticism and, in part, by those of cultural anthropology, has sought to read American law as a cultural text and to explore American law as the specialized conversation of a community—an ongoing conversation about the meaning of our society. Along with legal scholars concerned with what makes law successful, such as Edward Levi, and moral, such as Lon Fuller, these scholars have tried to see American law as a practical discourse, historically located, like literature, and to do so in conscious opposition to those on the right and left who would see law chiefly as an exercise of reason or of power. Lon Fuller characterizes this cultural view of law as one which sees law as "a purposeful enterprise," to be distinguished from one that sees law as "a manifested fact of social authority or power."[40]

Preeminent among these scholars of law and literature is James Boyd White, who may be said to have begun this conversation with his book, *The Legal Imagination*.[41] *The Legal Imagination* is in the form of a law school case book and is designed to be used in law school classes. Included, however, in addition to the traditional selection of excerpts from American and British judicial opinions, are textual excerpts ranging across classics of Western literature from Icelandic sagas to Norman Mailer. In his notes and questions on the texts, White urges the law student reader to expand his or her understanding of the relationship of law to language and culture and to give careful attention to how words are used, by lawyers and by others. A lawyer—indeed

[40] Fuller, *The Morality of Law*, 145.
[41] White, *The Legal Imagination*.

any professional who uses words—has a professional ethical obligation, in White's view, to give attention to how those words are used and to their effect on other individuals and on the community as a whole.[42] For White, law is "a culture of argument" that "creates a world of meaning."[43] Those who participate in it have a responsibility for the nature of that culture and the world it creates.

White's concerns about the relationship of law and language in legal writing are most fully laid out in his *Justice as Translation*, in which he analogizes the practice of law, in the broadest sense, to translation. Like translation, he argues, law involves interpretation and is ethical as well as intellectual. It is practice as well as theory. It is ongoing and needs to be continually revised and redone, like English translations of the Bible and of foreign literary classics. It is a process and a project that is never finished. For White, law, like translation, inhabits a marginal position between worlds, "tentative, suggestive, incomplete."[44] We have to keep working on it.

Other important influences on the law and literature movement include Robert Cover and John T. Noonan. Robert Cover, in a widely cited article entitled *"Nomos* and Narrative,"[45] argues that the norms of a community and the narratives of a community depend on one another for being and coherence. He looks at and evaluates judicial decisions in terms of what he calls their jurisgenerative or jurispathic (or statist) potential, depending on their correspondence with the narratives of the many included jurisgenerative communities.

---

[42] See Milner Ball, *Lying Down Together: Law, Metaphor and Theology* (Madison: University of Wisconsin Press, 1985), suggesting that the use of fluid metaphors, such as those arising out of the international law of the sea, rather than metaphors of defense, such as "bulwark," would lead the law toward a more positive role in the creation of community.

[43] White, *Justice as Translation*, ix, xiii.

[44] White, *Justice as Translation*, 259.

[45] Cover, *"Nomos* and Narrative," 4–68. For a careful analysis of Cover's work as it relates to an ongoing effort to use Jewish law as a solution to interpretation in American law, see Suzanne Last Stone, "In Pursuit of the Counter-Text: The Turn to the Jewish Legal Model in Contemporary Legal Theory." *Harvard Law Review* 106 (February 1993): 813–94. Stone argues that Jewish law is inescapably religious and that the attempt by American lawyers to use Jewish legal models in interpreting American law reconstructs and secularizes Jewish law in unacknowledged and contradictory ways.

John Noonan, in his *Persons and Masks of the Law,* criticizes lawyers and judges from Thomas Jefferson to Benjamin Cardozo for using legal language to avoid dealing with people as fellow humans.[46] He calls Jefferson to account for his unwillingness to rewrite the laws of Virginia, using Blackstone's *Commentaries*[47] as a basis, because, as Jefferson said, the result would be to "render property uncertain."[48] Jefferson and his friend and teacher, George Wythe, used the technical words of property law when referring to slaves as a way of distancing themselves from the humanity of the slaves and from their own destructive actions toward that humanity. Noonan asserts that without the complicity of lawyers slavery would not have survived:

Without their professional craftmanship, without their management of metaphor, without their loyalty to the system, the enslavement by word more comprehensive than any shackles could not have been forged.[49]

It was, in his view, the willingness of lawyers, even enlightened lawyers like Jefferson and Wythe, to use the language of property law to talk about people which allowed slavery to continue.

Noonan is also critical of Benjamin Cardozo, a distinguished member of the New York Court of Appeals from 1917 to 1932, both for obscuring the social situations of the parties in the famous *Palsgraf* case[50] and for his contemporaneous involvement in the drafting of

---

[46] John T. Noonan, *Persons and Masks of the Law: Cardozo, Holmes, Jefferson, and Whythe as Makers of the Masks* (New York: Farrar, Straus and Giroux, 1976).

[47] William Blackstone, *Commentaries on the Laws of England* (1765).

[48] Noonan, *Persons and Masks*, 50.

[49] Noonan, *Persons and Masks*, 60–61.

[50] Palsgraf v. Long Island Railroad Co., 248 N.Y. 339 (Court of Appeals, 1928), "[t]he most famous tort case of modern times," in Noonan's words, concerned the extent of liability for injury to an unforeseeable plaintiff in a negligence case.

The facts in *Palsgraf*, as stated by Cardozo, were as follows: "Plaintiff was standing on a platform of defendant's railroad after buying a ticket to go to Rockaway Beach. A train stopped at the station bound for another place. Two men ran forward to catch it. One of the men reached the platform of the car without mishap, though the train was already moving. The other man, carrying a package, jumped aboard the car, but seemed unsteady as if about to fall. A guard on the car, who had held the door open, reached forward to help him in, and another guard on the platform pushed from behind. In this act, the package was dislodged, and fell upon the rails. It was a package of small size, about fifteen inches long, and was covered by a newspaper. In fact it contained fireworks, but there was nothing in its appearance to give notice of its contents. The fireworks when they fell exploded. The shock of the

model legislation which would have governed the *Palsgraf* case.[51] A judge of the United States Court of Appeals for the Ninth Circuit and a Roman Catholic canon lawyer, Noonan shows how Cardozo streamlined the facts to serve the rule he sought to promote and to elucidate. Mrs. Palsgraf and her injury as a result of the railroad's obvious negligence were ignored, Noonan argues, in Cardozo's drive for a more perfect legal science. Quoting Cardozo on Oliver Wendell Holmes, Noonan summarizes Cardozo's purpose, as follows:

"Many a common law suit can be lifted from meanness up to dignity," so Cardozo wrote of Holmes, "if a great judge is by to see what is within." As "a system of case law develops," so Cardozo declared at Yale, "the sordid controversy of the litigants are the stuff out of which great shining truths will ultimately be shaped." The particular facts which interlocked [in *Palsgraf*] were not all the circumstances of the case but the construction of events he made as he molded his opinion to lift the case to dignity, to create a great and shining truth.[52]

Noonan, in contrast, makes a strong appeal for "a shift to a less rule-focused jurisprudence"[53] and for a legal process modeled on the Augustinian ideal of justice defined as "love serving only the one loved"[54]—law as love, rather than as "shining truth."

These American theorists, White, Cover, and Noonan, are reformers. Their goal is the remaking of American law and American lawyers through a strategic retrieval of humanistic traditions in law and the selective use of various forms of discourse criticism. As reformers, they give greater agency to the historical actor than would an anthropologist or an historian.[55] Noonan does not acknowledge, furthermore, although

---

explosion threw down some scales at the other end of the platform many feet away. The scales struck the plaintiff, causing injuries for which she now sues." 248 N.Y. at 340. The Court determined that the railroad was not liable for Mrs. Palsgraf's injuries.

[51] For another view of Cardozo's opinion in *Palsgraf*, see Richard A. Posner, *Cardozo: A Study in Reputation* (Chicago: University of Chicago Press, 1990).

[52] Noonan, *Persons and Masks*, 150.

[53] Noonan, *Persons and Masks*, 142.

[54] Noonan, *Persons and Masks*, xii.

[55] See, for example, on slavery and the cultural and economic reasons for its persistence in eighteenth-century America, David Brion Davis, *The Problem of Slavery in the Age of Revolution: 1770–1823* (Ithaca: Cornell University Press, 1975).

White and Cover do, that the problems he sees in legal language are part of a larger problem about the nature of language and the possibility of accurate and authentic representation.[56] As with many prophets, however, the warning that all three give is both penetrating and timely.

Another result of their reforming zeal is that these American lawyers, while purporting to talk about law generally, have in fact talked only about American law and have assumed the existence of American legal institutions. Cover speaks of "law and narrative" and Noonan of "the central purpose of the legal enterprise." White says, without qualifying the word "law," that "[t]he activity of law is in the interpretation and composition of authoritative texts. . . ."[57] None of the three gives explicit recognition to the larger global comparative context in which American law exists and functions and with which it has always interacted. Unless the words "law" and "text," as these reformers understand them, are greatly expanded, their conclusions are less clearly relevant or pertinent for many oral cultures and cultures in which law operates without formal precedent.[58] Furthermore, in civil law jurisdictions legal texts are arguably created in a very different way.[59]

Another leading voice urging reform of the language of American law is Mary Ann Glendon, a scholar of comparative law[60] and a student of Max Rheinstein, a pioneer in the comparative study of family law. Glendon argues that if American law on abortion and divorce is compared to European law on these matters, the perniciousness of "rights talk" can be seen.[61] Citing Geertz and White, Glendon espouses a view of law as educational, in a classical sense. She argues that, whereas in the American context political positions on abortion and divorce have become so polarized as to paralyze public debate, in

[56]See, for example, among others, Michel Foucault, *The Order of Things: An Archaeology of the Human Sciences* (New York: Vintage Books, 1970).

[57] White, *Justice as Translation*, 95.

[58] See, for example, Rosen, *Anthropology of Justice,* and Fallers, *Law Without Precedent.*

[59] See John Henry Merryman, *The Civil Law Tradition: An Introduction to the Legal Systems of Western Europe and Latin America*, 2d ed. (Palo Alto: Stanford University Press, 1985).

[60] The field of comparative law has been largely focused on comparison among Western legal systems, although that is beginning to change.

[61] Glendon, *Abortion and Divorce.*

England, France, and Germany middle positions have been successfully negotiated and legislated. Analogizing to the Platonic dialogue, she argues that law on these subjects in Europe works better because it has more successfully negotiated with cultural needs and expectations.

The often isolated position of these critics—and the frequent misunderstandings of their position—reveals what currently seems to be a genuine split in the American academic legal community between two at times incompatible and antagonistic understandings of what law and legal language are and what they can do, emblematic perhaps of a wider cultural split.[62] On the one hand are those, neorealists perhaps, who view law as a formal, technical exercise of reason, an exercise in which legal language and legal institutions are simply propositional vehicles for the clean, refined, and rational power of the intellect.[63] On the other are those who wish to focus on the symbolic texture and cultural embeddedness of legal language and institutions and their engagement with other social and cultural languages and institutions— believing that in that texture and in the possibilities of that interrelationship lie the real richness and power of the law.[64] In resisting a technocratic view of law, these theorists suggest that the success of the law is derived from its sometimes fragile and always changing cultural expression and its correspondence with the aspirations of those who participate in it. Law works when it successfully talks about and acts in correspondence with a culture we recognize. The failure of such cultural correspondence can result in law doing violence to the people

---

[62] Not everyone would regard the two understandings of law as irredeemably incompatible in practice. For example, White, though harshly critical of economic reductionism, acknowledges the importance and power of economic analysis for lawyers, *Justice as Translation*, 46–86.

[63] See Morton J. Horwitz, *The Transformation of American Law 1870–1960: The Crisis of Legal Orthodoxy* (New York: Oxford University Press, 1992), for an analysis of the history of legal realism and of the oscillation between utilitarian and natural law theories in American law.

[64] Criticizing legal realists through the use of the critical methods of the humanities and social sciences, as those in law and literature do, is to be distinguished from the use and promotion *by* legal realists of the tools of social sciences in the service of utilitarian ends.

and situations for whom and in which it practices and can contribute to contempt for the law.[65]

Although these American lawyer/reformers share with anthropologists of law a more culturally embedded understanding of law than most legal academics, they have, in contrast, as has been mentioned, largely confined themselves to talking about Western law. And, when they talk about religion, which they do—often—they talk Western theology. Three of the American lawyers mentioned, White, Cover and Noonan, as well as other reforming critics of American law, such as Sanford Levinson, Milner Ball, and Joseph Vining, use Christian or Jewish theological references and analogies as strategic resources for the critique of American law. There is thus a parallel and unacknowledged[66] parochialism both in their use of the law to mean Western law and in their use of religion to mean Jewish or Christian theologies.

An example of this parochialism can be seen in Milner Ball's work. His book, *Lying Down Together*, urges the use of metaphors of interdependence and of cooperation rather than of separation and of defense in describing law[67] and explores how such metaphors can serve as models for international cooperative legal efforts. The fascinating complexity of his critique of American law and his "thick description" of the law of the sea and its development, is, however, marred by the

---

[65] See, for example, Justice Scalia's opinion in Employment Division v. Smith, 494 U.S. 872 (1991), in which he harshly and abstractly announces a new rule of law which effectively outlaws a central religious practice of the Native American church (the sacramental use of peyote). He does this almost without mention of the persons or religious beliefs affected. Half a sentence is devoted to a reference to the respondents' religious beliefs and to their motives for using a controlled substance. I would argue that it is the inhumanity of the language rather than the outcome of the case that fuels the tremendous outcry over this case. Like the lawyers and the judges that Noonan criticizes, Scalia distances himself from the respondents and refuses to admit them and their religion into the time and space of his opinion.

[66] It is this lack of acknowledgment that I wish to criticize. It is the purporting to talk about Law or Religion or Theology without acknowledging that one is talking about American law or about only one of a variety of Judaisms and Christianities, and without acknowledging the limitations those contexts imply, that concerns me. Like these other authors, I, too, am trained as an American lawyer and have studied largely, although not exclusively, American religion. I believe that it makes a difference, however, if that study is done within the context of a cross-cultural understanding of each.

[67] Ball, *Lying Down Together*.

narrowness of his theological conclusions. Ball wishes to oppose "The Peaceable Kingdom" as a set of metaphors about law to "Fortress America" as a set of metaphors about law. He insists that, in this effort, the theology of Dietrich Bonhoeffer is simply his personal way of finding a "better way to talk about these things."[68] The reader is free to find her own. Yet, the secret tentativeness of Bonhoeffer's "religion-less religion," as understood by Ball, still narrows the conversation about religion by attempting to avoid the problems religion presents.

Ball's own project could benefit from a more inclusive religious understanding. His admiration for Bonhoeffer's "religionless Christianity" seems to cut off and exclude in the same way as the law he criticizes.[69] Ball's insistence on the need "to protect the world from violation by religion," while understandable in Bonhoeffer's context, is oppressive in ours. Moreover, Ball's professed Calvinist allergy to the movement of the spirit is in fact belied by the very watery metaphors he admires. For those who would bring religion into dialogue with law, Ball's Calvinism reveals the larger problem of acknowledging the multiple theologies within American Christianity, as well as those of other religious traditions, and of acknowledging the inescapable tension between religion and law.

It *is* interesting that these critics of legal realism, like many postmodern critics of a sterile rationality, do seem to gravitate almost inevitably to religion: religion as the other of the Enlightenment.[70] In this, these lawyers form a part of another conversation about the validity and/or necessity of moral and theological arguments in debates on American public issues.[71] There appears to be, in fact, a structural

[68] Ball, *Lying Down Together*, 138.

[69] See, for example, Ball, *Lying Down Together*, 181–82, nn. 14, 15.

[70] See Ernst Gellner, *Postmodernism, Reason and Religion* (London: Routledge, 1992).

[71] See, for example, Michael Perry, *Morality, Politics and Law: A Bicentennial Essay* (Oxford: Oxford University Press, 1988), Kent Greenawalt, *Religious Convictions and Political Choice* (New York: Oxford University Press, 1988), and other writings in the exponentially growing law and theology field.

See, also, Stephen L. Carter, *The Culture of Disbelief: How American law and Politics Trivialize Religious Devotion* (New York: Basic Books, 1993). For a critique of Carter's book, see my forthcoming review article in *Journal of Religion* 75 (January 1995).

See, also, Franklin I. Gamwell, *The Divine Good: Modern Moral Theory and*

connection such that a cultural understanding of law leads to a view that insists on the close relationship of law to religion or theology.[72] The argument seems then to be that if law is not a utilitarian exercise of power and reason, it must be an exercise in theological ethics. The third position would seem to tend toward the nihilistic. Law is simply and inexplicably there. It has no purpose or meaning.

Religion, oddly perhaps, does seem to be an inevitable part of the conversation about law. If the members of the law and literature movement, however, in their interest in theology, are not going to become parochial within the larger academic community and captives of the political right, I would argue that they, like the Supreme Court, need to expand their understanding of theology, of religion, and of the respective relationship of each to law. In order to avoid excluding those who are not members of their religious communities, religion should be seen as culturally various, as inescapably compromised, and as structurally related to law, not simply as a personal or cultural resource for mending law. Religion can then be seen as a problem for law as well as a solution.

Drawing then from these many students of the culture of law and looking at the decisions of the United States federal courts in *Lynch*, law will be here understood to be a specialized and privileged location for a changing cultural discourse and practice about public issues, including religion. Judges and lawyers engaged in interpreting the First Amendment will be viewed as creators and participants in a shared public language and practice about the relationship of law and religion in American life. The assumption will be made that laws *and* religions

---

the *Necessity of God* (San Francisco: Harper, 1990), for the argument that ethics presupposes a transcendent reference.

[72] One parallel between the study of religion and the study of law can be seen in the fact that the skeptical reductionists in each field are greater fideists than those who insist on talking about truth and morality. See, for example, Robert A. Segal, "In Defense of Reductionism," *Journal of the American Academy of Religion* 51 (March 1983): 97–124, and Sanford Levinson, *Constitutional Faith* (Princeton: Princeton University Press, 1988). Levinson raises the question of the place of truth in teaching law. He asks the question, parallel to one often raised in the study of religion, as to whether you can study and teach law if you do not believe in it.

are distinctive and changing ways of, in Geertz's words, "imagin[ing] principled lives [people] can practicably lead."[73]

TALKING ABOUT RELIGION

What is religion? If law seems an elusive and elastic concept, locating religion can be even more bewildering. To what does the word refer? To one of a number of world ideologies and institutions? To a natural human propensity? To an expression of an encounter with the holy? Is it universal? Is it eternal? Is it increasing? Or declining? Is it good or bad? Is it about groups or individuals? Is it public or private? Are these peculiarly American or Western questions to ask? Is religion even a useful word?

The academic study of religion in the West, along with the other social sciences, is a child of the Enlightenment. Its practitioners, painfully conscious of the difficulty of these questions and concerned to avoid theological presuppositions, try to find a way to talk about religion which authentically describes human religiousness, its cultural expression, and its role in society. Although the academic study of religion takes place across humanistic and social scientific disciplines as diverse and, at times, as mutually antagonistic as anthropology, sociology, psychology, history, literature, philosophy, linguistics, and theology, it finds a particularly intense expression in the field of history of religions.

History of religions itself covers a wide range of academic approaches. In what follows I shall try to articulate a vision of what history of religions can offer to other disciplines as a way to think and talk and act about religion. Notwithstanding the notorious diversity of voices within history of religions over the last two centuries (within the rarefied circles in which such notoriety is possible!), I see the following characteristics as unifying ones in the discipline of history of religions.

The distinguishing characteristic of history of religions is an almost naïve insistence on seeing humans as inescapably religious. If anthropologists see humans as irreducibly cultural, sociologists see humans as members of groups, and economists see them as rational choice makers, historians of religion are committed to the *epistemo-*

---

[73] Geertz, "Local Knowledge," 234.

logical value of seeing humans as religious. Seeing humans as inescapably religious does not imply that self-proclaimed atheists, for example, are necessarily anonymous persons of faith or that all people participate in the same way or with equal intensity in their religious traditions.[74] It implies that creating religion is something people do. Religion is not good or bad. It is not increasing or decreasing. It is there and it is there in extraordinary variety.

Not only do human societies, indeed all human groups, have inherent religious aspects as projections or human constructions of social identity, in a Durkheimian sense, but, more broadly, a religious aspect can be a distinctive property of all human creations. All human creations, individual and social, both of the ruling majority and of the critical minorities, are, or can be, locations for religious expression.[75] As Mircea Eliade said, "We must get used to the idea of recognizing hierophanies absolutely everywhere."[76]

There is, in consequence, a willingness, even a need, on the part of most historians of religion, in contrast to some other academics, to use the word "religion," while at the same time trying to expand and refine its meaning. In spite of enormous frustration with the word, its Western cultural location, its etymology, history of usage, and the uncertainty of its reference,[77] there is a commitment, a stubborn and almost existential commitment on the part of historians of religion to the value of trying to understand religion as an identifiable and universal human creation. Taking this stance toward religious phenomena does not presuppose a phenomenological approach to religion or a reification of the sacred.[78] It does, however, regard with suspicion those theories

[74] See Nancy Jay, *Throughout Your Generations Forever: Religion, Sacrifice and Paternity* (Chicago: University of Chicago Press, 1992), in which she discusses the difficulty of understanding the meaning of any ritual, given the different perspectives and degrees of involvement among different participants.

[75] See Bruce Lincoln, *Discourse and the Construction of Society* (Oxford: Oxford University Press, 1985).

[76] Mircea Eliade, *Patterns in Comparative Religion*, trans. Rosemary Sheed (New York: Sheed & Ward, 1958; reprint, New York: New American Library, 1963), 11.

[77] See Wilfred Cantwell Smith, *The Meaning and End of Religion* (New York: Harper & Row, 1978).

[78] See Hans H. Penner, *Impasses and Resolution: A Critique of the Study of Religion* (New York: Peter Lang, 1989), criticizing phenomenological approaches to religion and advocating a structural approach.

of human religion which explain it away[79] or assume that secularization is all but complete.

Some contemporary sociologists of religion have argued that one of the reasons for the inadequacy of secularization theories is that theorists have failed to see that there is a dynamic relationship between social and religious change. As societies change, religion necessarily changes too. As societies fragment, religion also fragments. As ethnic strife increases, religion defined along ethnic lines increases. In the contemporary context, as issue-specific social groupings occur along a liberal/conservative divide, religious groupings are also seen to be issue specific and grouped along such a divide.

According to these sociologists, the decline of community has not resulted in the decline of religion, as secularist theories would have it, but in the transformation of religion. James Beckford concludes his *Religion and Advanced Industrial Society*:

> [I]t is nowadays better to conceptualize religion as a cultural resource or form than as a social institution. As such, it is characterized by a greater degree of flexibility and unpredictability. For the decline of the great religious monopolies in the West has been accompanied by the sporadic deployment of religion for a great variety of new purposes. Religion can be combined with virtually any other set of ideas or values and the chances that religion will be controversial are increased by the fact that it may be used by people having little or no connection with formal religious organization. The deregulation of religion is one of the hidden ironies of secularization.[80]

Beckford and others, while focused on the social dynamics of contemporary religion, seem to agree with historians of religion that religion is not going to go away and therefore cannot be ignored.[81] Historians of religion might add to Beckford's insight that there is a sense in which religion has always been "deregulated," and that the reification of the "great religious monopolies in the West" as monolithic conceals the

---

[79] But, see Terry Godlove, Jr., "Interpretation, Reductionism, and Belief in God," *Journal of Religion* 69 (April 1989): 184–98.

[80] James Beckford, *Religion and Advanced Industrial Society* (London: Unwin Hyman 1989), 171–72.

[81] See, for example, Robert Wuthnow, *The Restructuring of American Religion: Society and Faith since World War II* (Princeton: Princeton University Press, 1988), and N. J. Demerath III and Rhys Williams, *A Bridging of Faiths: Religion and Politics in a New England City* (Princeton: Princeton University Press, 1992).

always enormous "flexibility and unpredictability" of religion over both space and time.[82]

It is easy to mock the tortured self-consciousness of history of religions today and to reject the irenic ecumenicism and romantic dreams of some of its forbears, both those with explicit theological agendas and those with more general humanistic ideologies. Many historians of religion, among them Mircea Eliade and Joachim Wach, have seen in the discipline a hope of transcending religious differences and answering secular despair.[83] In my view, both ecumenicism and romanticism stem, however, from this commitment to talking about religion as something real. Both arise from a conviction that something can be learned by taking religion seriously, by respecting human religious creations as rational and as genuine efforts at understanding.[84]

Although, as Jonathan Z. Smith insists, the possibility of talking about religion without making theological presuppositions is a serious question,[85] romantic dreams do not seem to me to be a necessary result of viewing religion as real. Religion can survive as a useful intellectual category with a much more open-ended, critical, and ambiguous

[82] See, for example, Ioan P. Culianu, *Eros and Magic in the Renaissance*, trans. Maragaret Cook (Chicago: University of Chicago Press, 1987).

[83] See the article by Gregory Alles, "Wach, Eliade and the Critique from Totality," *Numen* 35 (July 1988): 108–38.

[84] Jonathan Z. Smith, *Map is Not Territory: Studies in the History of Religions* (Leiden: E. J. Brill, 1978), and *Imagining Religion: From Babylon to Jonestown* (Chicago: University of Chicago Press, 1982).

The need for this seriousness as a basis for a productive conversation about religion also finds expression in the conversation about the possibilities of inter-religious dialogue. For example, Paul J. Griffiths, in his *An Apology for Apologetics: A Study in the Logic of Interreligious Dialogue* (Maryknoll: Orbis Books, 1991), insists on the need to regard religious doctrine as making truth claims, in order to have a fruitful dialogue. See, also, David Tracy, *Dialogue with the Other: The Inter-religious Dialogue* (Louvain: Peeters Press, 1990).

[85] Jonathan Z. Smith has suggested in class and elsewhere that it may be impossible to divorce history of religions from the Protestant theological assumptions with which it was created. It is necessary, however, he argues, to strive for thought without privileging any material. See, also, on the theological handicap to the study of religion, his *Drudgery Divine: On the Comparison of Early Christianities and on Religions of Late Antiquity* (Chicago: University of Chicago Press, 1990); and Peter Brown, *The Cult of Saints: Its Rise and Function in Latin Christianity* (Chicago: University of Chicago Press, 1981).

reference. Moreover, the attempt to use history of religions as a practical political discourse does not have to be romantic.

I want to insist that this is an epistemological stance, not an ideological or theological one, on the part of historians of religion. The key value of history of religions in my mind lies in its insistence that humans cannot be understood completely without understanding them as religious as well as social, cultural, and economic beings. The data look different if one is open to the possibility of a religious under-standing of them. One sees other things.[86]

The epistemological value of history of religions can be seen in contrast to the sometimes flattened picture of religion which exists in some other social scientific descriptions of religious phenomena. I think this value can be seen by comparing, for example, two recent readings of South American religion. The urgency, intensity, and density of the way Tod Swanson, a student of religion, talks about Ecuadorian religion,[87] his openness to and familiarity with the syncretistic texture of religious symbols and experience, is more successful, to my mind, than the detached, theoretical way Joseph Bastien, an anthropologist,[88] talks about South American Indian religion in his *Mountain of the Condor*.[89] Swanson's interlocutors appear to be alive and engaged participants, active agents in the modern project of understanding in a crazy-quilt culture, while Bastien's seem captives of their culture and victims of the colonial West.

In tension with this expansive view of religion, a view which looks to move beyond reductionist explanations and to understand human culture as universally religious, is a more bounded and dynamic understanding of religion. Sometimes historians of religion want to talk

---

[86] For a similar position about the value of the study of religion, see Daniel Pals, "Reductionism and Belief: An Appraisal of Recent Attacks on the Doctrine of Irreducible Religion," *Journal of Religion* 66 (January 1986): 18–36; and "Is Religion a *Sui Generis* Phenomenon?" *Journal of the American Academy of Religion* 55 (summer 1987): 259–82.

[87] Oral presentation at the University of Chicago Divinity School, spring 1992. See also Lawrence E. Sullivan, *Icanchu's Drum*.

[88] I do not mean to suggest that all anthropologists are tone deaf to religion or that only historians of religion understand religion. The openness of members of both disciplines to the religious imagination is idiosyncratic.

[89] Joseph W. Bastien, *Mountain of the Condor: Metaphor and Ritual in an Andean Ayllu* (Prospect Heights: Waveland Press, 1978).

about all human activity as having religious aspects, of the religiousness of human beings. At other times they want to refine the word "religious" by focusing narrowly on what distinguishes the religiousness of human activity from other social facts and how those different social events interact. This might be a more Weberian view of religion.[90]

Moving from an attempt to designate with great precision the nature and location of the "holy" or of the "sacred," whether humanly or divinely constructed or produced, the question is asked: how does that dynamic quality, as manifested in human creations, operate historically in and through and in relation to other human institutions?[91] What does religion do in history? Indeed, the need to see structures of meaning as historically situated is urgently felt in all cultural studies at the present.[92]

History of religions is reluctant to give up on the apparent tension between the universality and the locatedness of religion. Both views express a truth about human religiousness. The disciplinary role of history of religions might be seen to exist, thus, in mediating the tension between a functional reduction of religion and a theologically totalizing one. Peter Brown's rereading of early medieval Christianity might be seen as an example of such a strategy.[93] A similar approach can be productive in understanding radical or marginal religious groups in the United States and elsewhere, groups that have tended to be regarded and explained by journalists and academics as political rather than as

---

[90] See Beckford, *Religion and Advanced Industrial Society,* for a discussion of the sociology of religion beginning with Durkheim and Weber.

[91] See, for example, Joachim Wach, *Sociology of Religion* (London: Kegan Paul, Trench, Trubner, 1947); Joseph Kitagawa, *Religion in Japanese History* (New York: Columbia University Press, 1966); Edward Shils, *The Center and the Periphery: Essays in Macrosociology* (Chicago: University of Chicago Press, 1975).

[92] See, for example, Sahlins, *Islands of History*, which discusses the need for history in anthropology, and Daniel Gold, *Comprehending the Guru: Toward a Grammar of Religious Perception* (Atlanta: Scholars Press, 1988), which seeks a typology for understanding the history and context of religious personalities and their relation to their traditions. See, also, Comaroff and Comaroff, *Ethnography and the Historical Imagination.*

[93] Brown, *The Cult of Saints.* Thanks to Anne Blackburn for suggesting this insight about Brown's book.

William James's *The Varieties of Religious Experience* (New York: Longmans, Green & Co., 1902; reprint, Middlesex: Penguin Books, 1982) endures as a religious classic, in part, because James takes this existential stance toward religious data.

religious. That a more complex and sympathetic understanding of one of these groups can be had by seeing it as religious and as comparable to other religious phenomena is evident in Jonathan Z. Smith's article on the Jonestown massacre.[94]

A third characteristic of historians of religion may be found in their effort to be open to all religious traditions, an effort to which often only lip service is paid and which may perhaps ultimately even be impossible to achieve, but which is nonetheless of continuing value. This effort may be seen in a constant striving to avoid or to rework Western categories and to understand religion by finding family resemblances rather than through hard-edged distinctions—a commitment to comparison while holding conclusions open and provisional—which implies an acknowledgment of the materiality and contemporaneity of the other. This effort is, of course, part of a larger enterprise within the Western academy to acknowledge the cultural locatedness of its discourse and the political implications of talking about other peoples and cultures using this discourse.[95] Charles Long and Lawrence Sullivan, among others, have made continuing efforts to use history of religions as a location for expanding the conversation about human religion to include previously excluded voices.[96]

The deconstruction of Western religion is part of this project and one strategy for acknowledging the materiality of the other.[97] In the recent past Western religion has been studied primarily by church

[94] "The Devil in Mr. Jones," in his *Imagining Religion*. See, also, Lawrence E. Sullivan, "Recommendations to the U.S. Departments of Justice and the Treasury concerning Incidents Such As the Branch Davidian Standoff in Waco, Texas, September 12, 1993," Harvard University Center for the Study of World Religions, 1993.

[95] See, for example, Edward Said, *Orientalism* (New York: Vintage Books, 1978); and Johannes Fabian, *Time and the Other: How Anthropology Makes Its Object* (New York: Columbia University Press, 1983).

[96] Charles H. Long, *Significations: Signs, Symbols, and Images in the Interpretation of Religion* (Philadelphia: Fortress Press, 1986); and Lawrence E. Sullivan, *Icanchu's Drum: An Orientation to Meaning in South American Religion* (New York: Macmillan, 1988).

[97] See Jean Comaroff and John Comaroff, *Of Revelation and Revolution: Christianity, Colonialism, and Consciousness in South Africa* (Chicago: University of Chicago Press, 1991), for the view that one strategy for addressing the politically compromising aspects of anthropology is to use anthropology on the colonial encounter.

historians. Structural and phenomenological studies of Western religion are beginning, however, and Western religions are being seen as having structural and phenomenological aspects that are comparable to "other" traditions. "Other" religious traditions, meanwhile, are now recognized as having histories.

Taking religion as the subject matter for history of religions while expanding the meaning of "religion" has led more and more toward a view of human religiousness which must consider the whole person, within the context of historical and material culture and events. Religion cannot be reduced to faith or conscience.[98] The word "religion" for history of religions, in this mode, insists on acknowledging the embodiedness of the human spirit, its materiality. History of religions has an inclusive impulse, both toward the physical expression of religion and toward the material and changing circumstances of people's lives.[99]

The peculiar attachment of history of religions to the word "religion" may be seen, in part, as an attempt to affect the meaning of the word. For most English speakers, "religion" seems to refer to organized religious institutions. To be "religious," then, means to belong to a recognized, named religious body with a definable ideology. "Spiritual," in contrast, seems for some now to be a more comfortable means of self-identification, more open-ended, a way, perhaps, of avoiding the ambiguous humanness of religion. Like these latter-day spiritualists, history of religions, too, is committed, I think, to broadening the word "religion" to cover human religiousness in a more inclusive way. However, for historians of religion, the goal is not simply to broaden it, as "spiritual" does, to cover a more elusive set of positive religious

---

[98] This is a Protestant and Enlightenment tendency that is revealed, among many other places, in the title of John T. Noonan's book, *The Believer and the Powers That Are: Cases, History, and Other Data Bearing on the Relation of Religion and Government* (New York: Macmillan, 1987). What about the Actor and the powers that are?

[99] See, for example, Caroline Walker Bynum, *Holy Feast and Holy Fast: The Religious Significance of Food to Medieval Women* (Berkeley: University of California Press, 1987), and *Fragmentation and Redemption: Essays on Gender and the Human Body in Medieval Religion* (New York: Zone Books, 1991), and Jean Comaroff, *Body of Power, Spirit of Resistance: The Culture and History of a South African People* (Chicago: The University of Chicago Press, 1985).

orientations and practices but also to be more comprehensive and less squeamish than "spiritual" is in the kind of human activity which is covered. Rather than abandon the word, history of religions seeks to expand its reference to include a wider range of human activities, many of which are deeply compromised.

This inclusiveness has many effects. It makes it difficult to look away from the often destructive historical and economic consequences of religious activity and from issues of gender.[100] Religious practice and experience is taken seriously. Religion is an affair of the whole person, mind and body, individually and in community. Myth and ritual are related. Religion can neither be reduced to conscience nor to a text. And it is acknowledged as extremely varied.

The tendency to reduce religion to words, or indeed to reduce life to words, exists in both legal and religious studies. Neither law nor religion is just about the construction of discourses or about conversations. Neither can be completely understood as texts, nor can the idea of a "text" be so expanded as to take in the materiality of human culture. This temptation is rife in all cultural studies. Law and religion have real power and real effects on people's lives and bodies.

There is also, thus, an attempt on the part of history of religions to acknowledge that *all* religion, like all human activity, is deeply compromised and can be dangerous. It cannot be safely contained. It cannot be viewed and appropriated as a useful public and social good or as safely domesticated, as many political philosophers have sought to do. The violence of religion has been most obsessively considered by Rene Girard in his *Violence and the Sacred*,[101] but it is at the center of a vigorous debate on the part of students of religion.[102]

---

[100] See Jay, *Throughout Your Generations Forever.*

[101] Rene Girard, *Violence and the Sacred*, trans. Patrick Gregory (Baltimore: Johns Hopkins University Press, 1972).

[102] See, for example, Robert Hammerton-Kelly, ed., *Violent Origins: Walter Burkert, Rene Girard and Jonathan Z. Smith on Ritual Killing and Cultural Formation* (Stanford: Stanford University Press, 1987); Smith, "The Devil in Mr. Jones"; and David Carrasco, *Quetzalcoatl and the Irony of Empire: Myths and Prophecies in the Aztec Tradition* (Chicago: University of Chicago Press, 1992). See, also, for additional sources: Christopher Candland, *The Spirit of Violence: An Interdisciplinary Bibliography of Religion and Violence* (New York: The Harry Frank Guggenheim Foundation, 1992).

Finally, it is not irrelevant that historians of religions often start by defining themselves in relation to other disciplines—for example, that history of religions is not history or theology or comparative religion.[103] Notwithstanding history of religions' own origin in the modern Enlightenment, some of history of religions' most powerful voices have been deliberate critics of modernity and, as a result, of the academic disciplines which are the products of modernity. This ambivalence toward the Enlightenment produces a sort of double consciousness, in the sense of W. E. B. DuBois.[104] History of religions exists and derives its energy and voice, in part, from this role as a location for cultural criticism. It does this by insisting on the reality of what the modern Enlightenment rejects. It insists on talking about what is considered in Enlightenment circles to be in rather poor taste. Yet it does this with one foot in the Enlightenment,[105] resisting theological totalizing at the same time.[106]

Charles Long is particularly eloquent about this role for history of religions. In the first essay of *Significations*, he explains the danger of signifying. "Signifying," as Long uses the term, means presuming to understand the significance of someone else's culture. Long says:

Signifying is worse than lying because it obscures and obfuscates a discourse without taking responsibility for so doing. This verbal misdirection parallels the real argument and gains its power of meaning from the structure of the discourse without taking responsibility for so doing.[107]

Signifying is, in effect, a sinister sleight-of-hand that denies another person's experience by substituting for it the signifier's own interpretation of that experience.

While implying by its title that signifying is a more general problem in the study of religion, Long argues, in a number of the essays in

---

[103] This is not to say these are not related endeavors. See Ninian Smart, "The History of Religions and Its Conversation Partners," in Joseph M. Kitagawa, ed., *History of Religions: Retrospect and Prospect: A Collection of Essays* (New York: Macmillan, 1985).

[104] W. E. B. DuBois, *The Souls of Black Folk* (Chicago: A. C. McClurg, 1903; reprint, New York: Bantam Books, 1989), 3.

[105] See, for example, Smith, "The Devil in Mr. Jones."

[106] Religion, as the other of the Enlightenment, is also represented in the fundamentalist critique of modernity. See, for a description of the contemporary role of religion, Gellner, *Postmodernism, Reason and Modernity*.

[107] Long, *Significations*, 1.

Significations, that the American black community has long been the victim of such a sleight-of-hand on the part of the white community. The white community, even when well-intentioned, has "signified" the black community by telling it what meaning and value it has in the American community as a whole. As Long points out, this can have an insidious effect because the signifier purports to be giving meaning when he is in fact denying it or ignoring it. Signification can have the effect on the signified of making him doubt his own experience or even of making him incapable of owning it other than in the categories of the signifier.

Charles Long's agenda for history of religions is imperial in its designs on intellectual understanding since the Enlightenment. According to Long, religious studies believes that religious meaning is *the* key to understanding what is authentically human:

New discourse concerning the meaning of religion—a discourse whose possibility is present in America in its departments of religion—will occur when Americans experience the "otherness" of America; only then will the scholars in religion be able to understand that human intercourse with the world of sacred realities is, hermeneutically speaking, one way, and probably the most profound way, of meeting and greeting our brothers and sisters who form and have formed our species for these several millennia.[108]

In my opinion, the locus of ideological issues has fallen within religious studies because religion is the only area within the humanities and/or the human sciences that could hold together authentically all of the varied orientations; also, it can best provide space for discussing what is *common* to all human beings in the late modern period.[109]

While I do not have Long's confidence in the apocalyptic intellectual power of history of religions, the complexity and inclusiveness of this way of looking at human religion—as universal, as dynamic, as embodied, as dangerous, and as a location for a critique of modernity— seems well suited, in my view, to the public discussion of religion in a pluralist world.

The self-conscious reflexivity about the value of talking about religion that is characteristic of much writing by historians of religions

---

[108] Long, *Significations*, 25.
[109] Long, *Significations*, 76.

is particularly useful as a resource for understanding the language about religion of an institution like the United States Supreme Court, an institution that is required by law to talk about religion but which has very little in its own history and sources to help it to do this. Radical changes have occurred during the last two hundred years, both in the nature of American religion and in how it is understood and in the power and pervasiveness of American government.[110] In spite of these changes and the inevitable effect they have on the words of the First Amendment, the Supreme Court has failed to be explicit about the assumptions concerning religion and society which underlie its opinions. Such explicitness, the kind of self-consciousness at which history of religions is expert, is a necessary step, in my view, before the Court can go forward productively with its legal analysis.

Attempting to articulate the value of history of religions as a resource for American lawyers in understanding American religion and in interpreting the First Amendment, may, in turn, give history of religions a look at itself which could be helpful. Seeing its categories in active practice in the culture that created them might usefully balance the tendency of history of religions, like that of anthropology, to create texts about the exotic.

LAW AND RELIGION

Very little general academic theorizing has been done about the structural relationship of law and religion. Any explanation of that relationship has been left to the study of particular religious traditions— indeed, has been seen as a problem peculiar to or inherent in those religious religions. The canon law of the Roman Church, *shar'ia*, and *dharma* are each seen as natural expressions of their own religious traditions. To the extent that they are compared, the conceptual model is usually that of the political/philosophical problem of the separation of church and state as it developed in the medieval West. The very subject matter seems caught in the web of the church-state controversy. The institutional academic location then appears as a reified form of that theoretical approach to the issues. The study of religion and law is usually conducted by historians, not by students of law or of religion.

---

[110] See Wuthnow, *The Restructuring of American Religion*, for one view of the effect of this change.

In the West before the Enlightenment, the relationship of law to religion has generally been seen to be represented in the relationship of the institutions and ideas of the state to the ecclesiastical institutions and ideas of Western Christianity. Historians since the Enlightenment have generally assumed an irreversible process of secularization. Those who are interested in religion at all in the West, in relation to law, have, in general, also been interested in that question in the context of the ongoing relationship between these institutions and ideas—the complex known as church and state.[111]

Other social theorists, following Marx and Weber, have, in general, also assumed an increasing secularization. Religion, on this reading, is an irrational remnant, an anachronism in the modern West. It has been replaced by law. In the United States this view has been seen by many as enshrined in the First Amendment.[112] Law was viewed as rational and secular and public, religion as something to be kept apart. Religion and law did not have a relationship at all except in the practical housekeeping around the wall of separation between church and state.

Now that religion is seen by many to be rather more persistent and more flexible in form than was formerly thought,[113] and now that structural social issues are seen in a comparative multicultural context, it makes sense to ask how law and religion—generally, not simply as church and state—interact in different cultural contexts and whether that interaction has a structure and follows a pattern.

What happens when a secularly trained lawyer or judge anywhere tries to talk about religion? Why draw attention to such an event? Why

[111] See, for example, Harold Berman, *Law and Revolution: The Formation of the Western Legal Tradition* (Cambridge: Harvard University Press, 1983); *Faith and Order: The Reconciliation of Law and Religion* (Atlanta: Scholars Press, 1993); and *The Interaction of Religion* (Nashville: Abingdon Press, 1974). The agenda of "reconciliation" is strong in Berman's work. He wishes to repair what he sees as the Enlightenment rift between law and religion.

[112] See, for example, Philip B. Kurland, *Religion and Law: Of Church and State and the Supreme Court* (Chicago: Aldine, 1961).

[113] For an early anticipation of this realization, see "Religion and the Intellectuals: A Symposium," *Partisan Review* 17 (February 1950): 103–42; "Religion and the Intellectuals II," *Partisan Review* 17 (March 1950): 215–56; "Religion and the Intellectuals III," *Partisan Review* 17 (April 1950): 313–39; "Religion and the Intellectuals IV," *Partisan Review* 17 (May-June 1950): 456–83.

speak of law *and* religion at all? Is it any different than when lawyers speak of anything else? Yes, it is different. The "and" is loaded. It implies a separation between the two, but, more than that, an insistence on a separation, which is by no means obvious from the words. Why the separation? And why the conjunction?

There is a sense in which the expression "law *and* religion" is merely a clumsy attempt to be politically correct, to expand the cultural reference of the Western philosophical problem of church and state so as to refer to all religions and to all secular authority. Like other currently fashionable "law and. . ." expressions, such as law and medicine, or law and economics, "law and religion" also seeks to see law as a cultural product in relationship with other cultural products.

But "law and religion" bears a heavier and often concealed rhetorical charge. The conjunction is provocative. It is a challenge to the secularists. It is a *religious* assertion. It makes a statement about the nature of things. "Law and religion" calls up a rich history of associations and antagonisms. It is a variation on Durkheim's sacred/profane dichotomy.[114] In this sense, to say "law and religion" is also to imply both that law and religion are somehow structurally autonomous—that law is secular—and that the two are in tension. It is to imply that these are two separate kinds of cultural artifacts which can, or perhaps must, be kept separate but which cannot get away from one another. Law, on this reading, is seen, by nature, in opposition to religion. They seem locked in combat.

"Law and religion," as a rhetorical device and as an intellectual problem, is thus *both* an acknowledgment of the human tendency to distinguish the sacred from the profane and a reification of the Enlightenment commitment to the separation of church and state. Law here means the secular law of modern industrial society and religion means religion in the context of modern pluralism. For the Enlightenment, to speak of "law and religion" is to imply that it is appropriate to keep the two distinct, that law is something we can all live together under, while religion is something we must tolerate differences about, that law is public while religion is private. Law. . . *and*. . . religion. That is the modern commitment. Law has succeeded religion. It is the

---

[114] Emile Durkheim, *The Elementary Forms of the Religious Life*, trans. Joseph Ward Swain (New York: The Free Press, 1918), 52.

first and more equal of the pair. Religious law is something of the past or of particular communities. *As religion* it is not useful to the modern secular state.

The opposition of law as secular and religion as sacred can be seductive and dangerous. While useful, one has to be conscious always of the opposition as a partial analytical representation, an historically conditioned reality, rather than as a transparent description of reality.[115] Thus, Louis Dumont's reification of hierarchy in his opposition of the roles of king and priest in Indian society,[116] while extremely helpful as an exploration of the human tendency to create hierarchy, has been subject to critique by anthropologists who have shown the considerably richer and more complex nature of those roles in Indian cultural contexts.[117]

As Nancy Jay has also convincingly shown, setting up dualist oppositions may lead one into ideological traps. From a feminist standpoint, for example, opposing law and religion may be part and parcel of buying into other patriarchal oppositions.[118] If, as Nancy Jay argues, sacrifice is men's childbirth, is it then also appropriate to regard, as she does, the abrupt end of the male Hawaiian sacrificial cult, apparently accomplished through the subversive and sacrilegious acts of women, as effecting the "*secularizing* of the Hawaiian polity?"[119] What about women's religion? Did the Reformation, similarly, by ending the male sacrificial cult of the Catholic Church, spell the inevitable secularization of Western society? It did so only if religion is regarded as inherently male.[120] The scholarship of most historians

---

[115] Jay, *Throughout Your Generations Forever*, 12ff.

[116] Louis Dumont, *Homo Hierarchicus: The Caste System and Its Implications*, trans, Mark Sainsbury, Louis Dumont, and Basia Gulati, rev. ed. (Chicago: University of Chicago Press, 1980).

[117] See, for example, Gloria Goodwin Raheja, "India: Caste, Kingship, and Dominance Reconsidered," *Annual Review of Anthropology* 17 (1988): 497–522.

[118] Patriarchial oppositions such as: sacred:profane, men:women, individual:community, immortal:mortal, culture:nature, order:chaos.

[119] Stephenie Seto Levin, "The Overthrow of the *Kapu* System in Hawaii," *Journal of the Polynesian Society* 77 (December 1968): 402–30, quoted in Jay, *Throughout Your Generations Forever*, 92.

[120] This is a position that some would certainly seem to take. Rene Girard, for example, in *Violence and the Sacred*, apparently equates religion and sacrifice. There are also feminist theorists who would take this position. See, for example, Mary Daly, *Gyn-ecology: The Metaethics of Radical Feminism* (Boston: Beacon Press, 1978).

of religions would suggest not, in both cases. The Reformation did not spell the end of religion, and religion is not usefully understood as limited to male sacrifice.[121] Religion does not end. It is transformed. It is useful to see religion and law as opposed, but this does not tell the whole story.

The rhetorical separation between law and religion in the Western context is only one instance of a much more extensive cultural phenomenon ripe for comparative study: the encounter between modern secular legal institutions and religion all over the world. Law and religion encounter one another in thousands of local contexts and courts in many countries.[122] There is always an oil and water nature to these encounters. In spite of the widespread existence of so-called religious law and the common ancestry of laws and religions, there *is* a sense in which all law is also always secular.[123]

I will assume here, then, that, while acknowledging the historical and ideological source of the distinction is important, and that there is a danger in reifying the distinction in particular instances, it *is* useful to see how law is different from religion. Law, like religion, will be held for the purposes of this conversation as distinct in its own right— whatever the historical source of its authority and symbols. Good government and justice, as well as the peculiar nature of legal discourse and practice, will be seen as distinct human goods, separate, to some extent, from religion or from tradition.[124] Such a position is also

[121] See, among burgeoning anthropological efforts to describe women's religion, Lila Abu-Lughod, *Veiled Sentiments: Honor and Poetry in a Bedouin Society* (Berkeley: University of California Press, 1986); Carol Delaney, *The Seed and the Soil: Gender and Cosmology in Turkish Village Society* (Berkeley: University of California Press, 1991); and Ann Grodzins Gold, *Fruitful Journeys: The Ways of Rajasthani Pilgrims* (Berkeley: University of California Press, 1987).

[122] See, for example, Gold, *Comprehending the Guru*, 73–74; and Marc Galanter, *Law and Society in Modern India* (Delhi: Oxford University Press, 1989), 237, 256.

[123] This does not exclude, in my view, the argument that all law is also religious, an argument espoused by natural law theorists, among others.

A dramatic example of law as religion is seen in the fact that on English naval vessels during the Napoleonic Wars, in the absence of a chaplain, the captain read the Articles of War as a substitute for a sermon. Dudley Pope, *Life in Nelson's Navy* (Annapolis: Naval Institute Press, 1981).

[124] See, for example, Elizabeth Colson, *Tradition and Contract: The Problem of Order* (Chicago: Aldine, 1974).

Failure to maintain this distinctness can result in a hold-all category of "human

consonant with the fact that the modern desirability of a secular state is widely presumed.

The distinctness of law and religion can be seen as a thread running through the classics of legal anthropology. This theme owes its origins, partly, no doubt, to Enlightenment presuppositions about the need for the separation of church and state and the subservient place of religion as well as to anthropology's nervousness about religion. There is, however, something more.

Henry Maine begins his history of European law by insisting that law, as it is understood in "progressive" societies, does not really exist until it is separated from religion. The failure to differentiate between law and religion, for Maine, is a characterizing feature of primitive society.[125] Malinowski, on the other hand, insists that law is also differentiated in primitive society, that law is "one well-defined category" which exists for Melanesians as a very practical everyday economic affair. It is "social" rather than "mystical."[126] He opposes the daily economic rationality of the Melanesians to their religious life. Llewellyn, too, carefully separates out the religious aspects of Cheyenne cases, seeking to identify the "law-stuff."[127] He notes in Chapter One that "[t]he law. . . is curiously secular in flavor for a deeply religious people."[128] In the last chapter he admires the Cheyenne for their resistance to the exploitation of religion by law.[129] Like Malinowski, Llewellyn is keen to reject Maine's suggestion that law does not really exist in primitive societies or that there is no separation between law and religion in such societies. All three agree that law is a distinct kind of social fact, distinct from religion.

In *The Judicial Process Among the Barotse of Northern Rhodesia (Zambia)*, Gluckman recounts the jurisdictional muddle which occurs

---

discourse" which submerges the differences in different kinds of social fact. See, for example, Bruce Lincoln, *Discourse and the Construction of Society: Comparative Studies of Myth, Ritual and Classification* (New York: Oxford University Press, 1989), in which religious and political discourses seem at times indistinguishable; and Girard, *Violence and the Sacred*, 23, in which law and religion are seen as functional (and interchangeable?) responses to original and primal violence.

[125] Maine, *Ancient Law*, 22.
[126] Malinowski, *Crime and Custom in Savage Society*, 54.
[127] Llewellyn and Hoebel, *Cheyenne Law*, 28.
[128] Llewellyn and Hoebel, *Cheyenne Law*, 17.
[129] Llewellyn and Hoebel, *Cheyenne Law*, 317–21.

when the Jehovah's Witnesses, called before the Barotse Court for failure to pay taxes, appeal to God. The response of the court is to dismiss the case. The judges say that they cannot talk in court to people who want to bring God into the conversation. It is the wrong forum. Although law may at times derive from religious sources, "[t]he law itself is for the Lozi. . .a different kind of social phenomena from religion."[130]

These authors speak of societies which we might consider "traditional" or pervasively religious in contrast to our own. Yet each author insists on the secularity of law, on seeing law as law and not as religion. They do this, clearly, in part, because of their commitment to disestablishment and because of a reification of the categories of law and religion. But they are also reporting on something they see.

In insisting, thus, on the secularity of law, I do not mean to suggest that the line between law and religion is not both blurred and constantly shifting. There might be times when it is useful to overlap the categories to a greater or a larger degree. For my purposes here, however, I think it is useful to hold the two apart, to go with the Enlightenment. One is able to see more clearly, then, what it means and wherein are the pitfalls when a lawyer talks about religion.

Marc Galanter, in "Hinduism, Secularism and the Judiciary," the last chapter of his book on law and society in India, discusses the difficulties of constitutional interpretation that have arisen in cases involving religion before the Supreme Court of India. Whereas the government of India is secular and freedom of religion is guaranteed by the Constitution, the Indian Supreme Court's mandate to abolish the legal effects of untouchability has resulted in the Court's involvement in the reform and remodeling of Hindu theology.[131] In a discussion of an Indian Supreme Court decision interpreting a law proscribing equal access of all Hindus to temples, Galanter constructs a typology of the possible stances of a court toward religion: separation, limitation, or intervention.

Whereas Galanter is very critical of the Indian Court's active involvement in the reform of Hindu theology with respect to untouch-

---

[130] Gluckman, *The Judicial Process*, 264.

[131] A parallel situation has arisen in the United States in the conflict between the constitutional values of religious freedom and of racial and gender equality. See, for example, Bob Jones University v. U.S., 461 U.S. 574 (1983). See chapter 4, below, for a further discussion of these issues.

ables, he is equally convinced that it is a delusion to think the two can be kept totally separate:

No secular State is or can be merely neutral or impartial among religions, for the State defines the boundaries within which neutrality must operate. For example, the First Amendment of the United States Constitution is often said to enjoin state neutrality in religious matters. But it is clear in the larger sense, American law is not neutral among religions except in a purely formal sense. In defining the boundaries within which neutrality must operate, the First Amendment is a charter for religion as well as for government.[132]

As Galanter makes clear, while law and religion are distinct, they cannot be neutral with respect to each other. They are structurally related and they construct each other.

That the Supreme Court of the United States should find itself in the position of interpreting American religion to itself is a situation full of irony and paradox. The Constitution of the United States which created the Supreme Court and which is, in turn, interpreted by the Court, was written by people of highly self-conscious ambivalence toward religion, particularly religion in public life. The Constitution itself is almost totally devoid of explicit religious reference. The only explicit religious reference in the Constitution itself is in the prohibition of a religious test for public office.[133] Many of the authors of the Constitution, as is well known, were suspicious of the negative effects of established religion on government and public life and well-being as well as of the negative effects on the church of enforced participation. Furthermore, their personal religion was of a rather thin, attenuated kind on the whole: formal, intellectual, rational. It was rather anemic if it was there at all.[134]

It is important to remember, however, that the writing of the Constitution and the subsequent history of its interpretation has taken

---

[132] Galanter, *Law and Society in Modern India*, 249.

[133] *U.S. Constitution*, art. 6. See Stephen Botein, "Religious Dimensions of the Early American State," in *Beyond Confederation: Origins of the Constitution and American National Identity*, ed. Richard Beeman, Stephen Botein, and Edward C. Carter, II (Chapel Hill: University of North Carolina Press, 1987), for a discussion of the reasons for this lack.

[134] Henry May, *The Enlightenment in America* (New York: Oxford University Press, 1976).

place within a constantly changing religious and legal culture. The end of the eighteenth century in America and Europe was a time of very low church attendance and of weak conventional religiosity, a civilizational pause, perhaps, before the great religious revivals of the nineteenth century. Population was booming, but many rural areas in Europe and America lacked churches. Parts of Europe and America were not evangelized at all, in any sense of the word, until the nineteenth century.[135] In France, the privileged legal position of the Catholic Church was abolished by the Revolution practically overnight, and almost accidentally. Virtually all of its property was confiscated. The astonishing fact is how few seem to have regretted the loss.[136] While the lack in religious culture was supplied for some in France and in America by revolutionary cults, organized religion seems to have been in momentary disarray along with society and politics. Law, however, was in the ascendancy. There was tremendous confidence in law.

In contrast, the nineteenth century was a time of religious revival and of church building. Dedicated and tireless evangelists sought to fill the vacuum left by the Revolution. Every new American settlement needed a church spire. Christianity moved west with the pioneers.[137] A new piety, a religion of the heart, replaced the rational Christianity of the eighteenth century.[138] And a new religious flavor infused the government, finding its most eloquent spokesman in Abraham Lincoln.

The early twentieth century brought new religious concerns to the American churches. To the Protestant mainstream it brought the Fundamentals and the Social Gospel. To the Catholics it meant the coming of age of immigrant Catholic communities. For the Court, as well as for the society at large, concern for the unfinished business of racial justice brought a growing obsession with political equality, an obsession that radically affected the public discourse about religion.[139]

---

[135] Hugh McLeod, *Religion and the People of Western Europe 1789–1970* (Oxford: Oxford University Press, 1981), 57.

[136] John McManners, *The French Revolution and the Church* (New York: Harper & Row, 1969).

[137] See Laurie Maffly Kip, *Religion and Society in Frontier California* (New Haven: Yale University Press, 1994).

[138] Jaroslav Pelikan, *Christian Doctrine and Modern Culture (since 1700)* (Chicago: University of Chicago Press, 1989), 118ff.

[139] See Howe, *The Garden and the Wilderness*, for a discussion of the effect of the Fourteenth Amendment on the jurisprudence of the First Amendment.

The Supreme Court thus finds itself conceived as an Enlightenment institution with not much of an ear for religion, having grown up in a culture of sometimes oppressive evangelical piety, and having begun to find a voice about the First Amendment in the 1940s when political rather than religious concerns were to the fore.[140] These three distinctive modern American modes of talking about religion—Enlightenment rationality, anti-intellectual pietism, and the politics of equality—have alternatively enriched and plagued both the Court and the academic study of religion for the last two hundred years.[141]

When an American lawyer talks about religion, then, it is in a highly charged cultural and political context. Transcending the boundary between law and religion—trespassing, if you will—is highly suspect. It is a professional faux pas. Acknowledging religion other than in a highly contained, distanced, historical frame is risky. That religion and law are usefully seen as distinct, however, and that they are politically to be kept separate does not exclude the possibility that they are related and that they continually interact. Separation does not and cannot mean total neutrality, if neutrality means lack of interest or lack of understanding. If a lawyer is to talk about religion, she should know what she is talking about, and what the "and" in religion and law means.

American courts do not have the option of ignoring religion. They are paradoxically required by the very amendment to the United States Constitution that is arguably intended to keep the two apart to talk to religious people and to talk about religion. I do not here propose that the Court adopt a definition of religion, Durkheimian or otherwise. I propose rather that it undertake to participate in a mode of discourse and practice about human religion that acknowledges the limits of secularism and employs a less impoverished religious anthropology.

Whereas, as Durkheim and others have observed, it is in the nature of the human religious imagination to distinguish between the sacred and the profane, legislating on the basis of that perception is extremely difficult because of the shifting and fertile nature of religion. The

---

[140] The creation of a First Amendment jurisprudence by the Supreme Court only began in the 1940s, after the First Amendment had been applied to the states through the Incorporation Doctrine. Further discussion of this point may be found in chapter 4, below.

[141] See the writings of Jonathan Z. Smith cited previously in nn. 84, 85, and 94.

structural possibilities of the coexistence of a secular state and of human religion in a situation of radical pluralism—plural religious and legal traditions, plural reading of those traditions, and plural experiences of those readings—are not obvious. While acknowledging that, broadly defined, religious and legal readings and accounts can be offered of all cultural phenomena, I will argue that the First Amendment requires that the Court, in religion cases, read law narrowly and religion broadly, to avoid establishing either.

In this book, using primarily one set of Supreme Court opinions as an example, I will argue that the encounter of American law and American religion will be more successful if American lawyers, judges, and legal scholars enrich their discourse about American religion by participating in and contributing to a larger conversation about the nature of human religion and of the relationship of religion and culture and society. Rather than focusing on the intellectual history of the relationship of Christian institutions to the development of law, either in the West generally or in the United States in particular,[142] I will focus on how law as a privileged location for a specialized practical and secular cultural discourse can and should talk and act about the religiousness of Americans. I will argue that viewing the Court as a location for a type of secular cultural discourse and practice and history of religions as a model for a discourse and practice about religion as a complex and universal human creation will be a starting place for the articulation of an appropriate relationship between law and religion in the modern state. Both arguments will assume that law and religion are constructed intellectual categories, not essentialist ones. The following chapters will explore the interaction of law and religion in relation to the opinions by the United States Supreme Court in the case of *Lynch v. Donnelly.*[143]

---

[142] I believe, though, that this is a necessary and useful exercise. See, for example, Harold Berman, *Law and Revolution.*

[143] 465 U.S. 668 (1983).

Chapter 2

Lynch v. Donnelly

It was as he suspected. The Sahibs prayed to their God; for in the centre of the Mess table—its sole ornament when they were on the line of march—stood a golden bull fashioned from old-time loot of the summer palace at Pekin—a red-gold bull with lowered head, ramping upon a field of Irish green. To him the Sahibs held out their glasses and cried aloud confusedly.

—Kipling, *Kim*[1]

Each one of us is entirely free to find his history in other places than the pages of the *United States Reports*.

—Howe, *The Garden and the Wilderness*[2]

On 5 March 1984, the Supreme Court of the United States announced its decision in the case of *Lynch v. Donnelly*, holding that the city of Pawtucket, Rhode Island, had not unconstitutionally established religion[3] when it included a life-sized crèche[4] as a central feature of

[1] Rudyard Kipling, *Kim* (London: Macmillan, 1901; reprint, children's edition, 1958), 118.

[2] Howe, *The Garden and the Wilderness*, 5.

[3] The establishment clause of the First Amendment to the United States Constitution provides that "Congress shall make no law respecting an establishment of religion."

[4] According to the *Encyclopedia Britannica*, a crèche is ". . . in Christianity, the crib showing the infant Jesus in a manger; beside Mary and Joseph, animals, shepherds, angels and the Magi are often added. St. Francis of Assisi is credited with popularizing the devotion, which probably already existed before his time." 15th ed., s.v. "Crèche."

Caroline Walker Bynum disagrees: "It was a low country woman, Mary of Oignies, not Francis of Assisi, who invented the Christmas crèche." *Fragmentation and Redemption*, 56.

its annual civic Christmas display. The importance of the decision was variously regarded by local officials, by the press, and by academic commentators. Mayor Kinch of Pawtucket termed the decision "a triumph for religious freedom."[5] The *Barrington Times* called it "a defeat for. . .religious freedom."[6] The *Wall Street Journal* entitled its editorial on the *Lynch* decision, "Trivial Pursuits?"[7] *Newsweek* announced: "This is one of those fights that can only make things worse no matter which side wins."[8] Legal scholars found the decision confused.[9] Why did the *Lynch* decision produce such varied and mutually contradictory reactions? Why do the Supreme Court decisions in this area generally produce mainly conflict and confusion, rather than either resolution or constructive dialogue?

The *Lynch* decision was widely viewed as a serious blow by political advocates of the separation of church and state and as a victory for the religious right.[10] But the most serious issue was raised by Meg

---

[5] Quoted in Wayne Swanson, *The Christ Child Goes to Court* (Philadelphia: Temple University Press, 1990), 159. Swanson's book is a sociological description of the *Lynch* litigation designed to be used as an undergraduate teaching text. I am indebted to Professor Swanson for his collection of many of the details of the litigation history of the case.

[6] Quoted in Swanson, *The Christ Child*, 160.

[7] *Wall Street Journal*, 7 March 1984, 30.

[8] *Newsweek*, 24 December 1984, 72.

[9] See, for example, Philip B. Kurland, "The Religion Clauses and the Burger Court," *Catholic University Law Review* 34 (fall 1984): 1–18; and "The Supreme Court, 1983 Term," *Harvard Law Review* 98 (November 1984): 1–314.

[10] Left and right are clumsy political labels, at best, but they are particularly inaccurate and inept terms in the area of religion. Left and right in politics does not necessarily correspond to left and right in theology, so that one must be careful to identify what is being modified by the adjectives left and right. It might be more accurate to say, with respect to religious attitudes toward the Supreme Court's First Amendment jurisprudence, that there exists a loose affiliation of religious groups, some—but certainly not all—of whom might properly be called fundamentalist and/or evangelical, and who, in reaction to what they see as an "establishment" of "secular humanism" and a general hostility toward religion by the federal government, seek a greater public expression of religious faith. Some of these groups espouse the teaching of creationism, the return of prayer to the public schools, public support for parochial education, and a greater explicit influence of religion in debate on public issues.

It would be fair to say, I think, that a very broad range of religious groups would agree that there should be a greater public acknowledgment of religion and that

Greenfield in the *Newsweek* editorial: the possibility of informed and constructive conversation on the subject. Greenfield quoted Gibbon to the effect that religious tolerance existed in ancient Rome because the people believed all religions to be true, the intellectuals believed all religions to be false, and the government believed all religions to be useful. This aphorism may have described American attitudes at one time. It seems inadequate now.

Whatever the correct result in *Lynch*, the litigation history of the case and the various opinions by the judges who deliberated on it present fertile ground for consideration of how religion in late twentieth-century American public life is represented in legal and other public discourse. As one listens to the many voices in the *Lynch* case, one hears a variety of competing discourses about religion. What is religion for each of these people and what role should law play with respect to religion? How are the two related?

In this chapter I will introduce the *Lynch* case, the social and cultural context in which it arose, the legal issues, and the opinions of the trial court and of the court of appeals. Later chapters will explore these issues in more detail with respect to each of the four opinions of the United States Supreme Court in *Lynch*. The *Lynch* case will be viewed both as an historical text to be decoded and as a legal document.

---

privatization of religious expression and a dogmatic Jeffersonian separation are inadequate bases for public policy. Fewer would agree on the actual solution being public display of religious symbols, government sponsorship of religious teaching, and government celebration of religious rites.

Amicus briefs filed in the Court in First Amendment cases reflect the shifting alliances of particular denominations on this issue. Religious groups that once would not give each other the time of day are finding themselves bedfellows in opposition to what they see as the arid ascendancy of secularism. The number of religious organizations filing "accommodationist" Amicus briefs in the Supreme Court has greatly increased since the *Lynch* case. In Board of Education v. Grumet, 1994 WL 279673 (U.S.N.Y.), Amicus briefs supporting an accommodationist position were filed by the United States Catholic Conference, the Rutherford Institute, the Christian Legal Society, the National Association of Evangelicals, the Southern Center for Law and Ethics, the Family Research Council, the Institute for Religion and Polity, the Southern Baptist Convention, the Christian Life Commission, the Knights of Columbus, the Archdiocese of New York, the National Jewish Commission on Law and Public Affairs, the American Center for Law and Justice, and the Catholic League for Religious and Civil Rights.

THE FACTS

The action against Dennis Lynch, then mayor of Pawtucket, and other city officials was filed in the United States District Court[11] in Providence on 17 December 1980, one week before Christmas, by Daniel Donnelly, a local member of the American Civil Liberties Union (the ACLU), and by the Rhode Island chapter of the ACLU. The complaint alleged that display of a crèche by the city, at taxpayers' expense, violated the establishment clause of the First Amendment. The action sought a temporary restraining order against the city requiring immediate removal of the crèche from its Christmas display.

Judge Raymond Pettine of the United States District Court for the District of Rhode Island postponed consideration of the matter until after Christmas because of "the emotional storm" raised by the filing of the suit:

The timing of the suit brought a swift and passionate response from the public. The reaction was almost universal outrage that the ACLU would challenge this longstanding community tradition.[12]

The three-day trial began on 3 February 1981.

The city of Pawtucket is a relatively old American city that was founded in the first half of the seventeenth century by religious dissenters fleeing Massachusetts Bay Colony. As the home of J. & P. Coats and Co., the thread capital of the world, Pawtucket flourished during the nineteenth century as an important mill town, but, like many New England mill towns, has since declined economically. Pawtucket is the fourth largest city in a largely urbanized state.[13] Founded by Puritans on land purchased from the Narragansett, Pawtucket is now more than 70 percent Roman Catholic, as it is largely inhabited by the

---

[11] The claim could be filed in federal district court rather than in the state courts of Rhode Island because the claim was founded in the United States Constitution rather than in the Rhode Island Constitution. Plaintiffs undoubtedly chose to do so in order to have the advantage of a presumably more impartial (favorable?) federal forum.

[12] Swanson, *The Christ Child*, 19.

[13] In 1980 the population of Pawtucket was 71,204. Department of Commerce. Bureau of the Census. *1980 Census of Population and Housing: Congressional Districts of the 98th Congress*, Pt. 41 Rhode Island (1983).

descendants of Catholic immigrants from French Canada, Ireland, Italy, Portugal, Poland, and Hispanic countries.

David R. Carlin, Jr., a Democratic member of the Rhode Island Senate and professor of sociology at the University of Rhode Island, grew up in Pawtucket. He described Pawtucket in his article on the *Lynch* case for *Commonweal*:

> Pawtucket is a heavily Catholic city in a state which has a higher percentage of Catholics in its population (nearly 65 percent) than any other in the union. . . . It is a working-class and lower-middle class town, with the former more numerous than the latter. . . . The city is utterly devoid of elite amenities but abounds in proletarian comforts. . . . Though of course I didn't realize it at the time, Pawtucket was a kind of protective ghetto when I was growing up. . . . Being Catholic, it seemed, was the most normal thing in the world.[14]

Virtually every person involved in this case at the trial court level was Roman Catholic: the plaintiff, the defendants, the lawyers, and the district court judge.[15]

At the time of trial, the city of Pawtucket had, for over forty years, sponsored a Christmas display in a park on the outskirts of town. The city-owned display had been moved to a private park in the center of town in 1973 to give a boost to downtown merchants who had lost business to the shopping malls in a time of economic recession.[16]

Approximately a year after the suit was filed, Judge Pettine, a lifelong resident of Rhode Island and a graduate of Boston University,

---

[14] David R. Carlin, Jr., "Pawtucket and Its Nativity Scene," *Commonweal*, 16 December 1983, pp. 682–84.

[15] The local director of the ACLU, not a party to the litigation, was raised Jewish. Donnelly v. Lynch, 525 F. Supp. 1150, 1157 (1981). (The names of the parties are reversed on appeal because defendants, having lost in the lower court, were the initiators of the appeal. The appellants' names then appear first in the style of the case.)

I do not wish to suggest that the appellation Roman Catholic is necessarily determinative of a particular religious or political attitude. The Roman Catholic cultural context of this dispute is relevant, however, and helps to explain some of the cultural misunderstandings in this case. The Catholicisms in this case will be discussed further in chapters 5 and 6.

See also Demerath and Williams, *A Bridging of Faiths*, for a sociological analysis of religion and politics since the Vietnam War in Springfield, Massachusetts, another New England town which, like Pawtucket, went from being a Yankee town to a Roman Catholic city during the nineteenth century.

[16] Swanson, *The Christ Child*, 11–12.

issued his decision in an exceptionally long and thoughtful opinion. His opinion opened with a description of the display:

Hodgson Park, the location of the Christmas display, is a privately owned open space area of approximately 40,000 square feet. . . in the heart of the downtown shopping district. . . . With the private owner's permission, the City enters Hodgson Park each year in November and erects a lighted Christmas display. City employees, or city-paid contractors, perform the setup work. The City owns the lights, figures, and buildings that make up the display; it reimburses the private owner for all the electricity used by the display. Subject to the final approval of the Director of Parks and Recreation, a City maintenance supervisor designs the layout of the display. The Mayor may make changes in the layout.

The 1980–81 display contained the following:
—a "talking" wishing well
—Santa's House, inhabited by a live Santa who distributed candy
—a grouping of caroler/musician figures in old-fashioned dress, standing
    on a low platform surrounded by six large artificial candles
—a small "village" composed of four houses and a church
—four large, five-pointed stars covered with small white electric lights
—three painted wooden Christmas tree cutouts
—a live, 40' Christmas tree hung with lights
—a spray of reindeer pulling Santa's sleigh, set on an elevated runway
—a long garland hung from candy-striped poles
—cutout letters, colored in fluorescent paint, that spell "SEASON'S
    GREETINGS"
—21 cutout figures representing such varied characters as a clown, a
    dancing elephant, a robot and a teddy bear
—the nativity scene at issue in this case. . . .

The nativity scene occupies the foreground of the display. . . .

The figures in the nativity scene are approximately life sized. They include kings bearing gifts, shepherds, animals, angels, and Mary and Joseph kneeling near the manger in which the baby lies with arms spread in apparent benediction. All of the figures face the manger in which the baby lies; several have their hands folded and/or are kneeling. The figures' poses coupled with their facial expressions, connote an atmosphere of devotion, worship, and awe. The stable is inexplicably shored up with two hockey sticks. Some of the figures are chipped, and the paint on several is peeling. (citations to the record omitted)[17]

Standing alone, this is a curious narrative. It is a model of studied ethnographic objectivity, even to being styled in the timeless ethno-

---

[17] Donnelly v. Lynch, 525 F. Supp. 1150, 1155–56 (1981).

graphic present.[18] Its meaning is strangely opaque. In his effort to present The Facts without bias, Judge Pettine has created a parody of anthropological field notes. He invites us to see our own culture as anthropologists "see" "other" cultures, without cultural preconceptions. He gives us the opportunity to "bracket" our own assumptions and to look with fresh eyes. Whether and how this can be done is a matter of some debate, however, among anthropologists. If we bring nothing to it, if we have no categories and no context, how can we understand it at all? As Nancy Jay says, a religious event can "mean" anything—or nothing.[19] How do we find what this display is about? What and how does it mean? And to whom? Why does "the city" go to so much trouble to erect this odd assortment of objects? Where do we go for the answers to these questions?

With a little history and a little theory of religious symbolism and folklore, one could construct a plausible "religious" story about each of the items in the Pawtucket display. A "'talking' wishing well" evokes European folk oracles of many kinds. A Santa distributing candy recalls a rich history of European folk celebrations of visitors bringing gifts. Candles, stars, trees, poles, the construction of temporary housing, the distribution of food, lights, dancing, and flying animals—all this, even without the nativity scene, is the very stuff of ritual and of religious symbolism. To a student of religion, this is a motherlode of sacred objects.[20] One might even construct a religious explanation to help Judge Pettine out of his puzzlement about the sacred quality of hockey sticks and their role in midwinter New England life.

All of the participants in the case, however, including Pettine, seem to have assumed that the sacred was located, if anywhere, in the crèche—notwithstanding the flat tone in which the crèche was added

---

[18] Both Fabian and Noonan have criticized the politically distancing effect of this mode of description, Fabian in anthropological writing and Noonan in legal writing. Fabian, *Time and the Other*, and Noonan, *Persons and Masks*.

[19] Jay, *Throughout Your Generations Forever*. In her first chapter, Jay discusses at length the subtle difficulties of interpreting religious rituals and symbols. See, especially, 13–16.

[20] See Eliade, *Patterns*, for one well-known attempt to account for and categorize many natural and constructed objects as locations for the sacred.

For one attempt to bring together and account for the diverse symbolism of Christmas, see, William Sanson, *A Book of Christmas* (New York: McGraw Hill, 1968).

to the list in Pettine's description. He made a valiant attempt to see the crèche as one more object, but, as is revealed in his later description of the figures in the crèche, the categories he and others brought to the trial seemed to derail that attempt. It is the figures themselves that, in Pettine's words, "connote an atmosphere of devotion, worship, and awe."

After his description of the display, Judge Pettine went on to summarize the testimony of the witnesses and the exhibits at trial before considering the applicable law. Witnesses for the plaintiffs, including plaintiff Daniel Donnelly, testified that the city's display of the crèche produced in them the conviction that its purpose was government promotion of the religious views of the majority. In other words, the city of Pawtucket had, through the display, officially endorsed Christianity as the city's religion. Donnelly himself "testified that his reaction was one of fear," and that such government support was "contrary to his own *belief* in the separation of church and state" (emphasis added).[21]

Witnesses for the defendants, on the other hand, including the mayor himself, testified that the purpose of the display of the crèche, as of the entire display, was to build community morale and bring commerce into the city. He analogized it to other cultural and traditional events sponsored by the city, such as the Fourth of July, Memorial Day, and Veterans' Day. The display, featured as a part of the downtown redevelopment effort, was intended to boost the city's economy.

The adversarial structure of litigation combined with the language of the First Amendment as interpreted by the courts thus reinforced an opposition between a "sacred" and a "secular" reading of the crèche. The plaintiffs' rendering of the intended effect of display of the crèche is of the celebration of a sacred object. The defendants' rendering is that the intention was secular. There is no room in the structure of a trial or of the First Amendment for a middle position. There is no room for the position that the crèche can be both sacred and secular at the same time.

Expert witnesses also testified for both sides. Michael Werle, a clinical psychologist, and Thomas Ramsbey, a Methodist minister and a professor of the sociology of religion, testified for the plaintiff. Werle

----

[21] 525 F. Supp. at 1156.

testified that the nativity scene was "a very powerful symbol of worship" and that the display could cause a crisis of identity on the part of non-Christian viewers, especially young children. The display, he said, "reinforces an already prevalent attitude in our country that we are a Christian country" and "leads to the view that non-Christians are 'somewhat less important and have less merit.'"[22]

Ramsbey, also testifying for the plaintiffs, affirmed the religiousness of the crèche as a symbol because of its close connection with Christianity. He adhered, he said, to a theory of symbols which held that "sacred" symbols are "those which are clearly associated with a particular group." "Profane" symbols, in contrast, "are not closely tied to particular groups."[23] "They 'belong' to everyone." In the Pawtucket case, moreover, he felt that the setting "demeaned the Christian symbol."[24]

Defendants' expert, David Freeman, professor of philosophy at the University of Rhode Island, testified that symbols "function contextually" and concluded that:

[a] symbol in a religious context would be a religious symbol and have a religious impact. A symbol in a non-religious context will not be a religious symbol and will not have a religious impact.[25]

In the context of the Pawtucket display, then, Freeman concluded, the crèche was not a religious symbol. Pettine quoted his testimony:

"[People] are not going there to worship or to pray, they're going there to shop, and the function the display would have for most people at least—the great majority, if not all—would seem to be to participate in the Christmas spirit, brotherhood, peace, and let loose with their money." Personally, Dr. Freeman does not attach any religious significance to the crèche; indeed, he finds the Hodgson Park display aesthetically displeasing.[26]

Dr. Freeman seems to have felt that the combination of commerce and ugliness excluded the sacred.

Finally, Judge Pettine summarized the many letters about the display

---

[22] 525 F. Supp. at 1159.
[23] 525 F. Supp. at 1160.
[24] Swanson, *The Christ Child*, 38.
[25] 525 F. Supp. at 1161.
[26] 525 F. Supp. at 1161.

received, after the suit was filed, by the ACLU, Mayor Lynch, and the local newspapers, all of which had been admitted as exhibits in the case:

Overall the tenor of the correspondence is that the lawsuit represents an attack on the presence of religion as part of the community's life, an attempt to deny the majority the ability to express publically [sic] its beliefs in a desired and traditionally accepted way. In the Mayor's words, "The people absolutely resent somebody trying to impose another kind of religion on them. . . . I think the denigration, trying to eliminate these kinds of things, is a step towards establishing another religion, non-religion that it may be."[27]

Mayor Lynch seems to have been beleaguered by conflicting constituencies. During the course of the litigation, he moved from a commercial-civic view of the display to a religiously sectarian one. While his initial response to the filing of the action was that it was not about religion, he was finally moved to act as a defender of the faith, rashly announcing to the press at a rally/news conference held by him in front of the crèche some time after the suit was filed, that his purpose was indeed to fight the ACLU's effort "to take Christ out of Christmas."[28]

One cannot help but agree, after this array of views, with those who find the use of competing expert witnesses in an adversary context unhelpful. It certainly does not increase the credibility of academic research.[29] The diversity of opinion does, however, dramatize the fact that it *is* hard to locate the religion and therefore the constitutional issue in this evidence. Who is doing what to whose religion here? If the state is to stay away from religion, how is it to know how to do that, unless the experts can agree on where and what religion is?

There is a considerable difference of opinion here as to what is or what is not a religious symbol, even among the experts. Werle seems to be concerned with the psychological effects of cultural imperialism, a problem which is, in a way, independent of the religiousness of the

---

[27] 525 F. Supp. at 1162.

[28] 525 F. Supp. at 1173.

[29] For views on the use of scientific evidence in the courtroom, see Sheila Jasanoff, "Acceptable Evidence in a Pluralistic Society," and Kristin Shrader-Frechette, "Reductionist Approaches to Risk," in *Acceptable Evidence: Science and Values in Risk Management*, eds. Deborah G. Mayo and Rachelle D. Hollander (New York: Oxford University Press, 1991); and Peter Huber, *Galileo's Revenge: Junk Science in the Courtroom* (New York: Basic Books, 1991).

crèche. Ramsbey attempts a Durkheimian reading of the crèche and its purpose. He sees the crèche as belonging to a community. Outside that community, presumably, it has no religious meaning. Freeman, on the other hand, sees the crèche in terms of its microsociological location. The commercial location seems to have the automatic effect of desacralizing the crèche. Moreover, he is aesthetically offended by the whole event. While they each make relevant comments about the nature of the display, together these experts are not particularly helpful to the Court. In a sense each of them is right. Although it can be argued that there are universal symbols whose meaning transcends particular cultural contexts, deriving their import from either cosmic or subconscious mental structures, and that human religion is dependent on such universal symbols,[30] most academic religious theorists would agree basically with Werle that cultural imperialism is a serious issue, with Ramsbey that groups invest symbols with meaning, and with Freeman that religious symbols do not have inherent "meaning" apart from the structure of the particular cultural context in which they are created and encountered. But this does not help us or the Court very much. Which group and which context is the appropriate one in this case?

Judge Pettine struggles heroically to understand the proffered theories of symbols and to apply them to the crèche, and, in the end, relies on his own instinct about the matter. Judge Pettine's symbolic theory seems to be that if a symbol is understood (by him) to illustrate a particular biblical narrative then it is an *inherently* religious symbol:

[U]nlike stars, or bells, or trees, the crèche is not a common, ordinary object that attains a religious dimension only if the viewer understands that it is intended to connote something more than its facial significance, and possesses the key to unlock that secondary meaning. The crèche is more immediately

---

[30] Is the nativity scene such a symbol? Perhaps. Biblical scholars certainly agree that neither the story of a virgin birth nor the incarnation of a divinity in the birth of a human child is original to the gospel stories. Such stories are widespread in ancient religious traditions. *Anchor Bible Dictionary,* s.v. "Infancy Narratives in the NT Gospels."

Some scholars would argue that the search for "meaning" is the wrong tack, that the import of symbolic structures is in their structures. Any "meaning" is embodied by the structures, which in turn reflect the structures of the human mind. See, for example, Claude Lévi-Strauss, *The Raw and the Cooked*, trans. John and Doreen Weightman, *Introduction to a Science of Mythology*, vol. 1 (New York: Harper & Row, 1969).

connected to the religious import of Christmas because it is a direct representation of the full Biblical account of the birth of Christ. . . .

In sum, the Court does not understand what meaning the crèche, as a symbol, can have other than a religious meaning. . . .

. . .the crèche does not lose its power to make a theological statement simply because it is removed from a Christian church, nor is it any less a religious symbol because it does not necessarily invoke a response of worship.[31]

The crèche tells the biblical story of the birth of Christ; it is, therefore, a religious symbol.

But the crèche *is* in fact composed of common ordinary objects, like stars, bells, and trees, to which Judge Pettine "possesses the key to unlock the secondary meaning." The crèche shows a family and animals gathered around a newborn baby. What can be more ordinary or more universal? Such a scene, just like a star or a tree, arguably *only* has "meaning" if it is viewed as religious either because of its historical and cultural context or because it participates in universal structures. It is religious, according to his theory, because he, Pettine, can understand its secondary meanings.

Pettine is surely right. A crèche is not really out of context in an American city unless it is displayed to people who have never heard the story of the birth of Christ. Such people may exist, but not in Pawtucket, Rhode Island, in 1980. Maybe Pettine does not go far enough. The crèche seems rather to have too many "religious" contexts—too many secondary meanings—rather than too few. The crèche "means" different things to different people, even, at times, different things to the same people at different times: to Lynch, to Donnelly, to Werle, to Ramsbey, to Freeman, to the shopkeepers, to the children, to Pettine. . . . The cliché that symbols are multivalent finds confirmation in this kaleidoscope of readings. More witnesses, one would guess, would only have produced more theories and new emotional reactions.

Among the participants to this litigation, the range of readings of the crèche is structured both by the person's religious attitudes and background and by the person's political convictions. Because of the heavy ideological load carried by any form of public religiosity in this country, whether or not one views the crèche as a religious symbol is

[31] 525 F. Supp. at 1167–68.

related to whether or not one thinks it is appropriately displayed. On the whole, the plaintiffs and Judge Pettine see the crèche as different from the rest of the display and as intensely religious in a sectarian sense, *both* because it tells a story from the Bible *and* because, in their view, government display of a Christian symbol is an oppressive majoritarian action. The defendants, in contrast, see the crèche as part of a larger, more diffuse whole, a celebration of a public holiday and of the municipality, which is open-ended and subject to many readings. They are also more comfortable with a majoritarian ideological establishment.

The structural connection between these two different cultural styles of combining religion and politics, individual religious particularism and religious establishments, is explored at length in Howe's *Garden and the Wilderness*. Howe believes that a *de facto* Protestant establishment is paired historically in the American context with a lowering of individual religious freedom while a high level of separation is conjoined with a greater concern for religious freedom. This pattern, Howe believes, can be seen in the history of the Court's religion opinions. It can also be seen in the two sides of this case.[32] It is a pattern the accommodationists are trying to break. It is an extremely tenacious cultural structure. Perhaps it cannot be broken. Perhaps a moderate, even tolerant, establishment and true religious freedom are incompatible.

THE LAW

Having summarized the evidence produced at trial, Judge Pettine then turned to the legal arguments in the case. In doing so he entered a confusing and murky area of constitutional interpretation.

The establishment clause of the First Amendment to the United States Constitution provides that "Congress shall make no law respecting an establishment of religion." Interpretation of the words of the Constitution is always a subtle and risky business. Like that of many other provisions in the Constitution, the meaning of the First Amendment is not self-evident. The words of the First Amendment, however, present particular problems. Does the First Amendment mean only that *Congress* may not establish a *national* church, while states

---

[32] Howe, *The Garden and the Wilderness*, 43.

may establish state churches?[33] Does it mean that neither Congress nor the states may institute single establishments but are free to institute multiple establishments as long as they are nonpreferential, as some have argued?[34] Or does it mean that multiple establishments were also specifically excluded?[35] Does it mean that government may "accommodate" religion as long as it is not coercive?[36] Does it mean that the two religion clauses should be read together to require that laws should be completely neutral toward religion, never making religion a legislative category, either to confer a benefit or to impose a burden?[37] Is non-religion protected by the First Amendment religion clauses? If so, does *any* government acknowledgment of or aid to religion or religious institutions offend a constitutionally imposed equality of believers and non-believers? What did the founders mean by religion? And, finally, how do we know the answers to any of these questions? Can we?

The proper method for interpreting the language of a written constitution is much debated and highly charged, politically. Two seductively simple methods, with great political appeal, are "original intent" and "plain meaning." Attempting to determine the "original intent" of the framers of the Constitution in the case of the First

---

[33] The First Amendment, which, by its terms, refers only to Congress, was made applicable to the states under the Incorporation Doctrine. Under the Incorporation Doctrine the Supreme Court has read the Fourteenth Amendment's due process clause to "incorporate" the First Amendment and thereby apply it to the states. Everson v. Board of Education, 330 U.S. 1 (1947). See chapter 4, below, for further discussion of the Incorporation Doctrine and its effect on First Amendment jurisprudence.

Some scholars continue to argue that the incorporation of the First Amendment religion clauses, particularly the establishment clause, into the Fourteenth was a mistake because it is not framed as a "right," as the Fourteenth Amendment is. See, for example, William K. Lietzau, "Rediscovering the Establishment Clause: Federalism and the Rollback of Incorporation," *DePaul Law Review* 39 (summer 1990): 1191–234.

[34] Robert L. Cord, *Separation of Church and State: Historical Fact and Current Fiction* (New York: Lambeth Press, 1982).

[35] Leonard Levy, *The Establishment Clause: Religion and the First Amendment* (New York: Macmillan, 1986).

[36] See Allegheny v. ACLU, 492 U.S. 573 (1989); and Lee v. Weisman, 112 S. Ct. 2649 (1992) (Scalia, dissenting).

[37] Philip Kurland, "Of Church and State and the Supreme Court," *University of Chicago Law Review* 29 (autumn 1961): 1–96.

Amendment has resulted in a monumental amount of scholarship about the historical context of its passage but no clear answers. All commentators argue that their interpretation is *proven* by history.[38] "Historical" support, whatever that is, can be found for all theories. It is like proof-texts in arguments over biblical interpretation. There is always one more piece of evidence. And, also like biblical interpretation, it is very difficult to see the words of the Constitution as new, apart from the interpretation and reverent ideology that encrust them.

The doctrine of original intent is based on a rigid and deterministic theory of history: that the words of the Constitution can be unambiguously understood by discovering the intent of the framers. But, how does one discover the intent about anything of legislators who lived two hundred years ago? And whose intent counts? What about the intent of the thousands who voted to ratify the Constitution?[39] And, is intent the issue? Perhaps intent should not matter in deciding what effect the words of legislators should have. Perhaps the words should stand on their own. It is they which have been enacted, not the minds of the legislators. It may in fact be the very ambiguousness of the words that permits legislative compromise. Thomas Jefferson was very nervous about legislating for the future, even suggesting that a new revolution and a new Constitution might be needed periodically, that "[t]he tree of liberty. . .be refreshed from time to time with the blood of patriots and tyrants."[40]

"Plain meaning" is appealing as an idea. How, though, can one determine the plain meaning of these words? And at what time? The

---

[38] Cord, *Separation of Church and State,* and Levy, *The Establishment Clause,* are good examples of this problem. With opposite conclusions, they both appeal to the historical record and declare it to be conclusive. The result is only to call into question the whole doctrine of original intent.

[39] See Edward Levi, *An Introduction to Legal Reasoning* (Chicago: University of Chicago Press, 1948), for a discussion of the difficulties of determining legislative intent in the case of the Mann Act.

See also Ruti Teitel, "Original Intent, History and Levy's *Establishment Clause,*" *Law and Social Inquiry* 5 (June 1992): 591–609, criticizing the use of original intent in the religion area and arguing that the Court has tended to be majoritarian in this area, looking to historical continuities and consensus. Teitel urges the Court to take a prophetic role in considering the difficult contemporary issues of diversity and difference.

[40] Thomas Jefferson to William S. Smith, 13 November 1787, *Writings of Thomas Jefferson* (New York: Library of America, 1984), 910–12.

meaning of words does not stand still. The problems of recovering the past are problems which all historians face in trying to understand causation in human history. The academic issues are given heightened emotional and political significance when projected onto the political arena.

Both of these methods of constitutional interpretation, if used exclusively and mechanically, attempt to avoid the inescapable and extraordinarily difficult job of interpreting and reinterpreting through time the broad words and principles of the Constitution.[41] Both, however, can contribute important insights to an understanding of the document and of its history, and thus to its interpretations. James Boyd White, in his *Justice as Translation*, offers a sustained critique of both original intent and plain meaning as methods of constitutional interpretation, suggesting that interpreting the Constitution is inevitably an exercise in constructing meaning, an exercise informed with the tools both of history and of textual criticism, all within the context of a changing cultural community. There is no short cut. It only works if it is difficult.

Most commentators agree that the First Amendment does more than prohibit a single national church,[42] but that it does not and cannot forbid *all* government action "respecting" religion. Many would also argue that there has to be some form of "acknowledgment" by government of the religiousness of Americans and of the importance of religion in American public life, whether or not that was the intention of all of the founders.

The Court has also chosen this difficult middle way but has found itself deciding each case with very little increase in principled interpretation of the constitutional language. Property tax exemption

---

[41] Howe, in *The Garden and the Wilderness,* is eloquent on the pitfalls of using history in understanding the First Amendment. See also Barry Sullivan, "Historical Reconstruction, Reconstruction History and the Proper Scope of Section 1981," *Yale Law Journal* 98 (January 1989): 541–64.

[42] Support for this position comes, in part, from the fact that the wording of the Bill of Rights section on religion was changed during the debates from "nor shall any national religion be established," as proposed by Madison, to "No religion shall be established by law," in the House Committee, and, finally, to its present wording in the Senate Committee. Levy, *The Establishment Clause*, 75–81.

for religious institutions and the existence of congressional chaplains has been held constitutional because religious institutions and chaplains, like the crèche, have supposedly been around since before the First Amendment.[43] Sunday closing laws are constitutional because their purpose, according to the Court, has become secular.[44] Aid to parochial schools continues to have a rocky career. At times it is permissible, at times not.[45] Prayer in public schools and at graduation, display of the Ten Commandments, and the teaching of creationism in public schools are not constitutional.[46] Courts, however, continue to open with appeals that "God save the United States and this honorable Court." Currency continues to announce "In God We Trust."

The first Supreme Court case testing the constitutionality of state action under the establishment clause was *Everson v. Board of Education of the Township of Ewing*,[47] decided in 1947. A New Jersey statute reimbursing the parents of both public and parochial school students for bus fare was challenged on the ground that such support for sectarian education violated the First Amendment. Justice Black's frequently quoted opinion for the majority announced an uncompromising loyalty to a Jeffersonian separation of church and state:

The "establishment of religion" clause of the First Amendment means at least this: Neither a state nor the Federal Government can set up a church. Neither can pass laws which aid one religion, aid all religions, or prefer one religion over another. Neither can force nor influence a person to go to or remain away from church against his will or force him to profess a belief or disbelief in

[43] Walz v. Tax Commission, 397 U.S. 664 (1970), and Marsh v. Chambers, 463 U.S. 783 (1983).

[44] McGowan v. Maryland, 366 U.S. 420 (1961).

[45] Anti-Catholicism has played a large part, here, historically. Whereas any government support of Catholic parochial education had been suspect, under the free exercise clause, the Amish of Wisconsin have been held to have a right to exempt themselves from compulsory high school attendance laws, a right which was arguably necessary to preserve the Amish religion. Wisconsin v. Yoder, 406 U.S. 205 (1972). Similar arguments have been made about Catholic parochial education.

The school cases present a special case in the religion area because of acrimonious political debates about the purpose and adequacy of the public schools. See, also, Board of Education v. Grumet.

[46] Engel v. Vitale, 370 U.S. 421 (1962); Lee v. Weisman, 112 S. Ct. 2649 (1992); Stone v. Graham, 449 U.S. 39 (1980); Epperson v. Arkansas, 393 U.S. 107 (1968).

[47] 330 U.S. 1 (1947). See chapter 4, below, for further discussion of this case.

any religion. No person can be punished for entertaining or professing religious beliefs or disbeliefs, for church attendance or non-attendance. No tax in any amount, large or small, can be levied to support any religious activities or institutions, whatever they may be called, or whatever form they may adopt to teach or practice religion. Neither a state nor the Federal Government can, openly or secretly, participate in the affairs of any religious organizations or groups and vice versa.[48]

A literal reading of this passage would, at the very least, condemn every public mention of God by any member of the government, all tax exemptions for churches, police and fire protection for religious buildings, conscientious exemption from the draft, army and prison chaplaincies, prayer breakfasts, etc. In the view of many, it would also lead to a sterile public space.

In spite of this ringing anti-establishment manifesto in the majority opinion, however, the Court's decision was in favor of the statute on the ground that it would benefit children, not churches! It is hard to see how any government practice would be condemned under that standard. People, rather than religion, would always benefit. Despite the frequent quotation of Black's dicta, its message has been often ignored and much of the statement remains controversial, particularly Black's putting of religion and nonreligion on an equal basis.[49]

While reconciling the Court's subsequent establishment clause decisions is not easy,[50] from 1971 until *Lynch*[51] the announced legal test in establishment clause cases was the *Lemon* test, outlined by the Court in *Lemon v. Kurtzman*.[52] *Lemon* was one of several cases considered simultaneously by the Court in which the constitutionality of various forms of state aid to parochial schools was at issue. Two statutes were challenged in *Lemon*: a Pennsylvania statute authorizing the state to "purchase" certain "secular educational services from nonpublic schools" (including teaching salaries and textbooks); and a

---

[48] 330 U.S. at 15.

[49] See Howe, *The Garden and the Wilderness*.

[50] For a good summary of the cases in this area, see Henry J. Abraham, *Freedom and the Court: Civil Rights and Liberties in the United States*, 5th ed. (Oxford: Oxford University Press, 1988), 325–92.

[51] Since *Lynch*, the issue has become considerably more complicated and the Court more fragmented on the issue.

[52] 403 U.S. 602 (1971).

Rhode Island statute authorizing a 15 percent state salary supplement to nonpublic school teachers of secular subjects.

Chief Justice Burger, writing for the majority in *Lemon*, considered the word "respecting" as it is used in the First Amendment:

> The language of the Religion Clauses of the First Amendment is at best opaque, particularly when compared with other portions of the Amendment. Its authors did not simply prohibit the establishment of a state church or a state religion, an area history shows they regarded as very important and fraught with great dangers. Instead they commanded that there should be "no law *respecting* an establishment of religion." A law may be one "respecting" the forbidden objective while falling short of its total realization. A law "respecting" the proscribed result, that is, the establishment of religion, is not always easily identifiable as one violative of the Clause. A given law might not *establish* a state religion but nevertheless be one "respecting" that end in the sense of being a step that could lead to such establishment and hence offend the First Amendment. . . .
>
> In the absence of precisely stated constitutional prohibitions, we must draw lines with reference to the three main evils against which the Establishment Clause was intended to afford protection: "sponsorship, financial support, and active involvement of the sovereign in religious activity." *Walz v. Tax Commission*, 397 U.S. 664, 668 (1970).[53]

He then announced the famous, but much criticized,[54] "*Lemon*" test:

> First, the statute must have a secular legislative purpose; second, its principal or primary effect must be one that neither advances nor inhibits religion. . . ; finally, the statute must not foster "an excessive government entanglement with religion."[55]

Both the Pennsylvania and Rhode Island statutes were declared unconstitutional under this test.

Judge Pettine felt bound to apply the *Lemon* test as the appropriate constitutional test. Before reaching the three parts of the *Lemon* test, however, Judge Pettine, in his decision in *Donnelly v. Lynch*, first addressed two preliminary arguments by defendants that a First Amendment claim was not properly made in the case because religion

---

[53] 403 U.S. at 612.

[54] See, for example, Michael McConnell, "Religious Freedom at a Crossroads," *University of Chicago Law Review* 59 (winter 1992): 115–94.

[55] 403 U.S. at 612–13.

was not involved. Defendants first argued that if there was no religion, then the court did not need to reach the First Amendment question. Because Christmas was a constitutionally approved national holiday, it could be constitutionally celebrated by the city with the erection of a crèche symbolizing its historical origins. The crèche was not part of religion. It was part of history. Pettine concluded that Christmas was both a religious and a secular holiday and that government must "be exceedingly careful that it indeed acts to advance only the secular elements."[56]

The city's second preliminary argument was that the crèche had been secularized by its context so that no First Amendment claim had been stated. In this connection, one of the legal issues between the parties was whether the constitutionality of the display of the crèche should be considered independently or only as part of the constitutionality of the whole display. In other words, was the crèche more or less religious, given its placement together with the reindeer and the wishing well? Plaintiffs were concerned only about the religiousness of the crèche and wanted to consider it separately.[57] They had no objection to the rest. Defendants argued that the presence of the other items secularized the message of the crèche.[58]

Dropping his ethnographic objectivity, Pettine gave a lengthy and impassioned disquisition on the religiousness of the crèche, essentially arguing that the crèche could not be secularized unless it was stripped of *all* historical and cultural context. The crèche, for Pettine, seemed to carry with it the "key" to unlocking its meaning. Its essence was religious. Pettine could not really conceive of it being otherwise.

[56] 525 F. Supp. at 1164.

[57] Plaintiff Donnelly testified that the crèche was the only religious symbol in the display because it is the only one described in the Bible.

[58] One might argue, alternatively, that all of the items together only intensified the religiousness of the display. David Carlin said that the whole display, all of it, was part of his religious formation as a Catholic child growing up in Pawtucket. Carlin, "Pawtucket and Its Nativity Scene."

In a subsequent case in the Supreme Court in which the constitutionality of a menorah displayed in front of City Hall—in this instance, next to a Christmas tree— was considered, Justice O'Connor read the fact of having one symbol for each religion, for Christianity and Judaism, as conveying a message of multiculturalism, not of religious endorsement. Allegheny v. ACLU, 492 U.S. 573 (1989).

Having decided that a crèche is "fundamentally" religious, Pettine then turned to the application of the three-part *Lemon* test. He concluded that inclusion of the crèche in Pawtucket's Christmas display:

(1) although having secular purposes as well, was not clearly motivated by a secular purpose, such as the museum display of a crèche as an *objet d'art* would be, but rather had the *purpose* of endorsing or promoting a religious message, namely, "to keep Christ in Christmas";

(2) had the primary *effect* of endorsing Christianity; and

(3) led to political divisiveness, as evidenced by the public outcry after the suit was filed.

Under *Lemon*, Pettine held, display of the crèche is unconstitutional.

Like almost everyone else in this case, Judge Pettine wanted to have a religious Christmas and a secular Christmas with a bright line distinguishing the two. In attempting that division he made distinctions of dubious validity: a crèche is religious, stars and flying reindeer are not; a crèche is only religious, Christmas can be secular; a crèche is religious, George Washington's birthday is not. *Can* you take Christ out of Christmas? What does that mean? What does it mean to keep him in? If the crèche is "*fundamentally* religious," as Pettine says, can the holiday be secular? Can holy days ever be wholly secular?

Pettine's opinion granting a permanent injunction against display of the crèche by the city concluded with a passage by Justice Douglas:

We are a religious people whose institutions presuppose a Supreme Being. Under our Bill of Rights free play is given for making religion an active force in our lives. But if a religious leaven is to be worked into the affairs of our people, it is to be done by individuals or groups, not by the Government. (citations omitted)[59]

The second two sentences considerably modify the impact of the declaration made in the first, often quoted sentence. Pettine's citation of these words is evidence of his commitment to the separation of church and state and thus to the possibility of distinguishing the two:

We have staked the very existence of our country on the faith that complete separation between the state and religion is best for the state and best for religion.[60]

---

[59] Engel v. Vitale, 370 U.S. at 443 (Douglas, J., concurring), in which the Court struck down the New York State Regents' school prayer as unconstitutional.

[60] 525 F. Supp. at 1180, Pettine quoting from Torcaso v. Watkins, 367 U.S. 488 at 493–94.

That commitment to the possibility of distinguishing the sacred and the secular will be echoed in the Court of Appeals and by the dissents in the Supreme Court.

THE APPEALS

Judge Pettine's decision enjoining display of the crèche was handed down in December 1981, two weeks before the Christmas display was scheduled to be reinstalled in Hodgson Park. Stay of the order pending appeal was denied by both Judge Pettine and the United States Court of Appeals for the First Circuit. Public protest supporting the display, however, led to the sale of the crèche to a private group which installed it in the same location, next to the city-owned portion of the display.

On 3 November 1982, almost exactly a year after Pettine's decision, and again just before Christmas, the United States Court of Appeals for the First Circuit affirmed Judge Pettine's ruling in a two-to-one decision. All three judges filed opinions. Judge Fairchild's opinion for the panel held Pawtucket to an even higher standard than Judge Pettine had, declaring that in a case such as *Lynch,* in which a particular religion was favored rather than religion generally, the "strict scrutiny" test, rather than the *Lemon* test, was required. The "strict scrutiny" doctrine requires, in certain types of constitutional challenges involving fundamental rights or suspect classifications, that the government show a "compelling state interest" to overcome a charge of unconstitutionality. The city of Pawtucket, according to the First Circuit Court of Appeals, had failed to show such an interest.[61]

Judge Bownes of the Court of Appeals for the First Circuit concurred in the result but wrote a separate opinion detailing the history of Christmas as a public holiday beginning with its pre-Christian Roman predecessor and emphasizing its checkered history. He concluded that the holiday is both religious and secular. However, he added:

Unlike today's Christmas holiday, the crèche is not the result of the combination of folk culture and tradition. The crèche is *purely* a Christian religious symbol. (emphasis added)[62]

---

[61] Lynch v. Donnelly, 691 F. 2d 1029, 1034 (1981). See Larson v. Valente, 456 U.S. 228 (1982), in which the strict scrutiny test was first used in a religion case.
[62] 691 F. 2d at 1037.

He agreed with Pettine that the crèche is somehow different. It stands apart from the working of history.

Judge Campbell of the First Circuit, dissenting, disagreed with both Judge Fairchild and Judge Bownes. Campbell argued that since all the parties agreed that Christmas was a constitutionally permissible public holiday, display of the crèche must also be constitutional:

As the nativity scene is *prototypically* symbolic of Christmas—and as Christmas is itself a legal holiday whose constitutionality is not here questioned—I think the court errs in holding that the display in a public park during the Christmas season of characters and animals associated with that scene constitutes "an establishment of religion" within the first amendment. Unassociated, as they were, with the performance of any religious rites, the figures did not "establish" religion in the context in which they were presented. They simply contribute to the message that the holiday they represented was at hand. . . .

. . .It seems a little like maintaining a holiday known as "Washington's Birthday," while extirpating all reference to George Washington. (emphasis added)[63]

For Campbell, it is "rites" that make the context religious. The simple display of objects associated with religion does not. His argument is that if the public celebration of Christmas is constitutional, how can the crèche logically be excluded from the public celebration, as long as there are no "rites"?[64]

In their efforts to decide the issue in the absence of a workable First Amendment jurisprudence, these appellate judges, like Pettine, resort to intuition and hyperbole. The crèche is "purely" a religious symbol. It is "prototypically" symbolic. As if saying so would make it so.

How can a court be expected to fix the public meaning of any symbol?[65] The closer one looks at the history of and the diversity of cultural contexts surrounding the crèche, or surrounding any important religious or cultural symbol, the more its meaning seems to dissolve.

---

[63] 691 F. 2d at 1038.

[64] This is an interesting argument with some support in the academic study of religion. However, Judge Campbell perhaps underestimates the ritual nature of the display and of Christmas shopping.

[65] A similar issue is raised in the flag cases. See, for example, West Virginia State Board of Education v. Barnette, 319 U.S. 624 (1943) and Texas v. Johnson, 491 U.S. 397 (1989).

The shifting, multilayered significance of the crèche seems a risky foundation for constitutional interpretation. Even Mayor Lynch, its sponsor, seems uncertain either of its meaning or of his own purpose.

On 18 April 1983, the Supreme Court of the United States granted certiorari in the case of *Lynch v. Donnelly*.[66] The questions presented for review by the petitioners (Lynch et al, the losing defendants in the trial and appellate courts), were:

I. Does Municipal Sponsorship of a Traditional and Dominantly Secular Christmas Display Which Includes a Crèche Violate the Establishment Clause?

II. Does the Establishment Clause Require the Elimination From Publicly Sponsored Christmas Celebrations of All Religious Symbolism Associated With the Holidays?

Amicus briefs[67] supporting the petitioners and urging reversal of the lower courts were filed by the United States, the Coalition for Religious Liberty and the Freedom Council,[68] the Legal Foundation of America,[69] and the Washington Legal Foundation.[70]

The brief filed by the solicitor general of the United States in support of the petitioners' brief asserted that the United States had "a substantial interest in the matter":

The United States has a substantial interest in this matter, which raises the question whether the Constitution requires us rigidly to exclude from our

[66] The granting of certiorari is a discretionary one with the Court. Only in certain kinds of cases, of which *Lynch* was not one, must the Supreme Court review the case. 28 U.S.C. 1253, 1254, 1257.

[67] An Amicus brief is a brief filed, with the permission of the Court, by a non-party who has a "substantial interest" in the matter.

Briefs in important Supreme Court cases are published in Philip B. Kurland and Gerhard Casper, eds., *Landmark Briefs and Arguments of the Supreme Court of the United States: Constitutional Law* (Washington: University Publications of America, 1975–). Copies of the briefs and a transcript of the oral argument in *Lynch* may be found in volume 151.

[68] According to their briefs, the Coalition for Religious Liberty and the Freedom Council are organizations founded to promote religion in American life and to oppose the imposition of "secular religion" on American society.

[69] According to their briefs, the Legal Foundation of America is a public interest law firm which promotes states' rights.

[70] According to their briefs, the Washington Legal Foundation is a libertarian organization.

public ceremonies and celebrations all acknowledgments of the religious elements in our national traditions.

The United States, like the City of Pawtucket and countless other state and local governments, has long participated in the celebration of the Christmas season. Congress has declared Christmas to be a national holiday, and the United States has in past years sponsored Christmas pageants that included nativity scenes. Since the days of the Pilgrims, we have devoted, as a Nation, one day every year to giving thanks to God. More broadly, the federal government has, from the earliest days of the Republic to the present, felt free to acknowledge and recognize that *religion is a part of our heritage and should continue to be an element in our public life and public occasions. The United States has a deep and abiding interest in maintaining this longstanding tradition.* (citations omitted and emphasis added)[71]

One cannot help but wonder about the behind-the-scenes negotiations in the Department of Justice and with the White House that led to the composition of this statement. This statement and its assertion that religion is and should be a part of American public life raises serious issues about the obligations of the executive branch to uphold the Constitution.

Amicus briefs supporting respondents and urging affirmance were filed by the American Jewish Committee together with the National Council of Churches and by the Anti-Defamation League of B'nai B'rith together with the American Jewish Congress. Oral argument in the case was heard on 4 October 1983.

The Supreme Court's 5-4 decision for the petitioners, reversing the court of appeals decision, was announced in March of the following year. Four separate opinions were delivered. Chief Justice Burger wrote the opinion for the five-person majority. Justice O'Connor concurred in the result but not in the majority's reasoning and therefore wrote a concurring opinion giving her own reasons for the result. Justices Brennan and Blackmun wrote dissenting opinions. The majority opinion found that display of the crèche did not violate the First Amendment either because the Constitution permitted government sponsorship of a sectarian religious symbol or because it was not really a religious symbol. Justice O'Connor proposed a new "endorsement" test to replace the *Lemon* test. The dissenters harshly criticized the majority opinion and reaffirmed the *Lemon* test.

---

[71] Kurland, *Landmark Briefs*, vol. 151, 178–79.

Chief Justice Burger, in his opinion for the majority, and echoing the government's statement in its Amicus Brief, described the historical—and, impliedly, therefore, also the constitutional—relationship of religion and government in the United States as follows:

Nor does the Constitution require complete separation of church and state; it affirmatively mandates accommodation, not merely tolerance, of all religions. . . .

. . .accommodation of religious belief [was] intended by the Framers. . . .

There is an unbroken history of official acknowledgment by all three branches of government of the role of religion in American life from at least 1789. . . .

Our history is replete with official references to the value and invocation of Divine guidance. . . .

There are countless. . .illustrations of the Government's acknowledgment of our religious heritage and governmental sponsorship of graphic manifestations of that heritage.[72]

Display of the crèche, Burger argued, was simply a case in which government "respected the religious nature of our people."[73]

"Accommodation," "acknowledgment," "sponsorship," "respect" are the words Burger uses to describe government's proper attitude toward religion. The pseudosociological distance and irenic passivity of those words belies the passion of protagonists on both sides of this dispute. His further insistence on the existence of a single historical American attitude is emphasized by his rhetoric: "history is replete," "unbroken history," "from at least 1789," "countless illustrations." His language is relentless. Religion in America has always been sponsored by government. And yet, he also says that the crèche, as displayed by Pawtucket, is secular. History's "accommodation" of the crèche seems to have made it so.

The dissenters in the Supreme Court vociferously agreed with Judge Pettine and the court of appeals. The majority opinion had achieved the dubious distinction, according to Justice Brennan in dissent, of offending believers and non-believers alike.[74] Justice Blackmun, also

---

[72] 465 U.S. at 672–87 passim.
[73] 465 U.S. at 678.
[74] 465 U.S. at 712.

dissenting, called the city's victory "Pyrrhic": It had succeeded in keeping Christ in Christmas by declaring the crèche to be "devoid of any inherent meaning."[75]

Mayor Lynch's attitude toward religion, as confirmed by the Supreme Court in the *Lynch* decision, are in marked contrast to those of his earliest predecessor in Pawtucket. There is, in fact, a gentle irony to the fact that the *Lynch* case arose in Rhode Island. In October of the same year in which *Lynch* was decided by the Supreme Court, a national memorial was dedicated in Providence, Rhode Island, to Roger Williams, founder of Rhode Island and apostle of religious liberty and the separation of church and state. More than three hundred and fifty years separate Roger Williams, founder of Pawtucket, and Dennis Lynch, mayor of Pawtucket from 1973 to 1981. In their respective views on the appropriate relationship between church and state, however, the issue may be said to be joined.

Roger Williams is enjoying a modest renaissance in the popular imagination. He is one of those historical figures, strangely out of tune in some ways with his own age, who seems oddly consonant with ours.[76] In his many writings he is appealingly articulate and passionate about the need for the separation of church and state and for religious freedom. He is prophetic in his early espousal of Native American legal rights and religious freedom. He is also excitingly difficult to pin down. He is eagerly appealed to by advocates on both the Right and the Left of the establishment debate. Above all, he seems to provide a balance to the dry reserved rationality of Jefferson as *the* definer of the American experiment in religious freedom.

Roger Williams was a Puritan minister who, to escape religious persecution, left England in 1631 for the Massachusetts Bay Colony. In January 1635 Roger Williams was banished from the Bay Colony for his unorthodox views. He had challenged, on the basis of what he saw to be obvious Indian ownership, even according to English property

---

[75] 465 U.S. at 727.

[76] This can be vastly overdone, as many scholars have pointed out. He was in many ways the Puritan's Puritan—the very model of a Calvinist reformer—and intensely involved in Puritan politics. See, for example, Clark Gilpin, *The Millenarian Piety of Roger Williams* (Chicago: University of Chicago Press, 1979).

law, the validity of the King's Patent granting ownership of the land to the colony, and he had condemned what he termed the "unholy" union of church and state in Massachusetts.

After they left Massachusetts Bay, Williams and his family, with several other families, moved to and founded the first Rhode Island settlement on land purchased from the Narragansett. When the township was incorporated two years later, the agreement among the citizens of the town carefully provided that the laws of the town extended to "civil things" only.[77] Two years later a further agreement among thirty-seven families confirmed that "Wee agree, as formerly hath bin the liberties of the town, so still to hould forth liberty of Conscience."[78] Three hundred and fifty years later, the United States Supreme Court has found it permissible for the local Pawtucket government to extend beyond "civil things," to the sponsorship of sectarian religious symbols. After their move, Roger Williams continued his active involvement in Puritan politics both in England and in the colonies, both in person and through his writings.

Should we care what Roger Williams would have thought about the *Lynch* case? He is often invoked in the debate over the First Amendment. Accommodationists point to his faith. Separationists point to his fierce condemnation of religious establishments. How have things changed in the last three hundred and fifty years?

Things *have* changed. In 1636 Massachusetts was a Puritan theocracy. Roger Williams was also a Puritan, a fanatical Puritan by almost anyone's definition. As his life went on he became more and more puritanical, more and more fastidious about the sacrilegious presumption of man encompassing the things of God.[79] Christianity was to be found, if at all, Williams argued, in small, independent, separate, gathered congregations, not in national churches, whether in England or in Massachusetts Bay, establishments that he scornfully derided as

---

[77] John Russell Bartlett, ed., *Records of the Colony of Rhode Island and Providence Plantations* (Providence: A. Crawford Greene and Brother, 1856), 15.

[78] Bartlett, *Records*, 28.

[79] See Yeshayahu Leibowits, *Judaism, Human Values, and the Jewish State* (Cambridge: Harvard University Press, 1992) arguing for the separation of synagogue and state out of concern for the synagogue. See also the review article by Menachem Kellner, *New York Times Book Review*, 19 July 1992, 7.

"Christendome."[80] His was an exceedingly narrow definition of religion—and of the possibility of salvation.

Chief Justice Burger's latitudinarian enthusiasm for the religiousness of Americans would likely have been repellent to Roger Williams. The words Roger Williams used to describe the alliance of church and state leap up from the page. He reviled the compromise and corruption of "Christendome" and so-called "Christian" princes, "the bloudy tenent of persecution," "the spiritual rape [that] forces the consciences of all to one worship." He advocated "soul freedom" for all, even Jews, Catholics, and Indians, all of whom he considered heathens, as he considered most Protestants heathens, too. He was very suspicious of earthly religious institutions of any kind, perhaps even more suspicious than Thomas Jefferson. But Williams's views about Christianity did not prevent him from believing that people should—and could—live together in civility and that good government was necessary and possible without the establishment of religion.[81]

In the seventeenth century the Rhode Island of Roger Williams was a haven for religious dissenters and for independent political thinkers from all over New England. These free thinkers had difficulty agreeing with each other and were never accepted in the United Colonies of New England. Rhode Island in the eighteenth century was the site of the first act of outright violence against England, and, in 1772, was the first colony to declare its independence from England. It was also the last state to join the Union. Its internal scrappiness continued to be represented in the fact that it had two capitols until the twentieth century.[82]

The nineteenth century, however, brought a new political and religious climate to Rhode Island, as it did to the rest of the United

---

[80] Roger Williams, *Christenings make not Christians, or A Briefe Discourse concerning that name Heathen, commonly given to the Indians. As also concerning that great point of their conversion* (London, 1645), in *The Complete Writings of Roger Williams*, ed. Perry Miller (New York: Russell & Russell, 1963), 7: 29–41.

[81] William Lee Miller, *The First Liberty: Religion and the American Republic* (New York: Paragon House, 1985), pt. 2.

Williams was also not alone. The accommodationists are right to point to the largely Baptist tradition of Protestant ideological support for the separation of church and state. See J. R. Pole, *The Pursuit of Equality in American History* (Berkeley: University of California Press, 1978), 71–78.

[82] *Encyclopedia Britannica*, 15th ed., s.v. "Rhode Island."

States. Catholic immigrants from Ireland, Germany, and French Canada contributed to create in Rhode Island the most Catholic state. Industrialization, urbanization, and voting disputes led to Rhode Island becoming heavily Democratic. The Second Great Awakening and revivalism brought a distinctive American religious piety to all Christian churches which, in turn, created the *de facto* Protestant religious establishment Chief Justice Burger is so intent on accommodating.

We are indeed a long way from seventeenth-century Puritanism, but it must help us in interpreting the Constitution to understand that the religious history of Rhode Island, as well as of the rest of the country, has gone through radical changes while, at the same time, it throws up perennial problems. We see in Rhode Island changing religion as well as changing understanding of what religion is and what relationship it has to government.

In *The Meaning and End of Religion*,[83] Wilfred Cantwell Smith, professor emeritus of religion at Harvard University, argues that the word "religion" should be abandoned because its referent is a reified construction which is the product of apologetics and therefore of no real use in considering religious phenomena as they are known and experienced in the world. While this position has considerable value for the reorientation of scholarly thought, the Supreme Court does not have the luxury of abandoning the word. Unless the First Amendment is repealed, interpretation of the Constitution in particular cases requires consideration of the word and of its possible referents. Given this necessity, can the Court find a better way to talk about religion?

The opinions by the Supreme Court reveal remarkably different understandings of religion and of the role of religion in public life. They typify, in some ways, the different options available to Americans to talk about American religion. Each is characterized by a particular understanding of the nature of religion and of the role religion should play. Each also demonstrates the limitations of that mode of discourse and points to some of the reasons why that discourse is foundering. Looked at carefully, the four opinions can be used as a gateway into a larger issue: How can Americans talk about and give value to the

---

[83] Wilfred Cantwell Smith, *The Meaning and End of Religion* (New York: Harper & Row, 1978).

remarkable diversity of American religions? How can they take religion seriously without establishing it?

When the Court agreed to hear *Lynch*, it agreed to participate at a number of levels in a number of different and ongoing discourses about American religion. Each of these discourses has both its own historical origin and a parallel within academic discourse. A close reading of the opinions of Chief Justice Burger, Justice O'Connor, and Justice Brennan will be used to display these discourses. (Justice Blackmun's dissent was, in effect, only a one-page footnote to Justice Brennan's opinion in which he joined, so his opinion will be considered together with Justice Brennan's.)

Speaking historically, these discourses are located and find a rhetorical source in three distinct moments of American history. The rhetorical moments do not determine constitutional interpretation, in the original intent sense, but provide the historical and cultural context of their articulation:

1. Chief Justice Burger's opinion is of its own time—the time of *Lynch* itself, the 1980s—a period of world-wide religious revival and the presidency of Ronald Reagan.
2. Justice O'Connor's opinion recalls the period of the incorporation of the First Amendment into the Fourteenth—the 1940s—the beginning of modern First Amendment jurisprudence.
3. Justice Brennan's opinion emphasizes a traditional Jeffersonian reading of the period of the founding—the 1790s—and of the promulgation of the First Amendment.

Each of these historical moments is characterized by its own mode of religious discourse, both about religion generally and about American religion specifically. Each received its articulation in a particular construction of the First Amendment by members of the Court in *Lynch*.

The Court's opinions also show relationship and affinity to three different academic and legal discourses about religion (which are historically keyed to the above periods):

1. Chief Justice Burger: accommodationist—or nonpreferential— Durkheimian.
2. Justice O'Connor: procedural—post-religious—law as religion— focus on neutrality and equality.

3. Justice Brennan: Catholic and separationist—expressed in Jefferson's wall metaphor.

The following chapters will examine the three discourses displayed in *Lynch*.

Chapter 3 will consider the majority opinion as an exemplar of the accommodationist discourse of the 1980s. The discourse about religion exemplified by Chief Justice Burger's opinion combines a Durkheimian reading of religion as integrating and unthreatening with the ascendant political sensibility and religious rhetoric of the 1980s.

Chapter 4 will consider Justice O'Connor's concurring opinion as an exemplar of the neutrality position first articulated in the 1940s. Justice O'Connor's opinion combines a religiously neutral constitutional theory with a political commitment to procedural justice and equality originating in the rhetoric about racial integration.

Chapter 5 will consider Justice Brennan's opinion as an exemplar of the separationist discourse which finds its inspiration in a reading of Jefferson and Madison and the Enlightenment discourse of the Founding. It is here interestingly espoused in the case of Justice Brennan by a religiously orthodox spokesperson, resulting in a Roman Catholic reading of Jefferson and of the crèche.

Each chapter will also engage in a form of comparison to highlight that discourse. Chapter 3 will compare Justice Burger's language with that of the Japanese Supreme Court in a similar case. This "horizontal" comparison will acknowledge and reflect the internationalization of issues for postmodern industrial society. Chapter 4 will compare Justice O'Connor's language about religion with that of Justice Black and his era. Chapter 5 will place the dissenters in relation to Jefferson and Madison and to Roman Catholic public and sacramental theology. Chapter 6 will return to a comparison of the Court's discourse with that of the academic study of religion and an examination of why the Court's discourse, in each of its modes, is inadequate to its task. Chapter 6 will also make an effort to contribute to the construction of a new discourse about religion in American public life.

Chapter 3

Discourse I: Chief Justice Burger

But I am sure I have always thought of Christmas time, when it has come round—apart from the veneration due to its sacred name and origin, if anything belonging to it can be apart from that—as a good time: a kind, forgiving, charitable, pleasant time.

—Dickens, *A Christmas Carol*[1]

The prosperity of England depends on the Church of her people.

—Trollope, *Phineas Redux*[2]

[F]or purposes of free exercise religion is defined by the nonconformist, but for the purposes of establishment it is defined by the dominant consensus.

—Freund, "The First Amendment: Freedom of Religion"[3]

All public issues in the 1990s are international ones. To talk of religion and law in the United States without reference to the rest of the world is anachronistic. Nevertheless, cross-cultural comparison is a difficult business.[4] In this chapter, after offering a critical reading of Chief

---

[1] Scrooge's nephew in Charles Dickens, *A Christmas Carol* (London, 1843; reprint, Boston: The Atlantic Monthly Press, 1920), 8–9.

[2] Mr. Browborough in Anthony Trollope, *Phineas Redux* (London, 1873; reprint, London: Oxford University Press, 1973), 35.

[3] Paul A. Freund, "The First Amendment: Freedom of Religion," in Virginia Van der Veer Hamilton, ed., *Hugo Black and the Bill of Rights: Proceedings of the First Hugo Black Symposium in American History on "The Bill of Rights and American Democracy"* (University: University of Alabama Press, 1978), 83.

[4] Jonathan Z. Smith, among others, has given a great deal of thought to the hazards of comparison. See, for example, "Adde Parvum Parvo Magnus Acervus Erit," *History of Religions* 11 (August 1971): 67–90; and "In Comparison a Magic Dwells," chapter 2 in Smith, *Imagining Religion*.

Justice Burger's opinion for the majority in *Lynch*, I will compare it with the opinions of the Japanese Supreme Court in the Nakaya case. While my choice of the Japanese case is partially a result of serendipity, it turns out to be a helpful one. Although many differences could be found between the two cultures and although Japanese and American religions are strikingly unalike in many ways, Japan and the United States have participated in important ways in the same history during the last fifty to one hundred years. They have shared in the spread of modernity and presently inhabit the same postmodern industrial world. Further, the Japanese Constitution was written by American lawyers and consciously modeled on the Constitution of the United States.

THE AMERICAN MAJORITY

Chief Justice Burger's opinion for the majority in *Lynch*, reversing the two lower court decisions and vindicating Mayor Lynch and his crèche, is a powerful example of instinct in search of a legal theory. The tension between Burger's tenacious commitment to a vision of America which includes the constitutionality of Pawtucket's action is at times in almost surreal contrast to the confusion of his reading of history, his theory of constitutional interpretation, and his understanding of religion. The tortured rhetoric of the opinion is easy to satirize. The perception which drives the argument should not be dismissed so quickly. Underlying his opinion, as with the other opinions in *Lynch*, is an anthropology and a view of religion that needs to be made explicit.

The major discourse about religion, of which Burger's opinion and Mayor Lynch's trial testimony may be seen as clumsy examples, might be loosely termed Durkheimian. Burger and Lynch see, like Durkheim, that the community is constituted in part by a need to express its unity and celebrate its identity with public symbols. It is what people do. For Burger and Lynch, it is what Americans do, and, therefore, it must be constitutional. They see the Pawtucket crèche and, indeed, the whole complex of the American celebration of Christmas, as a symbol of American culture, a location for the expression and celebration of American unity—of the best aspects of being American.

But Burger and Lynch are also participants in, or perhaps captives of, a political discourse which advocates a return to a dominant sectarian religion—to a Christian nation—a political discourse which was created in the 1980s in reaction to a perceived hostility to religion on the part of the media and the national government. What appears irenic and celebratory in one context is found as a prop for a hard-edged programmatic agenda in another. At times both Burger and Lynch seem caught between these two often contradictory political discourses about religion.

Burger's sixteen-page opinion is divided into six sections. It begins with a short, one-and-a-half-page section summarizing the facts. Pawtucket's Christmas display and its crèche are presented by Burger as familiar, ordinary, and unthreatening—even inexpensive:

The display is essentially like those to be found in hundreds of towns and cities across the Nation—often on public grounds—during the Christmas season. The Pawtucket display comprises many of the figures and decorations traditionally associated with Christmas [brief description of larger display]. . . .

The crèche, which has been included in the display for forty or more years, consists of the traditional figures, including the Infant Jesus, Mary and Joseph, angels, shepherds, kings and animals, all ranging in height from 5" to 5'. In 1973, when the present crèche was acquired, it cost the city $1,365; it now is valued at $200. The erection and dismantling of the crèche costs the city about $20 per year; nominal expenses are incurred in lighting the crèche. No money has been expended on its maintenance for the past 10 years.[5]

How could anyone object? What Burger sees is a typical, modest, and frugal civic decoration. If "society is God," as Durkheim says, then such creations of the majority must be constitutional. The ongoing subtext of this opinion is that Burger cannot see what the fuss is about. Furthermore, he is convinced that his underlying instinct is the proper basis for his interpretation of the First Amendment, if only he can find a legal theory.

Beginning the next section with a brief acknowledgment of both the desirability and the difficulty of maintaining separation between church and state, Burger moves quickly to the announcement of an astonishing new legal theory: "[the Constitution] affirmatively mandates *accommodation*, not merely tolerance, of all religions" (emphasis added).[6] Whereas in most previous establishment clause cases the Court had struggled heroically, if often ineptly, to maintain separation between

[5] 465 U.S. at 671.
[6] 465 U.S. at 673.

government and religion—as it believed the First Amendment mandated—through the balancing of legitimate secular purposes and possible illegitimate entanglement with religion, suddenly the Constitution is seen to be positively in favor of religion.

Chief Justice Burger has difficulty assembling authority for this new "accommodation doctrine." He cites *Zorach v. Clauson*,[7] in which the Court upheld, in an expansive opinion by Justice Douglas which he later repented, the constitutionality of a program releasing public school children for religious instruction at their own religious institutions,[8] and *McCollum v. Board of Education*,[9] in which the Court held unconstitutional an Illinois program of optional religious education offered by religious groups in the public schools. The odd juxtaposition of *Zorach* and *McCollum* as support for a doctrine of "accommodation" is followed by a thin set of weak dicta in previous cases disclaiming any "hostility" to religion which are then elevated into constitutional doctrine requiring accommodation: "Anything less would require the 'callous indifference' we have said was never intended by the Establishment Clause."[10] The choice seems to be between hostility to or "accommodation" of religion. There is no middle ground.

Bypassing the bulk of First Amendment establishment clause cases calling for a strict separation of church and state and ignoring the words of the First Amendment that have been understood to prohibit any government sponsorship of religion, this new "accommodation" theory is further supported by a one-page section detailing "what history

[7] 343 U.S. 306 (1952).

[8] By far the greatest number of First Amendment religion cases concern school situations. The history of public schooling, the relationship of that history to sectarian religious controversy, and periodic crises in public education considerably muddy the discourse about religion in these cases. Public education did not exist in the eighteenth century, when virtually all schooling was accomplished in religious institutions. Furthermore, public schooling, when it did begin, was often perceived by Catholics as anti-Catholic due to the more or less explicit Protestant religious instruction which was a part of the public school curriculum. This perception helped to fuel the then nascent Catholic schools movement. The Court has struggled to find an appropriate constitutional stance towards religion and the schools. See Justice Brennan's opinion in Abington School District v. Schempp, 374 U.S. 203, 238–42 (1963), for one account of the historical development of public schools.

[9] 333 U.S. 203 (1948).

[10] 465 U.S. at 673.

reveals."[11] "History reveals," according to Burger, that the First Congress had paid chaplains for the House and Senate:

In the very week that Congress approved the Establishment Clause as part of the Bill of Rights for submission to the states, it enacted legislation providing for paid chaplains for the House and Senate.[12]

In other words, city display of a crèche is constitutional because the First Congress had paid chaplains. The First Congress is apparently shown to have given with one hand what it has just taken away with the other.

Burger makes no effort to reconcile these two apparently contradictory congressional actions. He simply allows his broad reading of the significance of the establishment of a congressional chaplaincy to modify both the apparent meaning and the received interpretation of the words of the establishment clause of the First Amendment. He concludes: "It would be difficult to identify a more striking example of the accommodation of religious belief intended by the Framers."[13] In a somewhat crude effort to rewrite history and in response to the then reigning separationist construction of the founders' intentions, Burger's "history" in *Lynch* represents a clumsy attempt to reinvent the founding and to recapture the First Amendment for religion.[14]

In the second part of section II, moving on from what he sees to be the First Congress's determination to accommodate religion, Burger offers evidence for what he sweepingly terms "an unbroken history of official acknowledgment by all three branches of government of the role of religion in American life from at least 1789."[15] He lists, without distinction or comment: the quote from Justice Douglas's opinion in *Zorach* that "We are a religious people"; political invocations of divine guidance; the public celebration of Thanksgiving; the use of "In God

[11] 465 U.S. at 673.

[12] 465 U.S. at 674.

[13] 465 U.S. at 674.

[14] Since *Lynch*, prodigious efforts have been made by academic legal scholars supporting the accommodation doctrine to challenge the separationist reading of First Amendment legislative history through retrieval of historical documents demonstrating support by religious persons and groups with allegedly religious intentions for the original passage of the First Amendment—to offer, in effect, a "religious" reading of the First Amendment. See, for example, Michael McConnell, "The Origins and Historical Understanding of Free Exercise of Religion," *Harvard Law Review* 103 (May 1990): 1410–517; and Cord, *Separation of Church and State.*

[15] 465 U.S. at 674.

We Trust"; the Pledge of Allegiance; the exhibition of art with religious subjects in the National Gallery; and national days of prayer.

This motley collection seems intended by Burger to show that we live in a paradise of ecumenical piety. He sums up:

> There are countless other illustrations of the Government's acknowledgment of our religious heritage and governmental sponsorship of graphic manifestations of that heritage. . . . One cannot look at even this brief resume without finding that our history is pervaded by expressions of religious beliefs such as are found in *Zorach*. Equally pervasive is the evidence of *accommodation* of all faiths and all forms of religious expression, and hostility toward none. (emphasis added)[16]

Where some would find a series of harmless, watered-down, politically opportunist nods towards conventional piety and others would see oppressive evidence of a stifling and unconstitutional *de facto* Protestant establishment, Burger finds precedent defining a constitutional mandate for the affirmative "accommodation" of religion, religion in general, by government.

Having attempted to convince the reader that the First Amendment intends the government to accommodate religion by erecting religious displays such as the crèche, Burger abruptly changes his view of the crèche in the next section. Reluctantly coming, at last, in section III, to the "three-pronged" *Lemon* test, with many caveats undermining its importance, and only after quoting Justice Story to the effect that, "'the real object of the [First] Amendment was. . .to prevent any national ecclesiastical establishment,'"[17] Burger finally considers the case before him—the purpose and effect of Pawtucket's display of the crèche.

Burger holds that the district court's factual finding that the city's purpose was to endorse Christianity was quite plainly in error because it was insufficiently "contextual,"[18] or, in other words, Judge Pettine somehow had gotten the wrong context:

> When viewed in the proper context of the Christmas Holiday season, it is apparent that, on this record, there is insufficient evidence to establish that

---

[16] 465 U.S. at 677.

[17] 465 U.S. at 678, from Joseph Story, *Commentaries on the Constitution of the United States* (Boston: Hilliard, Gray & Co., 1833; reprint, Durham: Carolina Academic Press, 1987), 701.

[18] Burger deftly finesses the fact that he is simply reversing the trial court on a finding of fact. As a matter of course, appellate courts pay great deference to the

the inclusion of the crèche is a purposeful or surreptitious effort to express some kind of subtle governmental advocacy of a particular religious message.[19]

While plaintiffs' witnesses had found the message conveyed by display of the crèche to be anything but subtle, Burger emphasizes that the governmental purpose is only suspect if "motivated *wholly* by religious considerations" (emphasis added).[20] Here Burger unobtrusively shifts the burden of proof to the plaintiffs, requiring them to show that the government's actions did not merely have *a* religious purpose, but was motivated *wholly* by religious considerations.

It is difficult to believe that the American government would ever be motivated "wholly" by religious considerations, whatever that means, unless the meaning of religion is greatly expanded. In any event, such a motivation was, according to Burger, anachronistic in Pawtucket in 1980:

The city. . .has principally taken note of a significant historical religious event long celebrated in the Western World. The crèche in the display depicts the historical origins of this traditional event long recognized as a National Holiday.[21]

The city's purpose in displaying the crèche, according to Burger, was the obviously secular and legitimate one of celebrating a secular national holiday. Any benefit to religion was "indirect, remote, and incidental,"[22] because the reason for or effect of the city's inclusion of the crèche "merely happens to coincide or harmonize with the tenets of some. . .religions" (ellipses in original)[23]—religions now outmoded. Under Burger's reading of the display and of the crèche, it would be

---

factual findings of trial courts. Appellate courts are supposed to review only *legal* error, except in egregious cases. The assumption is that the trier-of-fact, the judge or the jury, had the witnesses and evidence before them and thus were in a better position to weigh the value of the evidence than are the appellate courts. Appellate courts are supposed to accept the trial court's reading of the facts and to stick to reviewing the law.

[19] 465 U.S. at 680.
[20] 465 U.S. at 667.
[21] 465 U.S. at 680.
[22] 465 U.S. at 683.
[23] 465 U.S. at 682.

impossible to show the city's purpose to be unconstitutional because, Burger says, "[i]n a pluralistic society a variety of motives and purposes are implicated."[24]

In other words, in Burger's view, either the Constitution requires government accommodation of American religion, so display of the crèche as a common American religious symbol is constitutional, or, display of the crèche is constitutional because the Pawtucket crèche is not really a religious symbol. He concludes that "[any] notion that these symbols pose a real danger of establishment of a state church is farfetched, indeed."[25] Whether you regard the crèche as religious or as secular, it is constitutional.

Section IV of Burger's opinion, in answer to Justice Brennan's dissent, considers the nature of the crèche as a symbol. Like the rest of the opinion, this section is somewhat schizophrenic. On the one hand, Burger concludes that the Pawtucket crèche is "like a painting in a museum," "passive" and without "special meaning,"[26] a conclusion most art lovers would presumably view with astonishment. On the other, its display "engenders a friendly community spirit of goodwill."[27] He cannot decide whether the symbol is passive or engendering, but he is convinced that its connection with religion is remote. It is merely "a reminder of the origins of Christmas." It may have "religious implications" for those who "sense the origins" of Christmas, but it is only "one passive symbol." To worry about it would be "a stilted overreaction."[28] His is, indeed, a post-Christian world.

Section V reassures us that the Court has been vigilant in establishment abuses by listing cases in which government actions have been held to violate the First Amendment. Section VI announces the decision in the case.

Criticisms could be made of this opinion from many perspectives. Here I will confine myself to the rhetoric and internal logic of Burger's discourse; the following chapters consider the alternative discourses about religion in public life offered by Justice O'Connor in her

[24] 465 U.S. at 680.
[25] 465 U.S. at 686.
[26] 465 U.S. at 685.
[27] 465 U.S. at 685.
[28] 465 U.S. at 686.

concurring opinion and by Justices Brennan and Blackmun in their dissenting opinions.

The underlying assumption of Burger's opinion is that there are only two possible attitudes with respect to the relationship of government to religion: hostility or accommodation. If we shy away, as Burger would have us do, from any implication of a desire to be hostile to religion, we find that accommodation of religion is the only other possible position. The setting up of this opposition creates an atmosphere that pervades Burger's whole opinion, his reading of history, and his use of language. It also determines the nature of the "accommodation" he advocates. It must be broad and vague enough to include all who wish to avoid hostility.

Burger's elision of the words "acknowledgment" and "accommodation" increases the confusion. He uses the two interchangeably, sliding over and finessing the move from a more neutral "acknowledgment" of the religiousness of Americans—the need for which few would argue—to the more active need for "accommodation" of religion by government,[29] a move he seems to feel is necessary in order to avoid "hostility" to religion.

One of the reasons Burger can make this move so easily is because of what religion is for him. Religion, is for Burger, a Norman Rockwell-Hallmark card kind of sentiment; therefore, acknowledging and accommodating are very much the same thing and are equally harmless. The American religion Burger wishes to accommodate seems to lack all depth, danger, and particularity. He cannot see the crèche as more than another form of tinsel. The flatness of Burger's reading of American religion is in dramatic contrast to the rich variety and colorful intensity of American religion attested to by scholars of American religions. William James and Charles Long, among others, for example, write convincingly of the importance, distinctiveness, and vitality of religion in American culture.[30]

---

[29] William James urges "acknowledgment" of religion: "I think, therefore, that however particular questions connected with our individual destinies may be answered, it is only by *acknowledging* them as genuine questions, and living in the sphere of thought which they open up, that we become profound" (emphasis added); *The Varieties of Religious Experience*, 500.

[30] See, for example, Long, *Significations*, and James, *The Varieties of Religious Experience*.

One effect of Burger's confident and assiduous denial of any public sectarian religious symbolic meaning for the Pawtucket crèche is to "signify," in the sense used by Charles Long,[31] the religious community for whom the crèche has specific religious content. Burger's opinion purports to encompass and define for American culture the meaning of a publicly displayed crèche, while it denies the religious experience of millions of Americans, including the dissenting Justices Brennan, Blackmun, Marshall, and Stevens. Burger's opinion is, in effect, a "second creation," in Long's terms,[32] a new culture analogous to the new cultures created and imposed by powerful colonial empires. Display of the crèche, it is now ordained, is to communicate nothing more than a spirit of holiday goodwill. There need not be any separation of religious conduct from government because, as Burger understands religion, religion in America no longer poses the threat of divisiveness that the founders saw. It has no "otherness."

Burger also flattens and demystifies religious experience. He domesticates it, refusing to allow that it is a "live option," in William James's words.[33] If the cumulative effect of William James's *The Varieties of Religious Experience* is to provide a contour map of individual religious experience, the effect of Burger's opinion is that of a steam roller. Like the medical materialism James deplores, Burger's opinion reduces the meaning of the crèche to, in Justice Blackmun's words, "a neutral harbinger of the holiday season."[34]

Like Burger, both Long and James seek to acknowledge the role of religion in American life. In doing so, Long and James search for the particular and the powerful in religious experience, for that which makes a difference. Long's explication of the black experience in American history is analogous in some ways to James's heightening of the psychology of religious experience. They are both extraordinarily open to what Long calls the "opacity" of religious experience,[35] an experience which resists interpretation and reduction. Burger, on the

---

[31] Long, *Significations.*

[32] Long, *Significations,* 166.

[33] William James, *The Will to Believe and Other Essays in Popular Philosophy* (New York: Longmans, Green & Co., 1897; reprint, New York: Dover, 1956).

[34] 463 U.S. at 727.

[35] Long, *Significations,* 143.

other hand, wishes to accommodate a religion with no difference, no otherness. In doing so, he attempts to collapse the sacred and secular into one category.

If the crèche has no particular religious power for Burger, is religious power to be found anywhere in his reading of the facts of *Lynch*? The moving force behind the Pawtucket Christmas display, as described by Burger, the effervescence of which Durkheim speaks, is arguably not in the worship of Christ but in consumerism.[36] What Mayor Lynch and the shopkeepers who testified for him were trying to achieve through support of the Christmas display in the downtown business district was not a Christian revival but the economic revitalization of Pawtucket, a perfectly proper civic goal. All of the defendants admitted in Court that for their purposes the crèche itself was an optional and dispensable part of the display. The content of the display was unimportant. What was key was its capacity to attract shoppers.[37]

In his reading of the First Amendment and of the Pawtucket crèche, Burger depends for support on a particular reading of American religious history, a reading which sees American public religion, throughout its history, as irenic, celebratory, and unthreatening. Religious strife is part of the prehistory of America. It is part of the Old World that has been superseded. When the United States was created, on this reading, religion was reinvented.

Burger chooses, as early evidence for this reading, congressional authorization of paid congressional chaplains at the time of passage of the First Amendment. (The Supreme Court had held legislative chaplains to be constitutional in 1983, the previous term, with a 6-3 decision in *Marsh v. Chambers*.[38]) Burger's marking of the significance of the historical existence of paid chaplains in the First Congress and

---

[36] This thought was suggested to me in a conversation with Jonathan Z. Smith in which he described an exercise he does with his college students: they are asked to imagine that Emile Durkheim is a member of the Court in *Lynch*.

For a discussion of materialism as an element of the celebration of Christmas, see Part II, "Christmas and Materialism," in Daniel Miller, ed., *Unwrapping Christmas* (Oxford: Clarendon Press, 1993).

[37] See Miller, *Unwrapping Christmas*, for the argument that materialism and its redemption have always been central to Christmas and are a key, along with the theme of the family, to understanding Christmas in its present role as *the* global festival.

[38] 463 U.S. 783 (1983).

his choice of the *Marsh* case as *the* precedent for the *Lynch* decision raises several problems. The majority opinion in *Marsh* itself had emphasized the unique nature of that case. The *Marsh* decision was explicitly declared in the majority opinion to be outside the normal First Amendment jurisprudence and therefore to be of no precedential value.[39] While loudly disclaiming longstanding historical practice as a way of constitutionalizing what would otherwise be unconstitutional, the *Marsh* Court in fact allows just that. The Court concludes in *Marsh* that legislative chaplains must be constitutional because they were authorized by the First Congress, which must have intended congressional chaplaincy as either an exemption to the First Amendment or as a modification of the apparent meaning of its words.

Longstanding historical practice had also been held to validate tax exemption for churches. In the opinions in both *Marsh* and *Walz,* the Court appears to be acknowledging that the two decisions are aberrations. But for the longstanding historical practice, the two *would* have been unconstitutional under then current First Amendment religion clauses jurisprudence. Burger's addition of a third explicit[40] exception—Christmas—suggests a serious problem with the current application of the First Amendment and with the Court's understanding of religion. The exceptions seem to be swallowing the rule.

Burger's reliance on the First Congress's employment of chaplains as emblematic of the Constitution's intended accommodation of American religion at the time of the First Amendment, however, is also troublesome because of the historically changing nature of the congressional chaplaincy. In his article on the First Amendment, Stephen Botein persuasively argues that early congressional chaplains were not employed in order to celebrate public religiosity, as they much later came to be, but were needed because of the demands of congressional service on the representatives. Botein asserts that congressional chaplains served as personal counselors to members far from home, not as celebrators of a national commitment to religion:

It seems clear that the chaplains were not understood by most people to be ministering to the government at all. Instead, they were supplying personal

---

[39] See also Walz v. Tax Commission, 397 U.S. 664 (1970).

[40] There are clearly many state "accommodations" of religion of dubious constitutionality which the Court tolerates by not considering them.

pastoral assistance to individuals. . . . For the makeshift boardinghouse community that was Washington after the turn of the century, this was spiritual and not so greatly dissimilar to that provided by military chaplains.[41]

Congressional service, Botein implies, was at that time analogous to military service in the enforced isolation of its representatives.[42] The employment of chaplains by the armed forces is arguably constitutional because service men and women, like inmates of prisons, are removed by the state from access to religious associations of their choice. Failure to provide chaplains in either case arguably might even constitute a denial of a First Amendment right to free exercise of religion.

Botein makes this argument in the context of his larger point that the Federal government in 1789 lacked the attributes of a state that would have made it a natural locus for religious experience and expression.[43] The Constitution is overwhelmingly secular, he argues, partly because the religiousness of the American community was expressed at the state level, not at the federal level:

In view of the pattern of religious reference pervading the state constitutions, it is most curious, not that the United States Constitution was faulted for its secularity [which it was by a small minority], but that so few people appear to have cared. The problem, in other words, is to explain the prevailing indifference to the secularity of what was framed in Philadelphia. . . . Compared with the government of the several states, conceivably [the federal government] was too distant from the citizenry and too restricted in the scope of its responsibility to require an official religious dimension. By the very nature of its limitations, it did not have to be directly associated with "sacred things." It was not so much that church and state had to be separated at the federal level, then, as that there was no federal level to be kept separate.[44]

Botein goes on to point out that the rise in importance of the federal government in the nineteenth century coincided with a rise in the religiosity attributed to the federal government—including the establishment of regular Sunday services in the Capitol and an increase in the importance of the congressional chaplaincy—which rose to a peak

---

[41] Botein, "Religious Dimensions," 323.

[42] Botein, "Religious Dimensions."

[43] But, see Catherine L. Albanese, *Sons of the Fathers: The Civil Religion of the American Revolution* (Philadelphia: Temple University Press, 1976), for a lively and convincing description of the revolutionary civil religion of the new nation.

[44] Botein, "Religious Dimensions," 321–22.

during the Civil War. It is, thus, not surprising that the 1860s produced Abraham Lincoln, perhaps our greatest public theologian.

What Burger sees as an unbroken historical practice of public religiosity endorsing his view of the Constitution, a close-up look by an historian reveals to be a series of different practices with different purposes. As Botein concludes, and as Brennan emphasizes in his dissent in *Marsh*,[45] it seems unlikely that the First Congress intended by its establishment of the congressional chaplaincy to establish a precedent of generally endorsing public religious celebrations.[46] At the very least, however, it is a risky and questionable practice to use a selective reading of controversial history to validate constitutional interpretation.

It is even more risky in the case of Christmas. Burger characterizes Pawtucket's celebration as "tak[ing] note of a significant historical religious event *long* celebrated in the Western World" and as the observance of a "traditional event *long* recognized as a National Holiday" (emphasis added). This is an extremely problematic characterization of what Christmas is. Christmas, whatever else it may be, almost certainly does not commemorate an "historical event" in the sense Burger apparently means it—in the way the Fourth of July commemorates the signing of the Declaration of Independence. The infancy narratives, as the nativity story is known to biblical scholars, are among the most unreliable, historically speaking, of the gospel narratives.[47] The myths supporting the celebration of Christmas find their origins in the complex of ancient religions of the Mediterranean that predate the invention of Christianity and are the ongoing creation of a changing community over time. In a narrow sense, in any event, the doctrinal foundation for Christmas in most Christian traditions is that it celebrates the incarnation of God, not the birth of an historical figure. Trying to tame public religion by calling it history has the curiously reifying effect on historical narrative of denying the process by which such narratives are created. It cheapens history as well as religion.

Furthermore, as Justice Brennan notes in his dissent in *Lynch*,

---

[45] 463 U.S. at 795–822.

[46] Botein, "Religious Dimensions," 317, 330. Marsh v. Chambers, 463 U.S. 783, 813–21 (Brennan, J., dissenting).

[47] *Anchor Bible Dictionary*, s.v. "Infancy Narratives."

Christmas has not been *long* celebrated in the United States. The Puritans strongly objected to the celebration of Christmas, which they regarded as popish.[48] The celebration of Christmas was illegal in the Massachusetts Bay Colony from 1659 until 1681 and continued to be regarded with suspicion by many Protestant sects until well into the nineteenth century. Christmas was first recognized by Congress as a holiday only when it became a legal day off for the District of Columbia in 1870. It was not declared a holiday for federal employees until 1885.[49] Christmas as we know it is the invention of Charles Dickens, Washington Irving, and Victorian department stores.[50] Scrooge's nephew may well have been the first person to wish anyone a "Merry Christmas."[51] The celebration of Christmas cannot be constitutionalized by longstanding historical practice.

Burger's other historical "proof" is also unpersuasive. God was only added to the Pledge of Allegiance in 1892 as part of the quadricentennial of Columbus. National days of prayer have had an uneven and controversial career. Both Jefferson and Madison objected to proclaiming them. Like congressional chaplains, national days of prayer seem to rise and fall in status depending on the extent to which the union is sacralized. Burger's is a rather thin set of examples to support a generalized and unbroken national commitment to accommodate *religion*. It is not even clear that any of this is religion. Burger, like Dickens for England, is "inventing" tradition in order to support a version of what it means to be American.[52]

In spite of the inconsistency of his logic and the poverty of his historical evidence, Burger's opinion has a certain relentless power,

---

[48] Roman Catholic Pawtucket's celebration, if they knew of it, would presumably only confirm this prejudice.

[49] 465 U.S. at 720–21.

[50] J. M. Golby and A. W. Purdue, *The Making of Modern Christmas* (Athens: University of Georgia Press, 1986). Golby and Purdue note that Christmas fell out of favor as an English holiday at the end of the eighteenth century and in fact was not mentioned in the *Times* of London between 1790 and 1835. See, also, Miller, *Unwrapping Christmas*.

[51] See further discussion of the history of the celebration of Christmas and of the crèche in chapter 5.

[52] See Eric Hobsbawm and Terence Ranger, *The Invention of Tradition* (Cambridge: Cambridge University Press, 1983).

causing the reader to question his or her own experience. Perhaps Christmas and the crèche have indeed lost any religious content or reference. Perhaps Christmas is harmless. Perhaps, in some sense, we have always celebrated it. In taking this approach, however, in so rigidly ruling out alternative experiences of Christmas and the crèche, Burger, like White America for Black America, has marginalized the religious experience of a large and real community.

Burger also has a seductively benign view of the state's use of religious symbols. His blatant misuse of history and of precedent may be a little startling, but his genuine conviction and insistence that it is necessary and appropriate for government to celebrate people's religiousness cannot be so easily dismissed. He is right. Religion of all kinds, nationalist, sectarian, and capitalist, pervades American history, and Americans are arguably the most religious industrial nation in the world. Furthermore, if Durkheim is right, all nations must be religious. It is naïve and unrealistic to expect religion to vanish from public life. It will out. People in groups *will* generate religion.[53] But how is that ineradicable religiousness to be reconciled with the First Amendment? Perhaps what is first needed is an acknowledgment of that religiousness. In that, Burger and the accommodationists or nonpreferentialists provide a needed corrective to separationist rhetoric. Americans from the time of the Revolution have been creating American religion in many forms, whether or not it is called religion.[54] To deny that fact may lead, in part, to the vocal outrage of groups such as the Moral Majority.[55] Whether or not it should be "accommodated," religion should be acknowledged.

THE JAPANESE MAJORITY

The power of Burger's opinion is heightened by a comparison of the *Lynch* case with the Nakaya case, a recent case in the Supreme Court of Japan.[56] While the Japanese Supreme Court has a different consti-

---

[53] See Botein, "Religious Dimensions," 330.

[54] Albanese, *Sons of the Fathers*. See, also, Catherine Albanese, *Nature Religion in America: From the Algonkian Indians to the New Age* (Chicago: University of Chicago Press, 1990).

[55] See Carter, *The Culture of Disbelief.*

[56] Showa 63 [1988] June 1. The opinions of the Supreme Court of Japan are not routinely translated into English. As I do not read Japanese, I have had the help of

tutional and cultural role from the United States Supreme Court, and the Japanese Constitution is a different kind of constitution from the American Constitution,[57] making comparison tricky, it is still enlightening to compare the cases.

The story of the negotiations, both political and linguistic, which led to the promulgation of the present Constitution of Japan is a remarkable one.[58] When Japan surrendered to the Allied powers in 1945, Japan was governed by a constitution which the emperor had "bestowed upon the nation"[59] in 1889, as a part of the Meiji Restoration (which followed the defeat of Tokugawa feudal rule in 1868). The Meiji Constitution had been drafted by Japanese legal scholars working for the emperor after extensive study of Western government and politics, including tours of Europe, and consciously followed an authoritarian Prussian model.

Immediately after his arrival in September 1945, General MacArthur took it upon himself, personally, to advise the new Japanese Cabinet that it should prepare revisions for constitutional reform in line with the objectives of the Potsdam Proclamation. Several competing Japanese versions were prepared. On 3 February 1946, however,

---

James Squires, a member of the bar of the state of Virginia, in reading and interpreting these opinions. I have also relied on several English-language descriptions of these opinions: Higuchi Yoichi, "When Society Is Itself the Tyrant," *Japan Quarterly* (October–December 1988): 350–56; Sakai Takeshi, "A Matter of Faith," *Japan Quarterly* (October–December 1988): 357–64; Helen Hardacre, *Shinto and the State, 1868–1945* (Princeton: Princeton University Press, 1989); and Norma Field, *In the Realm of the Dying Emperor* (New York: Pantheon Books 1991). See also Ernst Lokowandt, *Die Rechtliche Entwicklung des Staats-Shintô in der Ersten Hälfte der Meiji-Zeit (1868–1890)* (Wiesbaden: Otto Harrassowitz, 1978).

[57] See Said Amir Arjomand, "Constitutions and the Struggle for Political Order: A Study in the Modernization of Political Traditions," *Archives européenes de sociologie. European Journal of Sociology* 33 (1992): 39–82, for a comparison of modern constitutions and their relationship to the prevailing international political climate at the time of their creation.

[58] See Kyoko Inoue, *MacArthur's Japanese Constitution: A Linguistic and Cultural Study of Its Making* (Chicago: University of Chicago Press, 1991). Inoue, a linguist, traces the exciting and surprising story of the creation of the language of the present Japanese Constitution.

[59] Carol Gluck, *Japan's Modern Myths* (Princeton: Princeton University Press, 1985), 43.

MacArthur, concerned that the Japanese proposals would not go far enough, and that his own power would be curtailed by the approaching meetings of the Far Eastern Commission and the Allied Council for Japan,[60] without waiting for an official Japanese proposal, directed three army lawyers on his own staff to draft a new constitution for Japan.

The American draft was presented to the Japanese Cabinet a week later. After threats by the Americans to take the draft to the Japanese people, the Japanese prime minister agreed to write a draft based on the American draft. That draft was delivered in person to general headquarters on 4 March 1946. When the Japanese lawyers arrived, they were told that the final version had to be prepared immediately. The American and Japanese lawyers were locked in a room guarded by military police and told to write a final constitution within twenty-four hours! The resulting document, which was basically a translation of the American draft, was released to the press the following afternoon.[61] After largely *pro forma* constitutional debates, the new Constitution of Japan, written by American army lawyers who were largely ignorant of Japanese language, history, and culture, was promulgated on 3 November 1946. Like the Meiji Constitution some fifty years earlier, the 1946 constitution was presented to the Japanese people by the emperor, a *fait accompli*, having had virtually no Japanese popular input.

In dramatic contrast to the long process of American constitutional formation conducted by a remarkably talented and thoughtful group of people, who had a large personal stake in its adequacy—a process enshrined in American history and regarded with awe and admiration by most Americans—the drafting of the Japanese Constitution, presided over by the extraordinary arrogance of MacArthur, seems an unbelievably hurried, awkward, and hugger-mugger affair. The process resulted, Kyoko Inoue argues in her book on the Japanese Constitution, in a series of cultural and linguistic misunderstandings, without which, ironically, the two sides would not have been able to agree.

Two crucial and underlying misunderstandings between the American and Japanese lawyers concerned the nature and location of

---

[60] The Far Eastern Commission and the Allied Council for Japan were committees of representatives of the Allied powers appointed to oversee the occupation.

[61] The part played by Americans in the creation of the new constitution was officially kept secret until the American occupation ended in 1952.

sovereignty and the concepts of rights and duties. The American Constitution begins with "We the People. . ." and is rhetorically positioned as an act of the American people. Sovereignty in the American Constitution explicitly rests with the people and is linked to limited government. This is true both in theory and in linguistic expression.

Many years of Japanese history and religiopolitical theory, including an ancient but enduring theocratic ideal and a view of Japan as a "natural community," supported a firm Japanese conviction that sovereignty rested in the government, not in the people. The Meiji Constitution explicitly affirmed this belief that the government ruled on behalf of the nation, granting rights as it saw fit.[62] The 1946 Constitution, after prolonged negotiation over the role of the emperor, only slightly modified this tradition by granting shared sovereignty between the emperor and the people.[63]

While the Americans who wrote the Japanese Constitution were partly inspired by the model of the American Constitution and were committed in theory to popular sovereignty, they were also immensely influenced by the New Deal. The American draft of the Japanese Constitution, therefore, was a hybrid, emphasizing popular sovereignty on the one hand, yet full of social welfare provisions exhorting the Japanese government to social reform. For example, Article 24 of the American draft read, "Laws shall be designed for the promotion and extension of social welfare." This effort to promote a "welfare state" only reinforced the paternalistic Japanese view of government.

In the United States Constitution popular sovereignty is further reinforced by the use of the English linguistic form "shall" as in "Congress shall make no law. . ."—a form which does not exist in Japanese. When translated into Japanese, the American draft articles which use this form were translated as simple assertions. Thus, for example, the American version of Article 32, "No person shall be denied the right of access to the courts," became, in Japanese, according to Inoue's translation, "No person is/will be denied the right of access

---

[62] Inoue, *MacArthur's Japanese Constitution*, 81.

[63] Inoue, *MacArthur's Japanese Constitution*, 82. Article 1 of the 1946 Constitution reads, "The Emperor shall be the symbol of the State and of the unity of the people, deriving his position from the will of the people with whom resides sovereign power."

to the courts." Inoue concludes that "[t]he extensive use of the simple nonpast tense form. . .[as well as the vocabulary choices in the translation]. . .have virtually eliminated the sense of the people's authority to command the government."[64]

It is also not clear in the Japanese Constitution who is commanding whom because the articles have no subjects. The inescapable effect of the situation of the drafting is that it reads as if the Americans are commanding the Japanese, not as if the Japanese people are commanding their government. The absence of agency on the part of the Japanese people is regarded by Inoue as an accurate reflection of the historically passive relationship of the Japanese people to their government, as well as to the power of an occupying force.[65]

The Japanese Constitution, thus, does not recognize any right in the people against the government. The people do not command the government, as in the American Constitution. What Inoue calls "the illocutionary force" of the Japanese Constitution is quite differently located:

The language of the new Constitution, in form and content, says that the government, joined by the people, undertakes the responsibility to create a democratic government, and to safeguard the citizen's rights and liberties.[66]

Japanese cultural emphasis on group loyalty, harmony, and conciliation is also a contributing factor in producing a very low level of "rights consciousness."[67]

In spite of the extraordinary circumstances of its promulgation, the Japanese Constitution of 1946 remains in place, and after forty-five years seems firmly so.[68] The "misunderstandings" noted by Kyoko Inoue, however, continue to affect recent cases. Japanese political

---

[64] Inoue, *MacArthur's Japanese Constitution*, 84–85.

[65] Inoue, *MacArthur's Japanese Constitution*, 102–3.

[66] Inoue, *MacArthur's Japanese Constitution*, 103.

[67] Dan Fenno Henderson, "Law and Political Modernization in Japan," in Robert E. Ward, ed., *Political Development in Modern Japan* (Princeton: Princeton University Press, 1968).

[68] In 1957 a commission was established by the National Diet to study the need for constitutional revision. An extensive review was conducted over seven years. Any actual revisions, however, seem unlikely for political reasons. John Maki, trans. and ed., *Japan's Commission on the Constitution: The Final Report* (Seattle: University of Washington, 1980).

history and theory, Japanese linguistic style, and the circumstances of the drafting of the Japanese Constitution, combined with the particular nature of Japanese religion, influence, for example, the nature of Japanese constitutional litigation and the role of the Japanese Supreme Court as an interpreter of the religion articles of the Constitution.

The American attempt to impose the First Amendment's prohibition of religious establishment and its guarantee of religious freedom on Japan—and the subsequent history of the results of that attempt—provides an interestingly compressed view of the modern interaction of religion and government. The richness and diversity of Japanese religious traditions and the very different social style of Japanese religion from American religion (which was shaped primarily by Protestant denominational cultural forms) were largely misunderstood by MacArthur's staff.[69] MacArthur himself saw his own role in somewhat apocalyptic terms. He believed that the Meiji government's

---

[69] Many authors have tried to describe the contours of modern Japanese religion. H. Byron Earhart, in *Religions of Japan: Many Traditions Within One Sacred Way* (San Francisco: Harper & Row, 1984), 22, sees it as many separate traditions, "within one sacred way." This characterization may suggest too monolithic a picture. Japanese religion seems somehow, though, to be an interestingly dynamic blend exhibiting both diversity and unity, across both space and time. Robert Bellah describes this blend as follows: "I would say that Japanese religion is fundamentally concerned with harmony—harmony among persons and with nature. Each strand of the tradition views harmony somewhat differently and offers its own peculiar approach." *Tokugawa Religion*, xix.

The different strands originated at different periods of Japanese history. The earliest strand is the prehistoric beginning of what is now called Shinto, which Joseph Kitagawa translates "the way of the kami": Kitagawa, *Religion in Japanese History*, 11. For most of Japanese history, Shinto was a loosely related set of indigenous and local nature cults centering in the *kami* (spirits or gods), which were, in turn, even more loosely related to the emperor cult. Very early in Japanese history, in the third to sixth century, however, Buddhist, Confucian, and Taoist ideas and cults were introduced into Japan. In the sixteenth century, the Jesuits brought Christianity to Japan.

Buddhism was in the ascendancy as a state religion for many centuries. However, as part of the Meiji Imperial Restoration at the end of the nineteenth century, Buddhism was disestablished as a state religion and some Shinto rites and shrines were consolidated and expanded to create a structure and mythology which could be consciously manipulated to support a national ideology. That ideology is known as State or Shrine Shinto (as opposed to what was distinguished by the Meiji

control and promotion of State Shinto was responsible for the oppression of the Japanese people. He encouraged the return of Christian missionaries to Japan after the war and frequently expressed his belief that Japanese religious freedom would lead to the mass conversion of Japan to Christianity.[70]

Religion was, therefore, high among the items on the American agenda for constitutional reform. The Meiji Constitution, partly as a result of pressure from Western nations with which the Meiji govern-

---

government as Cult, or sect, Shinto), and was explicitly designated as not religious by the Meiji government.

With the possible exception of Christianity, for most Japanese these different religious traditions are not regarded as necessarily mutually exclusive. Any one individual or family might participate in rituals of different traditions on different occasions or at different times in their lives and may study the writings and ideas of different traditions. (This may be true in the United States to a greater extent than is usually acknowledged, because of widespread intermarriage among religious traditions and because of the simultaneous practice of civil and sectarian religions.)

Like the religious traditions of other industrialized nations, those of Japan have been profoundly affected by urbanization, secularization, and economic vicissitudes. As Carol Gluck points out, the carefully constructed Meiji national ideology was already bankrupt by the time of the Second World War because of the many changes in Japanese society which belied the national portrait painted by the Meiji ideologues. Gluck, *Japan's Modern Myths*, 279–86. In addition to the changes within the long-standing traditions, there has been the emergence of the so-called New Religions of Japan, which since the early nineteenth century have called the Japanese to new religious consciousnesses adapted for a new society—religious consciousnesses which reinterpret the traditional strands and combine them with new elements. Kitagawa, *Religion in Japanese History*, 306–31.

Although State Shinto was abolished by special directive of MacArthur in 1945, and the emperor formally renounced his divinity shortly thereafter, Shinto remains a national symbolic source for the Japanese, as can be seen from the recent impressive enthronement of the new Japanese emperor in an elaborate Shinto ceremony. Even today, when the Shinto cosmogonic myth recounting the divine origins of the imperial family is relatively unknown to most Japanese, Shinto's great age and its association with what is indigenously Japanese gives it continued power in a country humiliated by military defeat and with a long history of foreign influences. There have been repeated unsuccessful conservative efforts to have certain national shrines declared non-religious so that they may be officially patronized and sponsored. For the Japanese dissenters, on the other hand, Shinto represents militarism and suppression. There are continued protests, for example, over tribute paid at shrines by Japanese prime ministers.

[70] William P. Woodward, *The Allied Occupation of Japan 1945–1952 and Japanese Religions* (Leiden: E. J. Brill, 1972), 78, 241–42.

ment wished to trade, had guaranteed religious liberty in these words:

Japanese subjects have freedom of religious belief, within limits not prejudicial to peace and order and not antagonistic to their duties as subjects.[71]

Under this provision Shrine or State Shinto was declared not to be a religion, but to be a suprareligious entity providing the nation's rites and creed. This decision permitted it to be used as a basis for nationalistic ideology and as an element in patriotic education without offending the separation of church and state and the secular ideal.[72]

At the same time, according to Helen Hardacre, the Meiji government privatized and controlled Buddhism, Christianity, and sect Shinto under the Religious Organizations Law of 1939. This law embodied a Protestant-derived division of doctrine and faith from rites that was expressed in the above constitutional guarantee of freedom of religious *belief*.[73] Prime Minister Kiichirō, presenting this law to the Diet, explained the policy:

In our country the way of the *kami* (Shintō) is the absolute way, and the people of the nation all must respectfully follow it. Teachings which differ from this and conflict with it are not allowed to exist.[74]

The Constitution and laws of the Meiji government had made a careful division of religion, drawing a line between the rites of the civil religion and private sectarian religion.

Article 20 of the 1946 American draft of the Japanese Constitution, which was unchanged in the final Japanese version, reads as follows:

Freedom of religion is guaranteed to all. No religious organization shall receive any privileges from the State, nor exercise any political authority. No

---

[71] Article 28. Inoue, *MacArthur's Japanese Constitution*, 115.

[72] This patriotic use of Shinto was effected partly through the Imperial Rescript on Education, which was venerated as a document embodying national ideals of filiality and loyalty derived from both Confucian and Shinto traditions. See Joseph Kitagawa, "Some Reflections on Japanese Religion and Its Relationship to the Imperial System," *Japanese Journal of Religious Studies* 17 (December 1990): 169–74, on his own memory of being required as a young student to memorize and venerate the Imperial Rescript.

An Imperial Rescript is a form of document originating as early as the sixth or seventh century which implies that the content is divinely revealed. Joseph Kitagawa, *On Understanding Japanese Religion* (Princeton: Princeton University Press, 1987), 73.

[73] Hardacre, *Shinto and the State*, 121.

[74] Quoted by Joseph Kitagawa in "Some Reflections," 164.

person shall be compelled to take part in any religious act, celebration, rite or practice. The State and its organs shall refrain from religious education or any other religious activity.

Article 89 also addressed religion:

No public money or other property shall be expended or appropriated for the use, benefit or maintenance of any religious institution or association, or for any charitable, educational or benevolent enterprises not under the control of public authority.

These articles expressed American concerns based on American experiences as well as largely uninformed American conclusions about the Japanese situation.[75] This is not to say that there was no Japanese support for religious freedom and the separation of church and state. There was and there existed a long history of discussion about the relationship of religion and the state in Japan. The American concerns were, however, often different from the Japanese concerns.

There was relatively little debate about Articles 20 and 89 in the National Diet at the time of ratification of the Constitution. There was also very little space given to these provisions by the recent commission to consider constitutional revision.[76] Most Japanese apparently regard these articles as having been the result of Western preoccupations necessitated by the imperial pretensions of the papacy and centuries of European religious wars. Inoue, too, regards religious freedom and the separation of church and state and their interrelationship as historically relatively unimportant issues for the Japanese people.[77]

The debate that did touch upon these articles did not address generally the need for religious freedom or for the separation of church and state[78] but concerned the effect of Article 20 on the legal status of national shrines and the effect on religious education. Legislators were

---

[75] Inoue, *MacArthur's Japanese Constitution*, 104–59.

[76] Maki, *Japan's Commission*, 283, 333–34. A total of one and a half pages out of four hundred are devoted to the subject of religion in Maki's abridged translation.

[77] Inoue, *MacArthur's Japanese Constitution*, 131, 158. See, also, Opinion of Justice Ito in the Nakaya case, Showa 63 June 1, p. 45.

[78] Inoue argues that this was partly because the emperor's renunciation of his divinity had already resulted in the disestablishment of State Shinto, as far as the Japanese were concerned. Inoue, *MacArthur's Japanese Constitution*, 158.

worried that Article 20 would negatively affect what they saw as critical for postwar Japan—the spiritual and moral education of children:

Sasaki: My point is whether it is possible to cultivate religious sentiment without referring to a particular religion. . . .

Kanamori: I don't know what educators think, but from my personal experience, I think it is possible. I don't believe in one particular religion, but I think I have gone through a few paths in cultivating religious sentiments. So I think it should be possible.[79]

Japanese legislators, like Japanese judges, make the distinction between the "particularity" of "religion," by which they seem to refer to exclusive religious traditions such as certain Buddhist sects and Christian churches, and a more diffuse immanent religious consciousness embodied in the common Japanese spiritual tradition. This theme reappears in the language of the Japanese Supreme Court.

Yasuko Nakaya, a Japanese Christian and the widow of a member of the Japanese Special Defense Forces (SDF), brought suit in 1973 against the SDF for violation of Articles 20 and 89 of the Japanese Constitution. (See the texts of these articles on pages 101–2 above.) The SDF is the name for what, in effect, is the Japanese army, and it exists in spite of (some would say in deliberate defiance of) Article 9 of the Japanese Constitution, which prohibits Japan from maintaining a standing army or engaging in war. Mrs. Nakaya's action alleged that the SDF, by apotheosizing[80] her husband as a military hero at a Shinto shrine, had violated the constitutional mandates proscribing the separation of church and state.

Mrs. Nakaya's husband, Takafumi Nakaya, who, according to the Court, ". . .did not observe any religion,"[81] had been killed in a traffic accident in 1973 while on duty. A Buddhist funeral, which Mrs. Nakaya attended, had been held for Takafumi Nakaya by his parents. Later, Mrs. Nakaya had part of his ashes interred at her church.

Several years later, the Taiyukai, a veterans' group interested in

---

[79] Inoue, *MacArthur's Japanese Constitution,* 155.

[80] According to the *Encyclopedia of Religion,* "[a]potheosis is the conferring, through official, ritual, or iconographic means, of the status of an immortal god upon a mortal person"; s.v. "Apotheosis."

[81] Showa 63 June 1, p. 36.

promoting the status of the SDF and in reviving the pre-surrender custom of enshrining servicemen, visited Mrs. Nakaya to obtain information about her husband and to ask her permission to arrange for his "apotheosis," or deification, according to Shinto ritual, at the local branch of Yasukuni Shrine,[82] along with other men who had died "in action." Mrs. Nakaya told the Taiyukai that she was a Christian and denied her permission, but the group, with the support and cooperation of the SDF,[83] carried out the apotheosis over her protest.

Yasukuni Shrine is one of a group of national shrines created as a part of the Meiji "nationalization" of Shinto at the end of the nineteenth century:

> The special status of this Shrine derived from the fact that the Emperor himself paid tribute there to the souls of the war dead. The significance of enshrining the soul of a human being in Yasukuni is that the rite of enshrining is an apotheosis symbolically changing the soul's status to that of a national deity. Accordingly, it ceases to be a mere ancestor of some household and instead attaches to the nation.[84]

Unlike the other national shrines which were administered by the Department of Interior, Yasukuni was under the supervision of the army.[85]

Mrs. Nakaya's action against the SDF sought damages for her mental suffering and sought to have her husband's name removed from the shrine.[86] The lower court ruled in her favor, awarding her one million yen. The award was upheld on appeal to an intermediate court.

---

[82] At Yasukuni, apotheosis is conferred through an elaborate ritual in which the spirits of the dead are transferred to the inner sanctuary of the shrine, and thus enrolled as national heroes. D. C. Holtom, *Modern Japan and Shinto Nationalism: A Study of Present-Day Trends in Japanese Religions*, rev. ed. (New York: Paragon Book Reprint Co., 1963).

[83] The extent of that support and cooperation was contested at trial, but most of the Japanese Court seems to have assumed that the SDF was actively involved.

[84] Hardacre, *Shinto and the State*, 90.

[85] An interesting cultural detail, cited by Helen Hardacre, illustrates the cultural status of Yasukuni Shrine. At the end of the nineteenth century there was a popular board game for children in Japan in which the quickest way to win was to land on a certain square. "Death" on that square provided instant enshrinement at Yakusuni. Hardacre, *Shinto and the State*, 91.

[86] This prayer for relief raises the interesting question of how a soul might be un-deified!

In 1988, however, fifteen years after Takafumi Nakaya died, the Supreme Court of Japan, in a fourteen to one decision, reversed the lower court decision and ordered Mrs. Nakaya to pay back the one million yen. There were six opinions filed by the Japanese Court, which, like the opinions in *Lynch*, reveal a range of readings of the facts and of the appropriate legal posture of the case.

The majority, in an opinion with no assigned author, held that the SDF was not jointly responsible with the private veterans' group for the petition to the shrine to apotheosize Mrs. Nakaya's husband. In any event, the Court held, the cooperation of the SDF with those who had filed the petition had a "weak relationship to religious consciousness,"[87] because the primary aim of the apotheosis was to elevate the social status of the SDF—to restore its tarnished image. Citing the earlier Tsu case,[88] the majority implied that, under these circumstances, apotheosis was not a religious act. Like display of the crèche in *Lynch*, the apotheosis was about celebrating civic pride and was not about religion.

The Japanese majority further held that, whereas a cause of action would lie between private parties for violation of religious freedom under the Constitution, such a cause would not lie in this case.[89]

---

[87] Showa 63 June 1, p. 38

[88] Showa 52 July 13. The Tsu case was decided by the Supreme Court of Japan in 1977. A Communist member of the Tsu City Council had brought suit against the mayor for violating Article 89 of the Constitution when he paid local Shinto priests to perform a grounds purification ceremony preceding the city's construction of a gymnasium. The city won in the trial court, but the judgment was reversed on appeal. The Supreme Court reversed again, holding that the ceremony was not religious but secular, so that its performance at public expense was not unconstitutional. There were five dissenters.

[89] A private cause of action between private parties could not be brought under the First Amendment to the United States Constitution. This aspect of the Nakaya case shows one difference between the American and the Japanese Constitutions. Suits for violation of either clause of the First Amendment to the United States Constitution are brought against the government. A suit against another private citizen or organization for infringement of religious liberty would have to be brought under a common law theory of intentional tort and would be very difficult to prove. In fact, it is almost impossible to conceive of such a suit in an American court. Religious liberty in the United States only exists in the relationship between the government and the citizens, not as among citizens. Interfering with another private party's religion would be considered a tort, not an infringement of religious liberty. Only the government can affect religious liberties. Recent complaints by Native American

Yasukuni Shrine, a private organization, had not violated Mrs. Nakaya's rights. There was no coercion of Mrs. Nakaya to practice a faith other than her own,[90] and she had no constitutional right to what the lower court had termed "tranquility of spiritual life."

Mrs. Nakaya's "religious human rights" were not violated, according to the majority, because freedom of religion requires "tolerance" toward action based on a faith which disagrees with one's own:

The freedom to undertake religious activities such as making someone the object of one's faith, memorializing people according to one's faith, or seeking serenity of souls, is guaranteed to all.[91]

"All" includes Yasukuni Shrine and the SDF, both of which seem to have a constitutional right to religious freedom under this theory. Mrs. Nakaya, in fact, far from having had her own rights violated, had, according to this theory, by filing this suit, run the risk of violating the rights of others. The Japanese majority moved quickly to the whole religious picture, with a greater sensitivity to the need for harmony in a situation of religious pluralism than probably would be seen in the American constitutional context, focusing, as it does, on individual rights. The appropriate American analogy might be the free speech doctrine that makes it extremely difficult to libel or to invade the

---

groups about "poaching" by New Age enthusiasts may raise a parallel situation. Michael Haederle, "Spirit in Disguise," *Chicago Tribune,* 4 May 1994.

In contrast, the language of Article 20 of the Japanese Constitution, as is borne out by all of the opinions in this case, does not necessarily give the Japanese citizen a right against the government. The government takes on a responsibility in the Constitution for ensuring religious freedom but the choice of how to do that rests largely with the government. The Supreme Court of Japan speaks with a paternalistic voice, seeking religious harmony, rebuking where necessary, but not seeming to feel called upon to recognize rights. The majority opinion emphasizes that "Article 20, Section 3, provides for a systemic guarantee of the separation of church and state, and does not directly secure the religious freedom of individuals." Showa 63 June 1, 38.

[90] The emphasis on lack of coercion as a key factor in the Court's decision finds an interesting parallel in the argument of the dissents in the recent United States Supreme Court case, Lee v. Weisman, 112 S. Ct. 2649 (1992). In his dissent in the *Weisman* case, Justice Scalia argued that, as long as the government did not coerce participation, it could engage in religious celebration.

[91] Showa 63 June 1, 39.

privacy of public figures. By dying, Mr. Nakaya had become public property.

A parallel in the American situation might be the recognition of the right of Arlington Cemetery or of the United States Armed Services to memorialize a serviceman whose family objected for religious reasons. It seems likely, in the American context, that the religious views of the family would be honored, as, for example, if there was a religious objection to including the name of a serviceman on the Vietnam Memorial. Is another parallel, perhaps, the Supreme Court's recognition of the religious rights of the city of Pawtucket? That may be changing, however, and the *Lynch* case may signal such a change. Mayor Lynch and others expressed a fear similar to that of the Japanese majority of repression of majority religious rights.

There are four opinions in the Nakaya case which agree with the majority holding but which offer modifications of the opinion. Justice Nagashima, in contrast to the majority, begins by stating that apotheosis *is* a religious ceremony, but, like the majority, he urges tolerance. After a long discussion of the need for forbearance among religions, he comes to the actions of the SDF and concludes, like the majority, that "the consciousness of the SDF's intent was worldly in nature with a weak religious dimension."[92] Justices Takashima, Yotsuya, and Okuno concentrate on censoring the SDF, through a rehearsal of the history of the Japanese relationship of church and state, and conclude that "officials should not do anything that might cast doubt on their religious neutrality."[93] Justices Shimatani and Sato conclude that, although the SDF did engage in religious activity, Mrs. Nakaya had no standing to bring a suit against the SDF. Justice Sakagami argues that Yasukuni Shrine, not the SDF, violated Mrs. Nakaya's "religious human rights."[94] These opinions, like the opinions of Justices Burger and O'Connor in *Lynch*, labor to exonerate the government.

All of the opinions in the Nakaya case display concern over the SDF's activities in the area; several, including the majority, directly censor the SDF for its involvement, but they are disinclined to see the issue as one involving citizen rights *against* the government. The focus

---

[92] Showa 63 June 1, 42.
[93] Showa 63 June 1, 42.
[94] Showa 63 June 1, 44.

is on the relationship among the various religious traditions. The emphasis is on harmony and tolerance. As in Burger's opinion, there is a certain disingenuousness in the Japanese Court's presentation of the unity and harmlessness of Japanese religion and in its impatience with "scrupulous" minorities.[95] Like Burger, the Japanese justices have great confidence in their ability to draw a line between a "worldly" and a "religious" consciousness.

Justice Ito, the lone dissent in the Nakaya case, argues for affirmation of the appellate court decision. He begins with Mrs. Nakaya's "spiritual pain and suffering" and goes on to argue that she has a right to "religious peace of mind." He urges that a minority perspective must be adopted when addressing human rights. His position might be analogized to the strict scrutiny doctrine in the American constitutional context. Justice Ito quotes the dissent in the Tsu case:

Even where there is a view which one might regard as based on the extreme scrupulousness of minorities, we must not upon the decision of the majority permit the violation of well-being and religious freedom.[96]

He then reviews at length the actions of SDF personnel and concludes that they *were* joint participants in the petition to the shrine.

Justice Ito finally considers the purpose of the petition to the shrine and whether the apotheosis should be considered religious activity. He distinguishes the enshrinement in the Nakaya case from the grounds purification ceremony in the Tsu case, which was held to be merely customary: "To view the apotheosis' aim as not having religious significance is to improperly make light of the act's objective meaning."[97] Ito concludes that the SDF's support of the petition was unconstitutional. Although Justice Ito affirms the separation of church and state as a systemic guarantee, he, too, emphasizes that no individual rights are guaranteed by that provision of the Constitution. Like the other opinions of the Japanese Supreme Court, he focuses on the desirability of social harmony and mutual tolerance. The goal is tranquility.

For left-wing and liberal critics of the Japanese government who

---

[95] See Field, *In the Year of the Dying Emperor*, for discussion of the difficulty of expressing dissent in Japan.

[96] Showa 63 June 1, 46.

[97] Showa 63 June 1, 48.

are concerned that the government is interested in promoting Japanese nationalism through a revival of certain Meiji-period customs, the Nakaya decision highlights serious issues about individual rights, the historic repression of minority religions in Japan, and Japanese militarism.[98] For most Japanese, one suspects that, like the crèche for Justice Burger, it is much ado about very little.

THE CASES COMPARED

Notwithstanding the historical, cultural, and legal differences between the Nakaya and *Lynch* cases, there are clear parallels between the arguments made by the Japanese and those made by the American majorities. It is true that the defendants in *Lynch* do not dispute the existence of state action. The crèche was clearly sponsored by the city. The involvement of the SDF in the Nakaya apotheosis is arguably more remote. However, conceding the SDF's involvement in and support of the enshrinement,[99] the majorities in each case focus on purpose or motive. In each case, the motive of the government is seen to be secular. The motives of Pawtucket, Tsu City, and the SDF are similar: to promote civic spirit. The fact that to do so they use religious symbols and ceremonies is viewed by the two courts as secondary.

Why do American and Japanese justices publicly affirm traditional religious forms, even if they do so by calling them secular? The problem for these courts is how to acknowledge, support, and celebrate the whole—"the inherent sacredness of central authority," in Geertz's words[100]—in the context of a religiously pluralistic but highly secular society. In the 1946 debate at the National Diet on ratification of the

[98] Yasukuni Shrine is a focus of post-war debate about Japanese nationalist ideology. The shrine includes apotheosized convicted Japanese war criminals and symbolizes for many in Japan the excesses of Japanese imperialism. A brochure given to Norma Field when she visited Yasukuni provides this description of the "Memorial to the Heroic Martyrs of the War Crimes Trial" at the local branch of Yasukuni in which Mrs. Nakaya's husband is enshrined: "Exalts the illustrious memory and comforts the souls of the martyrs from Yamagushi Prefecture who were executed, committed suicide, or died in prisons, their innocence unrecognized, due to the one-sided trial conducted by the victorious nations of the Greater East Asia War." Field, *In the Realm of the Dying Emperor*, 149.

[99] The Japanese opinions can be read, I think, to be doing this although they were unwilling to allow that concession to attain legal significance.

[100] Geertz, *Local Knowledge*, 146.

Japanese Constitution, Sato Gisen of the Liberal Party stated his position:

Of course, I go along with the notion that what belongs to God should be rendered unto God, what belongs to Caesar should be rendered to Caesar, and religion and state should be separated. But that does not mean that religion is not necessary for politics.[101]

The majorities on the American and Japanese Supreme Courts would agree, and they are willing to bend the words to their purpose.

In modern societies what appears, at least in Durkheim's work, to be the necessarily close coincidence between complete integration and religion is impossible.[102] Edward Shils seems to see it as characteristic of modern society (probably this is true of all societies) that there is a constant tension among "competing conceptions about the ultimate locus of charisma."[103] This tension is revealed in the strain these courts put on the language they use to talk about religion: How to represent and celebrate the unity when the diversity is so apparent and so constitutionally protected? The complexity of Shils's view of society is not easily adapted to the flexing of nationalist political muscle, to constitutional doctrine, or to its application in particular cases.

While less explicit than the Meiji government's careful appropriation and deliberate "secularization" of Shinto tradition, the aim of the American majority is the same. Justice Burger, in his "accommodation" theory, attempts the solution that Americans are "a religious people," in some general way, and that that very religiousness can be constitutionally expressed through the appropriation of sectarian religious— here Christian—symbols. The Japanese justices express the position that the use of religious symbols is permissible by emphasizing that the Japanese are *not* a religious people. While reserving "religious" as an epithet for those who are excessively "scrupulous," they affirm the Japaneseness of Shinto deification, as a symbol of national unity, in a generalized way. The religious nature of the Japanese people is to be not religious!

[101] Inoue, *MacArthur's Japanese Constitution*, 149.

[102] I would probably argue that this is true of all societies. See, also, Lincoln, *Discourse and the Construction of Society*, which argues that religious discourse is a strategy of minorities, as well as of majorities.

[103] Edward Shils, *Center and Periphery: Essays in Macrosociology* (Chicago: University of Chicago Press, 1975), 275.

Neither Burger nor the Japanese justices intend to establish a majority religion, in the traditional, coercive, and exclusive sense. Both would vehemently object to such a characterization of their opinions. They seem to be seeking a way to have their cake and eat it, too: a way to acknowledge, even accommodate, religious unity, while endorsing religious tolerance at the same time.

A similar argument apparently is being made by some of the theorists of the Hindu Nation movement in India: that to be Indian is, in some general cultural sense, to be Hindu—a sense that does not prevent one also being of a sectarian or non-Hindu faith as well. The theorists of the French Revolution made similar assumptions: that religion was necessary for good government and good citizenship. It was somehow essential to being French. They tried several variations: a remodeled Constitutional Church, a consciously invented revolutionary cult, and, eventually, dechristianization. None of the substitutes took. One of Napoleon's first acts was to reestablish the French Church.[104]

Both American and Japanese majority solutions, like the contemporary Hindu Nation movement in India and the religious experiments of the French revolutionaries, however, invite, no doubt unintentionally, manipulation from the right. Whereas Burger and the Japanese majority may wish to endorse a benign celebration of civic spirit, accommodation of nonsectarian religion or nonreligion may be appropriated as a battle cry for those whose purpose is more particular and divisive. The Hindu Nation movement has also led to violence against Muslims. Napoleon's strategic compromise with the Catholic Church only intensified the split between secular and ultramontane France. And, in the United States, the need to acknowledge religion is used as a foot in the door for a wide spectrum from the religious right who wish to put their God in the White House and in Congress. The same appears to be true in Japan. Accommodation is hard to contain.

What Burger and the Japanese Court are insisting on, however, with their Lewis Carroll-like language, is that writing separation into the

---

[104] By then, of course, the damage had been done. Disestablishment had divided the French populace, made secularism respectable, and insured the ultramontanism of the French Church, which thereafter looked to Rome rather than to Paris for leadership.

Constitution is not enough. We have to work together to create a new public language and practice about religion that will acknowledge the religiousness of people in a new way. Otherwise religion will be defined by the right, by those who seem to think that they have a monopoly on the "religious" perspective. The title of John Noonan's case book, *The Believer and the Powers That Are*,[105] suggests an adversarial relationship between the religious believer and the secular state. If the center is defined as secular and religion is by definition excluded from the center, religion will be defined by the extremes and will be limited to the prophetic voice.

---

[105] See above, chapter 1, n. 4.

Chapter 4

Discourse II: Justice O'Connor

Equal Justice Under Law.
—Carved over the entrance to the United States Supreme Court.

The concept of equality of conscience, which began as a claim for equal treatment between warring sects, thus ends by forming a perfect unity with the perfect equality of individuals. Whatever an individual's heritage, convictions, or associations, the government's only legitimate knowledge of him or her is as the sovereign possessor of autonomous moral being.
—Pole, *The Pursuit of Equality in American History*[1]

When the Law will come, it will do away with the Druid's magic spells that come from the lips of the false black demon.
—Irish Fairy Tale[2]

[T]he best way to take into account the full range of symbols, good and bad, noble and vain, is for the legal system to *ignore* them all—mine and yours alike.
—Epstein, *Forbidden Grounds*[3]

Justice O'Connor's concurring opinion introduces a new dimension to the discourse about religion in *Lynch*. It is a dimension that is articulated in and finds its origin in the political language of the 1940s and 1950s, the time in which the Court first began to articulate a modern First

---

[1] Pole, *The Pursuit of Equality in American History*, 111.

[2] The fairy maiden in "Connla and the Fairy Maiden," in Joseph Jacobs, ed., *Celtic Fairy Tales* (London: D. Nutt, 1892), 3.

[3] Richard Epstein, *Forbidden Grounds: The Case Against Employment Discrimination Laws* (Cambridge: Harvard University Press, 1992), 498–99.

Amendment jurisprudence. It is, in fact, not a discourse about religion. It is a discourse about law. It is a religious discourse about law, rather than a legal discourse about religion. Like Burger's, it blurs the distinctiveness of religion.

JUSTICE BLACK

In 1968, toward the end of his long career as an associate justice of the United States Supreme Court, Hugo Lafayette Black delivered the James S. Carpentier lectures at Columbia Law School. They were subsequently published under the title *A Constitutional Faith*.[4] In them Black expounded his "beliefs" about the United States Constitution, "the basic tenets of this faith," as he said.[5] He concluded with these sentences:

[The] Constitution is my legal bible; its plan of our government is my plan and its destiny my destiny. I cherish every word of it, from the first to the last, and I personally deplore even the slightest deviation from its least important commands. I have thoroughly enjoyed my small part in trying to preserve our Constitution with the earnest desire that it may meet the fondest hope of its creators, which was to keep this nation strong and great through countless ages.[6]

He might have left off the "legal" in the first sentence. The Constitution was his bible. Justice Black always carried a copy of the Constitution with him. He was buried with a copy in his pocket and at his funeral stacks of pocket copies of the Constitution were available as mementos for his mourners.[7]

The third of the three chapters of Justice Black's *A Constitutional Faith* is entitled "The First Amendment" and is devoted to an exposition of his views on the freedoms protected therein. Chapter 3 begins with the explanation that, as he cannot treat the entire First Amendment exhaustively in one chapter, he will limit himself principally to a

---

[4] Hugo L. Black, *A Constitutional Faith* (New York: Alfred A. Knopf, 1968).

[5] Black, *A Constitutional Faith*, xv.

[6] Black, *A Constitutional Faith*, 66.

[7] Henry J. Abraham, *Justices and Presidents: A Political History of Appointments to the Supreme Court,* 3d ed. (Oxford: Oxford University Press, 1992), 218.

discussion of freedom of speech and of the press.[8] Yet, curiously, he then immediately quotes, in full, his own views from the *Everson* case on the religion clauses.[9] He apparently does not need to talk about religion in this place, having conclusively disposed of religion in his *Everson* opinion.

Yet Chapter 3 then goes on to summarize his understanding of the amendment as a whole:

Since the basic theme of this book is my constitutional faith, I want to explain to you my belief that the First Amendment's guarantees of freedom of speech, press, and religion are the paramount protections against despotic government afforded Americans by their Bill of Rights and that the courts must never allow this protection to be diluted or weakened in any way. On the other hand, I want to emphasize that in harmony with my general views of faithful interpretation of the Constitution as written, which views I hope I have made clear in the preceding two chapters, I am vigorously opposed to efforts to extend the First Amendment's freedom of speech beyond speech, freedom of press beyond press, and freedom of religion beyond religious beliefs.[10]

For a self-proclaimed literalist in his reading of the Constitution, this is a carefully revisionist statement. In the first sentence he reverses the order of the freedoms as detailed in the amendment. Speech, which is second in the amendment, is first for Black. The concluding words of the last sentence are also curious. Whereas, according to Black, the First Amendment means "speech" when it says "speech" and "press" when it says "press," it means "religious beliefs" when it says "religion." The religion clauses, for Black, are about freedom of conscience; thus, they can be assimilated by him into the free speech and free press clauses as political freedoms and thereby be made redundant.[11] Black seems

---

[8] The First Amendment to the United States Constitution provides, in full, that, "Congress shall make no law respecting an establishment of religion, or prohibiting the free exercise thereof; or abridging the freedom of speech, or of the press; or the right of the people peaceably to assemble, and to petition the Government for a redress of grievances."

[9] Quoted above, 63, and below, 119–20.

[10] Black, *A Constitutional Faith*, 44–45.

[11] The meanings of "speech" and "press" are as highly debated, of course, as the meaning of "religion" and have been the subject of countless cases and articles. For discussions of the free speech and free press cases, see Abraham, *Freedom and the Court*, and Harry Kalven, Jr., *A Worthy Tradition: Freedom of Speech in America* (New York: Harper & Row, 1988).

to have chosen to begin his discussion of free speech with a quote from *Everson* in order to emphasize that, according to his faith, free exercise of religion has been subsumed under free speech.

This radical abridgment of the reference of the word religion affects both the establishment and the free exercise clauses. If religion means religious beliefs, then disestablishment is about not coercing religious beliefs and free exercise is about the freedom to believe and to express those beliefs in language. Both are arguably protected by the free speech clause of the First Amendment. Religious acts seem to be consciously excluded.[12] Religion is not different for Black. For Black, as is made clear in the rest of *A Constitutional Faith*, the First Amendment is about the centrality of free political expression to the government of a free people. Having made of his politics a religion, religion becomes a form of politics. Religious beliefs are a part of that political expression. Religious acts are not.

Justice Black is well-known for his view that when the Constitution says, "no law," it means "no law":

My view is, without deviation, without exception, without any ifs, buts, or whereases, that freedom of speech means that government shall not do anything to people, or, in the words of the Magna Carta, move against people, either for the views they have or the views they express or the words they speak or write. . . . Our Founding Fathers. . .wanted to ordain in this country that the new central government should not tell people what they should believe or say or publish.[13]

He also makes clear, however, that this absolutism is limited to free opinions and to free expression in words, and is not extended to free conduct, which was not necessary, in his view, to political freedom.

Known to be an absolutist in his literal reading of the language of the Constitution, Justice Black was ironically also a vociferous advocate of one of the most audacious examples of judicial expansion of the Constitution: the "nationalization" of the Bill of Rights. As written, the First Amendment religion clauses, like the rest of the Bill of Rights, apply only to the federal government. The prohibitions are addressed

---

[12] The line between speech and acts is a notoriously difficult one to draw in religion and in political expression. Justice Black's emphasis on belief is undoubtedly related to his own religious formation.

[13] Black, *A Constitutional Faith*, 45–46.

to Congress alone: "*Congress* shall make no law. . . ." Over the objections of Madison and Jefferson, the drafters of the Bill of Rights had explicitly limited its prohibitions to the federal government, leaving to the states the choice to grant or to withhold recognition of fundamental rights. At the time of the drafting of the Bill of Rights, most states had some form of religious establishment.[14] All eventually had some kind of state constitutional provision guaranteeing religious freedom and disestablishment.[15]

The First Amendment religion clauses as written and as originally passed were thus explicitly intended to limit only *federal* action. After the Civil War, primarily out of a concern that the civil rights of the new citizens, former slaves, be fully respected by the Southern states,[16] the Fourteenth Amendment to the United States Constitution was proposed and ratified, providing, in part, that:

No State shall make or enforce any law which shall abridge the privileges or immunities of citizens of the United States; *nor shall any State deprive any person of life, liberty or property, without due process of law*; nor deny to any person within its jurisdiction the equal protection of its laws. (emphasis added)

The precise significance of the words of these clauses have been the subject of extensive debate and litigation. Which particular privileges

---

[14] See Levy, *The Establishment Clause*, chaps. 1 and 2, for a description of colonial and state establishments.

[15] For example, the Rhode Island Constitution, adopted in 1842 and still in effect, provides: "Whereas Almighty God hath created the mind free; and all attempts to influence it by temporal punishments or burdens, or by civil incapacitations, tend to beget habits of hypocrisy and meanness; and whereas a principal object of our venerable ancestors, in their migration to this country and their settlement of this state, was, as they expressed it, to hold forth a lively experiment, that a flourishing civil state may stand and be best maintained with full liberty in religious concernments: We, therefore, declare that no man shall be compelled to frequent or to support any religious worship, place, or ministry whatever, except in fulfillment of his own voluntary contract; nor enforced, restrained, molested, or burdened in his body or goods; nor disqualified from holding any office, nor otherwise suffer on account of his religious belief; and that every man shall be free to worship God according to the dictates of his own conscience, and to profess and by arguments to maintain his opinion in matters of religion; and that the same shall in no wise diminish, enlarge, or affect his civil capacity." Art. 1, sec. 3.

Massachusetts was the last state constitutionally to disestablish religion. It did so in 1833.

[16] Abraham, *Freedom and the Court*, 41ff.

and immunities are intended? What process is due? What is equal protection?

One way of answering these questions has been to look at the specific provisions of the Bill of Rights to provide the detail missing in the general language of the Fourteenth Amendment. Henry Abraham expresses succinctly the problem of interpreting the Fourteenth Amendment:

> There is no disagreement that the [above italicized] portion of the Fourteenth, which was lifted verbatim from the language of the Fifth Amendment,[17] thus was intended to provide guarantees against *state* infringement supplemental to the Fifth's mandate against federal infringement. What does cause major disagreement, however, can be illustrated by two questions: first, *did* the framers of the Amendment intend to "incorporate" or "nationalize" or "carry over" the *entire* Bill of Rights through the wording of its "due process of law" clause, thereby making it applicable to the several states; and, second, regardless of their intention, *should* the Bill of Rights be applied to the states, given the nature of the rights involved and the demands of the democratic society in which we live?[18]

Justice Black's answer to the two questions summarized by Abraham was yes. He believed that the entire Bill of Rights, not just the Fifth Amendment, was incorporated into the Fourteenth Amendment through its due process clause.

Extensive legislative history and jurisprudential debate has been offered on the incorporation question. Over the course of the one hundred years following ratification of the Fourteenth Amendment in 1868, and in spite of continuing scholarly dissent,[19] the Supreme Court has gradually and selectively "incorporated" most of the provisions of the Bill of Rights, including the First Amendment, into the Fourteenth Amendment. As a result, states now, as well as Congress, "shall make no law respecting an establishment of religion or prohibiting the free exercise thereof." One consequence of this incorporation has been that when enforcing the First Amendment against the states, the Court is, as a result, also enforcing the Fourteenth Amendment and its concerns.

---

[17] The Fifth Amendment provides, in relevant part, that "No person shall. . .be deprived of life, liberty or property, without due process of law."

[18] Abraham, *Freedom and the Court*, 43–44.

[19] See, for example, William K. Lietzau, "Rediscovering the Establishment Clause: Federalism and the Rollback of Incorporation," *DePaul Law Review* 39 (summer 1990): 1191–234.

The Fourteenth Amendment has arguably thus also been "incorporated" into the First.

For the purposes of the religion clauses, it is critical to note, however, that it was not until the 1940s that the religion clauses of the First Amendment were "incorporated" into the Fourteenth. It was not until then that the Court began the serious business of interpreting and applying these clauses.[20] Only a handful of First Amendment cases had arisen before then that had raised religious objections to congressional action, and they were free exercise cases.[21] There had been no cases challenging the constitutionality of Congressional action under the establishment clause.

It was not until 1947, when an establishment clause challenge was made to the action of a state, that the Supreme Court began to address formally the meaning of the establishment clause. The jurisprudence of the religion clauses of the First Amendment is thus an eminently contemporary creation, and one created within the context of the contemporary politics of federal/state relations. The establishment clause as a judicial doctrine was invented in the last fifty years and should therefore be understood in the light of the history and culture of the last fifty years.

Everson v. Board of Education,[22] the first case to consider the constitutionality of a state statute under the establishment clause, was decided in 1947. The majority opinion in that case was written by Justice Black. His summary of the establishment clause in *Everson* has been cited countless times as *the* defining text interpreting the establishment clause:

The "establishment of religion" clause of the First Amendment means at least this: Neither a state nor the Federal Government can set up a church. Neither

[20] The Incorporation Doctrine received its first official judicial recognition in Gitlow v. N.Y., 268 U.S. 652 (1925), a free speech case.

[21] One example is Reynolds v. U.S., 98 U.S. 145 (1879), in which the Mormon defendant in a criminal trial for bigamy unsuccessfully defended on free exercise grounds. At the time Utah was still a federal territory and thus within federal jurisdiction.

Earlier cases in which the Court made comments about the separation of church and state were not First Amendment cases. See, for example, Watson v. Jones, 80 U.S. 679 (1871), which considered the appropriate test under federal common law for a judge to use in deciding between two factions for ownership of church property.

[22] 330 U.S. 1 (1947). This case is also discussed above at 86.

can pass laws which aid one religion, aid all religions, or prefer one religion over another. Neither can force nor influence a person to go to or remain away from church against his will or force him to profess a belief *or disbelief* in any religion. No person can be punished for entertaining or professing religious beliefs *or disbeliefs*, for church attendance *or non-attendance*. No tax in any amount, large or small, can be levied to support any religious activities or institutions, whatever they may be called, or whatever form they may adopt to teach or practice religion. Neither a state nor the Federal Government can, openly or secretly, participate in the affairs of any religious organizations or groups and vice versa. In the words of Jefferson, the clause against establishment of religion by law was intended to erect "a wall of separation between Church and State." (emphasis added)[23]

These words were written by a man of unshakable conviction.

In his remarkable little book on the religion clauses,[24] a cautionary tale, if you will, of constitutional interpretation, Mark DeWolfe Howe argues that the tone of establishment clause jurisprudence was enormously affected by its having developed in the 1940s, at a time when the Court and the country were preoccupied with issues of political equality. The Court's much-criticized concern to treat the believer and the non-believer alike, first articulated by Black in *Everson*, and evident in the portions emphasized above, arose, Howe argues, out of its general concern for political equality in the years leading up to the overturning of *Plessy v. Ferguson*[25] and would have been anachronistic in the eighteenth century:[26]

[T]he constitutional law of church and state which has been forming throughout the last quarter of a century has been shaped as much by collateral doctrines concerning the presuppositions of our society as it has been by political or theological principles concerning the two societies and their relationship. This century's theory of religious freedom was a by-product, as it were, of its theory of political liberty. The nation's growing awareness that

---

[23] 330 U.S. at 15.

[24] Howe, *The Garden and the Wilderness*.

[25] 163 U.S. 537 (1896). *Plessy* held that the Constitution permitted public facilities to be segregated if they were "separate but equal." *Plessy* was overturned by the Court in Brown v. Board of Education, 347 U.S. 483 (1954).

[26] Howe sees the rights of the unbeliever as being adequately and more appropriately protected by the First Amendment free speech clause.

the gravest brutality of our time is racial inequality had, I believe, important overtones in the evolving law of church and state.[27]

Howe seems concerned that the political and theological theory of church and state law should depend so much on social theory and conditions. The result, in Howe's view, of America's focus on equality in the 1940s and 1950s has been an unrecognized, illogical, and historically indefensible reading of the religion clauses which, combining Jeffersonian dogmatism with egalitarian impulses, denies any special place for religion in the Constitutional scheme. This reading is one that Howe views as politically understandable, and probably desirable, but as incompatible with constitutional history. Neutrality and equality are, in his view, bywords of the 1940s, not of the 1790s.[28] They were certainly paramount for Justice Black

JUSTICE O'CONNOR

Justice O'Connor's concurring opinion in *Lynch* shows her to be the natural heir to Justice Black and to the political language of the 1940s. It is interesting to note in that connection that both Justice Black and Justice O'Connor came to the Court from a previous career in a state legislature. Each is concerned with federal infringement of states' rights and with political freedom. In contrast to Burger, the federal government has, for Black and for O'Connor, a political rather than a religious identity.

O'Connor's opinion, from the first substantive sentence, reveals an understanding of the First Amendment and of the role of religion in American public life very different from that of Chief Justice Burger. Her opinion begins:

The Establishment Clause prohibits government from making adherence to a religion relevant in any way to a person's standing in the political community. Government can run afoul of that prohibition in two principal ways. One is excessive entanglement with religious institutions, which may interfere with the independence of the institutions, give the institutions access to government or governmental powers not fully shared by nonadherents of the religion, and foster the creation of political constituencies defined along religious lines. The second and more direct infringement is government

---

[27] Howe, *The Garden and the Wilderness*, 147–48.
[28] See also Pole, *The Pursuit of Equality*, for a fuller exposition of this idea.

endorsement or disapproval of religion. Endorsement sends a message to nonadherents that they are outsiders, not full members of the political community, and an accompanying message to adherents that they are insiders, favored members of the political community. Disapproval sends the opposite message.[29]

Disestablishment is, for O'Connor, a question of equality of the individual before the law, of political freedom, an issue which did not concern Chief Justice Burger in *Lynch*. O'Connor is concerned about discriminatory activity on the part of government, not about religion. For her, the First Amendment is about political and procedural justice, like the Fourteenth Amendment, not about the accommodation of religion. In fact, Justice O'Connor seems singularly uninterested in religion in this opinion. After the fuzzy sentimentality of the majority, her concern for "the political community" is bracing.

Affirming and restating the *Lemon* test, O'Connor asks whether Pawtucket has "endorsed Christianity," whether the government is aligning itself with one group and thus putting others at a constitutionally improper disadvantage, real or perceived. Under her scheme, unconstitutional endorsement can exist if the government intended to convey a message of either endorsement or disapproval of religion or if the government had that effect, whatever its intentions.

Like Burger, however, ignoring the district court's finding as a matter of *fact* that Mayor Lynch's display of the crèche had both the purpose and effect of endorsing Christianity, Justice O'Connor converts the question into one of *law* and holds that as a matter of *law*, Judge Pettine erred:

The evident *purpose* of including the crèche in the larger display was not promotion of the religious content of the crèche but celebration of the public holiday through its traditional symbols. Celebration of public holidays, which have cultural significance even if they also have religious aspects, is a legitimate secular purpose. (emphasis added)[30]

As to whether the display had the effect of communicating such a message, Justice O'Connor concludes:

Although the religious and indeed sectarian significance of the crèche, as the District Court found, is not neutralized by the setting, the overall holiday

---

[29] 465 U.S. at 687–88.
[30] 465 U.S. at 691.

setting changes what viewers may fairly understand to be the purpose of the display—as a typical museum setting, though not neutralizing the religious content of a religious painting, negates any message of endorsement of that content.[31]

The government's constitutional obligation is to treat its citizens equally. Pawtucket, according to O'Connor, has met that obligation.

O'Connor, as does Burger, analogizes display of the crèche to legislative prayers, Thanksgiving celebrations, the use of "In God we Trust," and the opening of court sessions with "God save the United States and this Honorable Court." Unlike Burger, however, she does not see these other apparent invocations of religion as evidence of a constitutionally permissible, intentional, and pervasive accommodation of public religiosity, but as serving wholly secular purposes:

These government acknowledgements of religion serve, in the only ways reasonably possible in our culture, the legitimate *secular* purposes of solemnizing public occasions, expressing confidence in the future, and encouraging the recognition of what is worthy of appreciation in society. (emphasis added)[32]

She acknowledges a thin and restrained role for what are only incidentally religious symbols.

The opinion finally, and rather weakly, concludes that display of the crèche does not constitute an impermissible endorsement of religion because "the overall holiday setting. . .negates any message of endorsement."[33] She does not minimize the importance of the establishment issue, as Burger does, nor does she deny the religiousness of the crèche as a symbol, as he does. She focuses instead on whether its inclusion in the display will be publicly interpreted as a government endorsement of religion.

O'Connor, like Burger, uses the analogy of a museum display but, unlike Burger, she does not use it as evidence of a permissible accommodation of religion by government. Her opinion is singularly lacking in conventional religiosity of any brand. For O'Connor, as for Black, the central meaning of the religion clauses is neither protection of religion nor protection of religious liberty for their own sakes, but

[31] 465 U.S. at 692.
[32] 465 U.S. at 693.
[33] 465 U.S. at 692.

protection of the political rights of individuals against despotic government. While her constitutional piety lacks the emotional intensity of Justice Black's, the location of her faith, like his, is in law, in the Constitution, not in religion. As Black does in his opinion in *Everson,* she too begins with a strong affirmation of disestablishment but ends by deferring to local government. Like Black, religion, as religion, does not interest or worry her much.

Justice O'Connor wrote a concurring opinion in a subsequent religion case—this time a free exercise case—in which she also concurred with the majority's judgment but dissented from their opinion. In *Employment Division v. Smith,*[34] the majority opinion, written by Justice Scalia, held that it was not unconstitutional for a state to deny unemployment benefits to members of the Native American Church who were terminated for cause because of their sacramental use of peyote, a controlled substance. Scalia wrote, in a harsh and much criticized opinion, that the First Amendment protects only beliefs, not acts.[35] Scalia's distinction between beliefs and acts, however, unlike Black's, does not proceed from a transcendent commitment to political freedom, but from a commitment to judicial restraint and to the police power of the state. Quoting *Reynolds*, the nineteenth-century polygamy case, Scalia says:

"Laws," we said, "are made for the government of actions, and while they cannot interfere with mere religious beliefs and opinions, they may with practices. . . . Can a man excuse his practices to the contrary because of his religious belief? To permit this would be to make the professed doctrines of religious belief superior to the law of the land, and in effect to permit every citizen to become a law unto himself."[36]

Many religious Americans would vigorously oppose Scalia's disingenuous equation of making "the professed doctrine of religious belief superior to the law of the land" with "every citizen becom[ing] a law unto himself." According to Scalia, it is simple. It is constitutional for the state to regulate narcotics, even narcotics whose only use is

---

[34] 494 U.S. 872 (1991).

[35] This decision resulted in a movement to legislate the meaning of the First Amendment through promotion of the Religious Freedom Act. Pub. L. 103–41 (16 November 1993).

[36] 494 U.S. at 879.

sacramental; therefore, the religious actor has no protection under the Constitution. And this is so in spite of the fact that there is, according to the Court, no market in or recreational use of peyote.

In her concurring opinion in *Smith*, Justice O'Connor begins with a literalism reminiscent of Justice Black by insisting that "the First Amendment does not distinguish between religious belief and religious conduct."[37] Arguing that previous cases have established that whereas belief is absolutely protected, acts are not, O'Connor advocates a balancing test to determine whether the state has a compelling interest sufficient to outweigh the respondents' constitutional rights. She eventually concludes that Oregon did have a compelling state interest (the war on drugs) which outweighed the respondents' First Amendment rights. However, in the course of the opinion, O'Connor rebukes the majority several times for its lack of concern for the political rights of persons before the Court:

[T]he Court today suggests that the disfavoring of minority religions is an "unavoidable consequence" under our system of government and that accommodation of such religions must be left to the political process. In my view, however, the First Amendment was enacted precisely to protect the rights of those whose religious practices are not shared by the majority and may be viewed with hostility. . . .

The compelling interest test reflects the First Amendment's mandate of preserving religious liberty to the fullest extent possible in a pluralistic society. For the Court to deem this command a "luxury," is to denigrate "[t]he very purpose of a Bill of Rights." (citations omitted)[38]

Justice O'Connor is outraged at the majority's easy dismissal of claims for political equality. But, as in *Lynch*, she is still inclined to give deference to the words and acts of state and local government.

It is easy to be cynical about these O'Connor concurrences, to conclude that "talk is cheap." A vote with the dissenters might be more

[37] 494 U.S. at 893.

[38] 494 U.S. at 902–3. It is ironic that Justice Scalia, a very conservative Roman Catholic, places so much confidence in the majority's protection of religious rights. Perhaps this is a further indication of the coming of age of the American Catholic community. No longer an immigrant community, the target of nativist anti-Catholicism, Catholics can be confident, as Protestants once could, that *their* "acts," *their* sacraments, will be protected as a part of the majority culture.

Another possibility is that Scalia, like Barth, sees no analogy between Christianity

welcome than some more words on political equality. But O'Connor's careful concurrences in each of these cases stand in sharp contrast to both the majority and dissenting opinions and highlight the importance of the language the Court uses in its opinions. O'Connor, like Black, thinks that the only religion the Supreme Court should be protecting is the religion of the Constitution.

For Justice O'Connnor, "[w]hat is crucial is that government practice not have the effect of communicating a message of government endorsement or disapproval."[39] Unlike both the majority and the dissent, she is uninterested in protecting, acknowledging, or accommodating *religion*. For her, it seems, religion *as* religion is irrelevant in the political community. She explains the *Marsh* Court's decision on the constitutionality of legislative prayers as political. The prayers have the secular purpose of solemnizing public occasions. Nothing more. Whereas Burger's opinion tends to trivialize religious symbols, O'Connor's simply ignores them, as religion. The central focus, the locus, as Phillip Hammond would say, of social integration in the Durkheimian sense, and the proper object of the Court's concern, is in the constitution of the political community.[40]

The extent to which law has superseded religion in this country is dramatically revealed in the confrontation between the values of religious freedom and of political equality that occurred in *Bob Jones*

---

and other religions (Karl Barth, *Church Dogmatics: The Doctrine of the Word of God, Pt. II*, trans. G. T. Thomson and Harold Knight [Edinbugh: T & T Clark, 1956], 344). Although, of course, if you had to classify it, the Native American Church is surely Christian.

In Texas Monthly v. Bullock, 489 U.S. 1 (1989), Justice Scalia, dissenting, announced: "And it is impossible to believe that the State is constitutionally prohibited from taxing Texas Monthly magazine more heavily than the Holy Bible. . . . It is not right—it is not constitutionally healthy—that this Court should feel authorized to refashion anew our civil society's relationship with religion, adopting a theory of church and state that is contradicted by current practice, tradition, and even our own case law." 489 U.S. at 45.

[39] 465 U.S. at 692.

[40] Phillip E. Hammond, "Religious Pluralism and Durkheim's Integration Thesis," in Allen W. Eister, ed., *Changing Perspectives in the Scientific Study of Religion* (New York: John Wiley & Sons, 1974), 115–42.

University v. U.S.[41] The question presented in *Bob Jones* was whether the Internal Revenue Service had acted properly in withdrawing tax exemption from Bob Jones University on the grounds that, according to the Internal Revenue Service, its racially discriminatory admission policies disqualified it from being "a charitable organization." The university had argued that it had a First Amendment right to be racially discriminatory because its policies were based on divine revelation. In an 8-1 decision (Rehnquist, dissenting), the Court, in an opinion by Chief Justice Burger, held that:

[the Government's] fundamental, overriding interest in eradicating racial discrimination in education. . .substantially outweighs *whatever* burden denial of tax benefits places on petitioners' exercise of their religious beliefs. (emphasis added)[42]

In fulfillment of Howe's thesis, racial equality, the value of the Fourteenth Amendment, is held to be a more fundamental interest than religious freedom.[43]

John Noonan, in a speech at Hamline University Law School in November 1990, challenged the audience to consider the possibility that *Bob Jones* is *the* test case for the continued existence of religious freedom in the United States. A largely liberal audience that had already shown itself to be outraged by the *Smith* decision, visibly balked at swallowing a denial of the correctness of the *Bob Jones* decision.[44]

---

[41] 461 U.S. 574 (1983).

[42] 461 U.S. at 604.

[43] There are those who would argue that the same should be true of sexual equality. See, for example, Mary Becker, "The Politics of Women's Wrongs and the Bill of 'Rights': A Bicentennial Perspective," *University of Chicago Law Review* 59 (winter 1992): 453–517.

In a recent case, the Court of the Appeals for the Tenth Circuit held that ordination, as a requirement for prison chaplaincy, if restricted to males, is invalid under Title VII of the 1964 Civil Rights Act. Murphy v. Derwinski, No. 91–1393 (1 April 1993).

A similar argument has also been made about animal rights: see the Supreme Court opinions in Church of the Lukumi Babalu Aye v. City of Hialeah, No. 91–948 (11 June 1993).

[44] Bob Jones University has changed its admission policies since this case to permit matriculation by non-white students.

Federal law can be a powerful incentive to changes in revelation. The Mormon

Presented with the choice in such stark terms, religious freedom proved
to be a secondary freedom.[45]

LAW AS RELIGION

Neutrality toward religion, elegantly and persuasively argued for by
Philip Kurland and others,[46] is not, however, simply the turning of
religious freedom into a question of political equality. It is the by-
product of a faith in law, law as a moral system. Liberal neutrality does
not mean that "government must be neutral as to questions of what
constitutes the good life," as Donald Beschle argues in his article on
Justice O'Connor.[47] Liberal neutrality for these thinkers means that law
is *the* location for thinking about the good life. Neutrality is based on
a faith in equality.[48] It shifts the rights from the individual as a member
of a religious community to the individual as a political individual,
consistent with the goals of the Fourteenth Amendment.

The commitment to the political rights enshrined in the Constitution
evident in O'Connor's opinions and in the writings of Justice Black
can be seen as an example of the kind of displacement of moral system

---

Church, in the time prior to the admission of Utah to statehood, partly in response
to pressure from the Federal government, changed its revelation with respect to
polygamy. Joseph Fielding Smith, *Essentials in Church History* (Church of Jesus
Christ of Latter Day Saints, 1950; reprint, Salt Lake City: Deseret Book Company,
1979), 491–500.

Howe argues that the form of all religious associations in the United States was
determined by the federal court decisions about ownership of church property that
established the congregational polity as *the* defining shape for religious institutions.
See *The Garden and the Wilderness,* 32–60.

[45] Hence the title of Richard Neuhaus's new journal attempting a restoration of
religion's place: *First Things.*

[46] Philip Kurland, *Religion and the Law: Of Church and State and the Supreme
Court* (Chicago: Aldine, 1961); Douglas Laycock, "Formal, Substantive and
Disaggregated Neutrality towards Religion," *DePaul Law Review* 39 (summer 1990):
993–1018.

[47] Donald L. Beschle, "The Conservative as Liberal: The Religion Clauses, Liberal
Neutrality, and the Approach of Justice O'Connor," *Notre Dame Law Review* 62
(spring 1987): 151–91.

[48] Kurland, *Religion and Law*, 112.

and meaning from religion to law discussed by Phillip Hammond.[49] It is Hammond's thesis that in a pluralistic society—one characterized by the existence of competing meaning systems—law takes up the slack left by the elimination of a single integrating religious establishment. He sees in the American context an increasing tendency, fulfilling the promise of the Reformation, to invest law with the responsibility for articulation of a common moral architecture. In his view, the experience of pluralism results in religion becoming less religious and law becoming more religious. The beginning of a full realization of the Reconstruction Amendments, including the Fourteenth, during and after the New Deal, as an historical location for the elevation of law as an integrating force like religion, had, in Hammond's view, a powerful effect on the Court's reading of the First Amendment.

The moral power of law is expressed also in the writings of the American lawyer-reformers discussed above.[50] Lon Fuller argues that the very procedural framework of law has a moral component and is not neutral:

[T]he internal morality of the law is not something added to, or imposed on, the power of law, but is an essential condition of that power itself. . . . Law is a precondition of good law.[51]

Natural law is a precondition of good law.[52] Furthermore, Fuller argues, law implies a community of persons of good will.[53] James Boyd White, too, argues that law is about creating a moral community, in John Dewey's sense.[54] Milner Ball and John Noonan argue that law is about love and should be used to create human community.[55] Justice O'Connor's concurrences show that she, too, is concerned, not with

---

[49] Hammond, "Religious Pluralism and Durkheim's Integration Thesis."

[50] See chapter 1, pages 15–23.

[51] Fuller, *The Morality of Law*, 155.

[52] For a full discussion of the relationship of natural law concepts to the Constitution, see Morton White, *Philosophy, The Federalist, and the Constitution* (New York: Oxford University Press, 1987).

[53] Fuller also argues that certain aspects of Nazi and Stalinist law would not qualify as law. Fuller, *The Morality of Law*, 54–62.

[54] White, *Justice as Translation*, 91.

[55] Ball, *Lying Down Together*, 119–36, and Noonan, *Persons and Masks*, xii, 165–67.

the law's attitude toward the religiousness of individuals, but with the kind of political community law constructs.

Although the Court's establishment clause jurisprudence has further splintered since *Lynch*, Justice O'Connor's efforts to create a new "endorsement" test for the establishment clause have continued. In *Allegheny v. ACLU*,[56] the Court considered the constitutionality of the display of a crèche on the "Grand Staircase" of the Allegheny County Courthouse and of the display of an eighteen-foot menorah next to a forty-five foot Christmas tree outside the city-county building in Pittsburgh. The judgment of the Court was that display of the crèche was unconstitutional but that display of the menorah with the Christmas tree was constitutional. Five opinions were filed, none of which represents a majority of the Court. The Syllabus in the United States Reports reads as follows:

BLACKMUN, J. announced the judgment of the Court and delivered the opinion of the Court with respect to Parts III-A, IV, and V, in which BRENNAN, MARSHALL, STEVENS, and O'CONNOR, JJ., joined, an opinion with respect to Parts I and II, in which STEVENS and O'CONNOR, JJ., joined, an opinion with respect to Part III-B, in which STEVENS, J., joined, an opinion with respect to Part VII, in which O'CONNOR, J., joined, and an opinion with respect to Part VI. O'CONNOR, J., filed an opinion concurring in part and concurring in the judgment, in Part II of which BRENNAN and STEVENS, JJ., joined, *post*, p. 623. BRENNAN, J., filed an opinion concurring in part and dissenting in part, in which MARSHALL and STEVENS, JJ., joined, *post*, p. 637. STEVENS, J., filed an opinion concurring in part and dissenting in part, in which BRENNAN and MAR-SHALL, JJ., joined, *post*, p. 646. KENNEDY, J., filed an opinion concurring in the judgment in part and dissenting in part, in which REHNQUIST, C.J., and WHITE and SCALIA, JJ., joined, *post*, p. 655.[57]

Justice O'Connor's partial concurring opinion in *Allegheny* argues vociferously against those who would read *Lynch* as permitting an "acknowledgment" of or an "accommodation" of religion. She argues at length that an endorsement test asks the proper question about government action, the goal of which should be *neutrality*. While

---

[56] 492 U.S. 573 (1989).
[57] 492 U.S. at 577.

agreeing that display of the crèche *alone* on the grand staircase of the county courthouse "has conveyed a message of governmental endorsement of Christian beliefs,"[58] her opinion argues that display of the menorah *and* the tree outside the city-county building does not convey such a message. Her opinion in *Allegheny* gives some positive emotional content to the somewhat sterile neutrality of her *Lynch* opinion:

[By] displaying a secular symbol of the Christmas holiday season rather than a religious one, the city acknowledged a public holiday celebrated by both religious and non-religious citizens alike, and it did so without endorsing Christian beliefs. A reasonable observer would, in my view, appreciate that the combined display is an effort to acknowledge the cultural diversity of our country and to convey tolerance of different choices in matters of religious belief or non-belief by recognizing that the winter holiday season is celebrated in diverse ways by our citizens.[59]

One cannot help thinking that it is easier to see someone else's religious symbol as merely a symbol of cultural diversity than it is one's own. Again like Justice Black she is, however, able to wax eloquent when she believes that the faith of the Constitution is being celebrated: multiple religious symbols celebrate the equality and neutrality of the political community, not of religion.

---

[58] 492 U.S. at 632.
[59] 492 U.S. at 634–36.

Chapter 5

Discourse III: Justice Brennan

Deus, qui hanc sacratissimam noctem veri luminis fecisti illustratione
clarescere: da, quaesumus; ut, cuius lucis mysteria in terra cogno
vimus, eius quoque gaudius in caelo pervamur: Qui tecum.
—Collect for Midnight Mass[1]

Jesus is the reason for the season.
—Sign on a church in Chicago[2]

The keeping of Christmas has origins far from the image of Christ.
It is an older habit caparisoned.
—Sanson, *A Book of Christmas*[3]

In 1951, a Japanese film entitled *Rashomon*, directed by Akira
Kurosawa, won the prize for best film at the Cannes Film Festival. The
film tells the story of a rape and murder from the viewpoints of the
three participants—a samurai, his wife, and a bandit—and from those
of three bystanders. Each of the six gives a different version of the
events. According to the bandit's story, he killed the husband in a duel
over the wife. In the wife's story, she killed her husband because he
despised her after the rape. The husband's story, related through a
medium, is that he killed himself in grief over his wife's betrayal. A

---

[1] *Roman Missal* (New York: Catholic Book Publishing Co., 1964). Translation:
"O God, you have made this most holy night shine with the brilliance of the true
light. Please enable us who have known this light of Christ on earth to enjoy his
happiness also in heaven. Who lives and reigns with you. . ." Thomas B. McDonough
and Joseph Marren, eds. *The Saint Jerome Daily Missal*, vol. 1 (London: Virtue &
Co., 1964), 38.

[2] Sign on St. Basil's Church, Chicago, December 1992.

[3] William Sanson, *A Book of Christmas* (New York: McGraw-Hill, 1968).

woodcutter, a priest, and a police agent recount their encounters with these principals. The viewer sees each version enacted. Through the testimony of the six witnesses, every detail of each of the versions is called into question. The viewer is left at the end of the picture unable to resolve the multiple stories into one.[4]

The ending of *Rashomon* sends the viewer back to the stories of the witnesses. In attempting to piece together the facts and sort out the true story, the viewer realizes that the film is about the witnesses rather than about what happened, that the truth is in the telling rather than in objective reality. *Rashomon* is not a murder mystery to which there is a solution. It is a film that explores the motives of its protagonists and the subjective nature of reality. Confusion arises when the viewer seeks an answer to the wrong question.

Rashomon-fashion, readers of the *Lynch* decision also move from opinion to opinion as if encountering in each a completely new story. Like the viewer of *Rashomon*, the reader is persuaded, in turn, by each new version but, finally, is left confused about the nature of what happened and even about why we care.

In the first take, Chief Justice Burger convinces the reader that display of the crèche is a harmless bit of post-Christian cultural tinsel celebrating our common heritage, "a neutral harbinger of the holiday season,"[5] in Justice Blackmun's words. Religious particularity and division, on this reading, is part of the prehistory of America, not of its present. Concern for the dangers of enforced religious conformity or for the protection of religious freedom is somehow un-American, "overscrupulous," in the words of the Japanese Supreme Court. The reader is made to feel slightly embarrassed by her oversensitivity.

Next, the reader is instructed by Justice O'Connor that it is not cultural Christianity but a faith in the Constitution, in political equality, that undergirds a great and free country. The crèche, whatever its meaning, and religion, whatever its kind, are not a proper part of the public conversation. In a very real sense they are irrelevant. What is relevant is how the government treats its citizens. The morality and the sacred are in the law, not in the religion.

---

[4] A transcript of the film and reprints of contemporary reviews may be found in Donald Richie, ed., *Rashomon* (New Brunswick: Rutgers University Press, 1987).
[5] 465 U.S. at 727.

The reader is finally left dazed by Justice Brennan's urgent and intense dissent. Once again she must shift gears. Now the crèche appears a glowing epiphany. It is a *mysterium tremendum*,[6] an encapsulation of the Incarnation, an object of sectarian devotion displayed with sensitive propriety only in the privacy of our homes and churches. The reader is startled to be reminded that religious awe is a part of Christmas—that, for some, the crèche embodies an entire cosmology. Here, with this infant, life is given meaning.

We have come full circle. With Justice Brennan's dissenting opinion we are back to the crèche witnessed to by Judge Pettine. We are reminded of Pawtucket's Roman Catholic piety. Ironically, perhaps, Justice Brennan also brings us back to Thomas Jefferson and James Madison, who have been oddly absent in the first two Supreme Court opinions.

A cynical and superficial reading of *Rashomon* is that Kurosawa intended to relativize truth in a nihilistic fashion. But the film can also be seen as putting into question the need to reconcile the stories. It is not that there is no truth, but that it is not found by reducing the six stories to one. The witnesses, on this reading, are an inescapable part of their testimony. Each reveals himself or herself, as well as what happened. Coming to the last two opinions in *Lynch*, the dissents, the reader realizes that in this set of opinions about a Christmas display in Pawtucket, Rhode Island, she learns more about the authors and the communal discourses of which they form a part, and about herself, than she does about the nature of the crèche. Our constitutional task is to find a language in which to acknowledge our religious diversity, not to give meaning to the crèche.

Lynch v. Donnelly was decided in the United States Supreme Court by a vote of five to four. Justice Brennan filed a long and detailed dissenting opinion—twice as long as that of the majority—that was joined in by Justices Marshall, Blackmun, and Stevens. Justice Blackmun also filed a short but passionate one-page dissent with which Justice Stevens joined. (Because Blackmun's dissent is so short and, in effect, forms an addendum to Brennan's opinion in which Blackmun also joined, I will not discuss it separately, but only as it relates to

---

[6] Rudolf Otto, *The Idea of the Holy*, 2d ed., trans. John W. Harvey (Oxford: Oxford University Press, 1950), 12.

Brennan's.) The dissents reveal an interesting marriage of religious intensity and particularity with a commitment to a Jeffersonian separation of church and state. Judicial dissents can take many forms. Here, Justice Brennan attempts an ambitious and comprehensive refutation of the majority's opinion on every point. Brennan's opinion is designed as a *complete* answer to the majority. It is intended to replace Burger's opinion, not simply to differ with it.

In this chapter I will consider Justice Brennan's Catholic response to display of the crèche in the context of a somewhat longer and broader Christian history than any represented in the Court, reaching back to the first celebrations of Christmas and to the Reformation. Then I will consider Justice Brennan as an heir to Thomas Jefferson and James Madison. Finally, I will ask how these two seemingly incompatible views of religion may be reconciled in a distinctively American Catholic sensibility.

A CATHOLIC CRÈCHE

Part 1 of Justice Brennan's opinion, more than half of the opinion, is a strong re-affirmation of the *Lemon* test, which had been explicitly undermined by the majority opinion as the appropriate standard of constitutional adjudication in establishment clause cases. Brennan begins:

[T]he Court's less-than-vigorous application of the *Lemon* test suggests that its commitment to these standards may only be superficial. After reviewing the Court's opinions, I am convinced that this case appears hard not because the principles of decision are obscure, but because the Christmas holiday seems so familiar and agreeable.[7]

He carefully considers the three parts of the *Lemon* test and then concludes, affirming the decisions of the lower courts, that, under the three prongs of the *Lemon* test:

1) Pawtucket's display of the crèche does not reflect a clearly secular *purpose*, because "[t]he inclusion of a distinctively religious element like the crèche. . .demonstrates. . .a narrower sectarian purpose";[8]

2) "The 'primary *effect*' of including a nativity scene is. . .to place

---

[7] 465 U.S. at 696.
[8] 465 U.S. at 700.

the government's imprimatur of approval on the particular religious beliefs exemplified by the crèche";[9]

3) There was "a significant threat of fostering 'excessive entanglement' between church and state."[10]

Throughout this section Brennan insists repeatedly that the crèche has a single meaning, and that the meaning is religious. Brennan repeatedly characterizes the crèche as irreducibly religious. He describes the crèche as "distinctively religious" and as "distinctively sectarian." He sees it as having "singular religiosity," "sectarian exclusivity," "clear religious import," and "inherent religious significance." For him the crèche is "a distinctively religious object" having a "clear religious effect" and "a specifically Christian religious meaning."[11]

At several points later in the opinion he summarizes the meaning of the crèche:

The nativity scene is *clearly distinct* in its purpose and effect from the rest of the Hodgson Park display for the simple reason that it is the only one rooted in a biblical account of Christ's birth. It is *the chief symbol* of the characteristically Christian belief that a divine Savior was brought into the world, that the purpose of this miraculous birth was to illuminate a path toward salvation and redemption. For Christians, that path is exclusive, precious, and holy. (emphasis added)[12]

For Christians, of course, *the essential message* of the nativity is that God became incarnate in the person of Christ. (emphasis added)[13]

[A] nativity scene represents far more than a mere "traditional symbol of Christmas." *The essence* of the crèche's symbolic purpose and effect is to prompt the observer to experience a sense of simple awe and wonder appropriate to the contemplation of one of the central elements of Christian dogma—that God sent His Son into the world to be a Messiah. . . . *[T]he crèche. . . is best understood* as a mystical re-creation of an event that lies at the heart of Christian faith. (emphasis added)[14]

[T]he message of the crèche begins and ends with reverence for a particular image of the divine. (emphasis added)[15]

[9] 465 U.S. at 701.
[10] 465 U.S. at 702.
[11] 465 U.S. at 694–726 passim.
[12] 465 U.S. at 708.
[13] 465 U.S. at 708.
[14] 465 U.S. at 711.
[15] 465 U.S. at 717.

Brennan is very clear that "the angels, shepherds, Magi, and infant of Pawtucket's nativity can *only* be viewed as symbols of a particular set of religious beliefs" (emphasis added).[16] Justice Burger, according to Brennan, is simply wrong about the crèche and about the city's intentions. The purpose *and* the effect of the city in displaying the crèche, under the *Lemon* test, can, according to Brennan, *only* be religious because of the inherent and essential nature of the crèche itself.

The devotional intensity with which Brennan invokes the crèche's meaning is in sharp contrast to Chief Justice Burger's easy, offhand, casual, and syncretic eclecticism. Justice Blackmun goes further in his dissent. He asserts that the majority "does an injustice to the crèche,"[17] and can be accused of heresy because of its "misuse" of a "sacred symbol." This is an extraordinary assertion for a federal judge to make: that the *crèche* has rights, including a right to justice. In our secular and person-centered culture, if the Constitution means anything, surely it means that it is constitutionally, even logically, impossible for the Court to do anything to the *crèche*.

In Part 2 of his opinion Brennan attacks the majority's accommodation theory. Reviewing earlier "accommodation" cases, he finds three exceptions to strict separation in those cases, but each is distinguishable from *Lynch*.

1. The government may constitutionally "act to accommodate to some extent the opportunities of individuals to practice their religion,"[18] as in *Zorach v. Clauson*, the released time case. He continues: "And for me that principle would justify government's decision to declare December 25th a public holiday."[19] It would not justify public display of a crèche.

2. The government may act for solely secular reasons even when the practice may have a religious past, as in the case of the Sunday Closing Laws or the celebration of Thanksgiving and thereby only

[16] 465 U.S. at 713.

[17] 465 U.S. at 726. Justice Blackmun's outrage in *Lynch* apparently led to his opinion in the *Allegheny* case, in which he attempted to do "justice" to Channukah by offering an extended cultural history of Channukah.

[18] 465 U.S. at 715.

[19] 343 U.S. 306 (1952).

incidentally accommodate religion.[20] A Christmas crèche, because of its inherent religiosity, cannot fall under this exception.

3. Finally, the government may engage, to a limited extent, in a "ceremonial deism," such as in the use of "In God We Trust."

Display of a crèche, in Brennan's view, fits into none of these exceptions to a strict separationist position:

> By insisting that a distinctively sectarian message is merely an unobjectionable part of our "religious heritage," the Court takes a long step backwards to the days when Justice Brewer could arrogantly declare for the Court that "this is a Christian nation." Those days, I had thought, were forever put behind us by the Court's decision in *Engel v. Vitale*, in which we rejected a similar argument advanced by the State of New York that its Regents' Prayer was simply an acceptable part of our "spiritual heritage."[21]

Throughout his careful limiting of the "accommodation" doctrine to the most attenuated and secularized examples of apparent public religiosity, Justice Brennan is confident in his ability to distinguish sacred and secular.

Part 3 of Brennan's opinion exposes the majority's ignorance of the history of the American celebration of Christmas, beginning with the Puritans. In response to Burger's assertion that Americans have always celebrated Christmas, Brennan observes that the Puritans outlawed the observance of Christmas Day as a popish practice, lacking scriptural warrant. He notes that in 1659 the Massachusetts Bay Colony made the observance of Christmas Day a punishable offense.[22] Although the law was repealed twenty years later, Puritan resistance to the celebration continued well into the nineteenth century.

Brennan further notes that during the eighteenth century, Anglican, German Protestant, and Roman Catholic immigrants brought Christmas traditions with them, while Presbyterians, Congregationalists, Baptists, and Methodists, the dominant American denominations, continued to regard the holiday with suspicion—a suspicion that continued well into

---

[20] McGowan v. Maryland, 366 U.S. 420 (1961).

[21] 465 U.S. at 718.

[22] Brennan cites Sanford H. Cobb, *The Rise of Religious Liberty in America: A History* (New York: Macmillan, 1902; reprint, New York: Burt Franklin, 1970), 209; 465 U.S. at 721.

the nineteenth century.[23] Brennan quotes Henry Ward Beecher, the great Congregational abolitionist:

> To me Christmas is a foreign day, and I shall die so. When I was a boy I wondered what Christmas was. I knew there was such a time, because we had an Episcopal church in our town, and I saw them dressing it with evergreens. . . . A little later I understood it was a Romish institution, kept up by the Romish Church. Brought up in the strictest State of New England, brought up in the most literal style of worship. . .I passed all my youth without any knowledge of Christmas, and so I have no associations with the day.[24]

Brennan also notes that the very sects that opposed Christmas were also vociferous proponents of the separation of church and state, seeing the celebration of Christmas and the union of church and state as a sinister and conspiratorial pair. Brennan uses his history to refute the majority's history.

The majority had argued that the celebration of Christmas, and, therefore, display of the crèche, is constitutionalized by its long history, as the Court had held with respect to legislative chaplains in the recent *Marsh* case. Brennan, quoting the Court's opinion in *Walz v. Tax Commission*, 397 U.S. 664 (1970), insists that:

> no one acquires a vested or protected right in violation of the Constitution by long use, even when that span of time covers our entire national existence and indeed predates it.[25]

Whatever the history, it is established constitutional doctrine that one cannot acquire an easement on constitutional property merely by force of habit.

Ironically, this section of the opinion subtly but surely undercuts Brennan's own reading of the crèche. While carefully laying out the Puritan antipathy toward the celebration of Christmas and the slow development of a public celebration of Christmas in nineteenth-century America, Brennan seems unaware that this very history displays a variety of orthodox Christian attitudes toward Christmas that belies the

---

[23] There were certainly regional differences here. The celebration of Christmas was more common, for example, in the South, which had originally had Anglican establishments, than in the North, which had had Puritan ones.

[24] Quotation from Robert J. Myers, *Celebrations: The Complete Book of American Holidays* (Garden City: Doubleday & Co., 1972), 315–16, cited by Justice Brennan; 465 U.S. at 722.

[25] 465 U.S. at 718.

dogmatic certainty of his own. While Brennan is right that Burger has his history wrong, he does not seem to realize that his history also relativizes his own reading of the crèche, setting it into a particular cultural framework. It opens the door to an even longer and broader "history" of Christmas that even further relativizes the crèches and the Christmases of the Court.

The celebration of Christmas has had a long and colorful history spread across both space and time. It is a holiday whose history vividly illustrates the meaning of syncretism through its intermingling with different and shifting "pagan" religious traditions and folk customs. More recently it has become *the* global festival, spreading inexorably into all corners of the globe, even into historically non-Christian areas. "By the 1990s we are faced with the extraordinary phenomenon of a global festival which seems to grow in its accumulated rituals and the extravagance of the homage paid to it, even as all other festivals and comparable events declined." [26] The holiday's celebration has also often fueled church/state controversy.

The Western Church's liturgical celebration of the Mystery of the Incarnation on December 25 likely began in the fourth century. "[F]or Augustine, Christmas was a *memoria*, a commemoration of a historical event, not a mystery feast such as Easter."[27] Apologetic motivations for its liturgical upgrading apparently included the anti-Arian and anti-Nestorian controversies, as well as a desire to coopt and eclipse the Festival of the Birth of the Sun celebrated by the popular Roman Mithraic cult on December 25. (For similar reasons, in the Eastern Church the Feast of the Nativity was and still is, in places, kept on January 6.) Another motivation of the Roman church in its promotion of Christmas appears to have been a desire to baptize and to Christianize the popular midwinter Roman festivals of Kalends and Saturnalia. Thus the mingled political, theological, and folk aspects of the celebration were present from the beginning.[28]

Christmas never had the dogmatic purity of Easter. The thin biblical

---

[26] Daniel Miller, *Unwrapping Christmas* (Oxford: Clarendon Press, 1993), 5. Miller's book is a fascinating attempt to account for why this is so.

[27] *New Catholic Encyclopedia*, s.v. "Christmas."

[28] The Roman origins of Christmas are cited by Judge Bownes of the First Circuit Court of Appeals in his Concurring opinion in *Lynch v. Donnelly*. He writes, "I concur

tradition in the infancy narratives seems, indeed, to have given licence to rich invention so that Christmas seems always to have gathered local folk culture to it. Sanson describes this multicultural aspect of Christmas:

Christmas, from whatever angle you look at it, is a complex. When the English-speaking countries sit down at lunch-time to a "traditional Christmas dinner," they eat an Aztec bird by an Alsatian tree, followed by a pudding spiced with sub-tropical preserves, while in England itself the most popular of Christmas carols still tells of the Bohemian King Wenceslas to music taken from a Swedish spring song.[29]

Whereas in the 1990s this observation seems to suffer slightly from a quaint Eurocentric pluralism, the crazyquilt texture of Christmas to which Sanson points could be repeated around the world with more exotic mixes.

The very global success of Christmas invites us to look beyond the Christian context. Seen at its most primordial, Christmas is a blaze of light in the dark of the winter solstice. It is Midnight Mass *and* Saturnalia *and* the Feast of Fools *and* the Teutonic Yule Feast— mummers, Druidic mistletoe, Rudolf the Red-Nosed Reindeer, and a thousand local customs with no specifically Christian content.[30] It is a celebration whose meaning and purpose is extremely difficult to fix or to confine to orthodox Christian dogma.

Daniel Miller, in his introductory essay to a recent anthropological study of Christmas as a global festival,[31] offers the following explanation of Christmas's survival:

[I]t is primarily concerned with the distance between the moral and normative order objectified in the domestic and family setting and the moral and normative order which is understood as pertaining to the larger universe within which we live, which itself, although vast, is also expected to share certain

---

fully in all of the majority opinion but write separately because I believe the dissent is incorrect when it says that Christmas originated as a religious holiday. Celebrations on or near the 25th of December predate the birth of Christ." 691 F. 2d at 1035. Religion, for Judge Bowne, apparently begins with Christianity.

[29] Sanson, *A Book of Christmas*, 10–11.

[30] See Sanson, *A Book of Christmas*, for a rich description of Christmas folk customs.

[31] Miller, *Unwrapping Christmas*.

social, affective, and 'human' properties. The birth of Christmas is itself an attempt to anthropomorphize the divinity in the form of the domestic family unit, and I would argue that we can interpret much of the associated ritual as an attempt to bring 'home' cosmological principles.[32]

The themes of the modern Christmas—materialism, the family, and the negotiation between global and local cultures—are ones which Miller both finds in the Roman context and which explain the importance of Christmas today around the world.

The crèche itself, as a religious object, has its own history, mostly lost. Even the history we "know" is so apologetically motivated as to be of questionable value.[33] Midnight Mass was apparently celebrated as early as the fourth century in the Church of St. Mary Major in Rome, in which had been built a reproduction of the Bethlehem grotto and which reputedly contained relics of the original crib.[34] The Beguines of the low countries and St. Francis of Assisi have both been credited with the medieval invention of the crèche as an object of folk piety.[35] Construction and display of nativity scenes may also have been popularized through the reenactment of the gospel stories of the birth of Christ in medieval mystery plays.[36]

The crèche, too, like other aspects of the celebration of Christmas, incorporates local customs and traditions in its iconography. Art historians have traced the cultural provenance of each of the figures of the nativity scene, their clothes, their attitudes, their relative positions. Traditions of their representation were specific to local cultures that, in turn, added their own figures and symbolism. Italian crèches included whole villages of Italian peasant types representing different occupations and crafts. For some, the stable/cave echoes the cave of Mithra's birth and the making of figures echoes Saturnalian or Druidic customs of doll-making and child sacrifice.[37] The crèche is not simply the transparent depiction of a Bible story. The stereotype many Americans

---

[32] Miller, *Unwrapping Christmas*, 29.

[33] See Smith, *Drudgery Divine,* and Brown, *The Cult of Saints.*

[34] *The Saint Jerome Daily Missal,* vol. 1, 37.

[35] See chapter 2, above, n. 4.

[36] Clement A. Miles, *Christmas in Ritual and Tradition: Christian and Pagan* (London: T. Fisher Unwin, 1912), 104–54.

[37] Sanson, *A Book of Christmas,* 126–28; Miles, *Christmas in Ritual and Tradition,* 113.

carry in their heads of Mary, in blue, kneeling by a manger, with Joseph standing has a cultural location:

La crèche appartient au folklore de Noël: dans certains milieux elle continue à nourrir la piété populaire; ailleurs, on peut la juger dépassé et craindre qu'au lieu de suggérer le mystère elle ne le voile sous l'anecdote; en certains cas elle risque même d'être vidée de tout contenu chrétien pour ne plus servir que d'illustration publicitaire, ce qui est évidemment le cas lorsqu'une bouteille de vin est couchée dans la mangeoire à la place de l'Enfant-Jésu.[38]

The French Catholic encyclopedia, from which this quotation was taken, like Justices Brennan and Blackmun, is clearly worried about desecration and secularization of the crèche. And while French sacrilege always puts American sacrilege to shame, the advertisement mentioned in the quotation might be said to be in the same spirit of Christmas as the Pawtucket crèche, a Christmas which both domesticates the cosmological and sacralizes a joyous mid-winter holiday.

In the United States, however, the crèche as an object of devotion is, or was, for most American Protestants, a Roman Catholic custom. The *Encyclopedia of Religion and Ethics*, published in 1911, describes the "cradle of Christ" as "the characteristic object of reverence in Roman Catholic churches on Christmas Eve."[39] In a recent book on the development of the modern Christmas celebration, the authors note that:

[t]he crib, which, at the turn of the century was confined to Roman Catholic and a few Anglican Churches, can now be seen not only in nearly all churches but also in department stores and numerous public buildings.[40]

Display of crèches came with Catholic immigrants and has represented and continues to represent, for many Americans, a distinctively Catholic

---

[38] "The creche belongs to the folklore of Christmas: in some places it continues to nourish popular piety; elsewhere, one could call it out of date, and one fears that, rather than suggesting mystery, it conceals it with anecdote; in some cases it runs the risk of being totally emptied of any Christian content in order to serve only as an advertising illustration, which is evidently the case when a bottle of wine rests in the manger in the place of the Infant Jesus" (author's translation). *Catholicisme hier aujourd'hui et demain: Encyclopédie publiée sous la Direction du Centre Interdisciplinaire des Facultés de Lille,* s.v. "Noël."

[39] *Encyclopedia of Religion and Ethics,* s.v. "Christmas."

[40] J. M. Golby and A. W. Purdue, *The Making of Modern Christmas* (Athens: University of Georgia Press, 1986), 109.

piety. Chief Justice Burger says dismissively of those who would defend the sacramental character of the crèche: "The crèche may well have *special meaning* to those whose faith includes the celebration of religious Masses"[41] (emphasis added). There is more than a little anti-Catholic tinge to his refusal to see the crèche as religious.

The contrast between the ways Burger and Brennan see the crèche is, in part the product of different sacramental theologies and different local cultural readings of the celebration of Christmas. Brennan is wrong. For many Americans, the crèche is not "clearly distinct" from the rest of the display. It does not cause them to experience "awe and wonder" as a "mystical re-creation" of dogmatic theology. It does not inspire "reverence." It does not have "special meaning." For many Protestants especially—as for Burger—the crèche, it seems, is either a simple illustration of a Bible story or one more Christmas decoration of vague cultural reference. It is not religious in Brennan's sense.

The differences between Catholics and Protestants in the celebration of Christmas are broad cultural differences in sensibilities and the differences vary regionally and vary depending on the national origins of local immigrant populations. It may even be too simple to dichotomize these views as Protestant and Catholic. It would probably be more accurate to see them as the two poles of a range of Christian attitudes toward the crèche and to include high Anglican and Lutheran with Roman Catholic theologies. It is also risky to essentialize any one person's religious attitudes based on that person's denominational affiliation.

It does help to sharpen the focus, however, if these poles are seen initially as deriving from two distinctive theologies. I would disagree with those who would overly downplay the contemporary theological and cultural differences between Protestants and Catholics. Theodore Caplow and his co-authors, in their Middletown study, seem to suggest, for example, that there are no real remaining differences between Catholics and Protestants.[42] That may be true to some extent for the kinds of things measured by their surveys and probably there is now greater tolerance between the two groups, but the opinions of Burger

[41] 465 U.S. at 685.

[42] Theodore Caplow and others, *All Faithful People: Change and Continuity in Middletown's Religion* (Minneapolis: University of Minnesota Press, 1983), 163–81.

and Brennan illustrate a real difference in the dimension of religious sensibility, at least for their generation.

If one characteristic can be said to distinguish American evangelical Protestant and Roman Catholic religious sensibilities, it is in their respective attitudes toward the possibility of God being revealed in the material world. For Catholics, the relationship between God and man is embodied in an intense sacramentalism. Beyond the seven canonical sacraments[43] that serve as signs of God's presence and involvement in the material world,

Catholicism recognized a humbler sacramentalism of the material world. Any natural object could become a sacramental, *a place where humans could meet and encounter the grace of God*. Thus, a priest could bless water to make it holy and confer a blessing, too, on a sacred painting or statue. People could wear commemorative medals dedicated to Jesus, his mother, Mary, or one of the saints. They could light candles in darkened shrines as signs of their prayerful remembrance of a loved one, receive ashes on Ash Wednesday to remind them that they would one day return to the dust, cherish rosary beads in a pocket or purse as talismans of the Virgin Mary's protection, acquire and venerate relics of the saints. (emphasis added)[44]

The crèche, too, can serve as such a meeting place. A consecration of time as well as of space also characterizes Catholic spirituality. The liturgical cycle inscribes salvation history into the annual round of feasts and fasts. Christmas fits into the liturgical calendar at the end of Advent, consecrating the winter solstice as the coming of the light of Christ.

In contrast, a nice appreciation for the dangers of idolatry combined with an austere devotion to the exclusiveness of God's revelation in the Word led Puritans to be highly suspicious of "popish" religious traditions and folk accretions, which they viewed as smacking of paganism and as lacking scriptural warrant. The multiplication of saints, sacramentaries, and feast days confirmed their suspicion that the Roman church was indeed the "Whore of Babylon." Only the Sabbath was ordained as a day set apart for Puritans. All other days were for sober attention to duty. Puritans prided themselves for working on Christmas

---

[43] Baptism, reconciliation, eucharist, confirmation, marriage, holy orders, annointing of the sick.

[44] Catherine Albanese, *America: Religion and Religions* (Belmont: Wadsworth, 1981), 67. Albanese speaks in the past tense. I am not sure that this sensibility is as much in the past as she seems to assume.

Day and other liturgically prescribed holy days. Pictures of Bible stories were for teaching children. Churches were for hearing the word and for praying. God's presence was in the heart of each member of the household and was invoked in prayers, Bible study, and devotion to duty, not in the presence of holy objects.

In his book on American Catholic art and literature, Paul Giles develops a typology that contrasts Protestant and Catholic sensibilities as they are revealed in the work of Protestant and Catholic artists and writers.[45] Whether or not they self-consciously regard themselves as religiously motivated and whether or not their work touches on explicitly religious themes, Giles sees in their work two contrasting and characteristic approaches to the world. From Orestes Bronson to Francis Ford Coppola, Catholic artists and writers display a characteristic Catholicity, one feature of which is a nitty-gritty materialism, a sacramentalizing of the world. For Giles, this is characteristic of the analogical imagination, an idea he borrows from David Tracy,[46] Peter Berger,[47] and indirectly from Thomas Aquinas, and which he contrasts to the allegorical in Protestant art and fiction.

Justice Brennan's reading of the crèche is, using Giles's typology, analogical and characteristically Catholic, and therefore necessarily in sharp contrast to that of the Protestant justices. It is Catholic in its cultural anthropology. The crèche for Justice Brennan is an instance of transubstantiation, not in the narrowly theological sense, but in a broadly cultural sense. As Giles points out, Jack Kerouac, in *On the Road,* similarly celebrates the Incarnation in the icon of the Greyhound bus station.[48] Ordinary objects have a tremendous revelatory power. Chief Justice Burger appears mystified by this view of the crèche revealed in Brennan's opinion.

The respective christologies of the two justices is also signaled in part by the chief justice's use of "Jesus" to refer to the founder of Christianity and Brennan's use of "Christ." A lower christology, a more human Jesus, corresponds in Burger's writing with a less charged

---

[45] Paul Giles, *American Catholic Arts and Fictions* (Cambridge: Cambridge University Press, 1992), 56.

[46] David Tracy, *The Analogical Imagination* (New York: Crossroad, 1981).

[47] Peter Berger, *The Sacred Canopy: Elements of a Sociological Theory of Religion* (Garden City: Doubleday, 1967).

[48] Giles, *American Catholic Arts and Fictions*, 56.

reading of display of the nativity scene. For many Protestants, for Burger, Jesus is first an historical figure. He is Jesus, "our brother," the Jesus of American Protestantism, who, in the words of the Methodist hymn, "walks with me and talks with me." His presence is in his individual encounter with a person of faith. The heart, not the crèche, is where that encounter takes place.

The Christ represented in Justice Brennan's crèche is, in Brennan's words, "His Son," "the Messiah," "a divine Savior," an "element of Christian dogma." Judge Pettine, too, speaks of "an atmosphere of devotion, worship and awe" surrounding the crèche and refers to the baby in the crèche as "Christ" or "the Son of God." Doctrinal theology is there embodied, given flesh every bit as real, if not more so, than at the actual historical birth.[49] The crèche is invested with meaning.

Many Protestants would find puzzling and unfamiliar an attitude of devotion toward a physical representation of the nativity scene. Such an attitude would be seen as idolatrous, or, at the very least, as misplaced devotion. Giles quotes Newman on this difference:

John Henry Newman suggested in 1864 that "the root of all controversies between the Catholic Church and Protestantism" lies in "whether it is of the essence of the church to be visible, i.e. to exist on the earth in the form of sacraments and a divinely instituted ministry, or to be invisible, consisting solely of the union of its members with Christ through faith."[50]

It is the very visibility of Christ in the manger that makes the crèche Catholic.

As Brennan notes at length, far from being a symbol of national unity from time immemorial, as Burger would have it, Christmas was one location for the battle between Protestants and Catholics. The religious celebration of Christmas was seen by American and English Puritans as one more dangerous Catholic innovation tied to a danger-ously high christology. This division, as Justice Brennan emphasizes, is played out in the history of the American celebration of Christmas.

---

[49] Brennan quotes Hans Kung: "Today, of course, it is admitted even by Catholic exegetes that [the biblical stories recounting Christ's birth] are a collection of largely uncertain, mutually contradictory, strongly legendary and ultimately theologically motivated narratives, with a character of their own. Unlike the rest of Jesus' life, these are dream happenings and angels constantly enter on the scene and leave it as heavenly messengers of God announcing important events." 465 U.S. at 711.

[50] Giles, *American Catholic Arts and Fictions*, 54.

Reformed churches did not celebrate Christmas until its secular revival or reinvention in the nineteenth century. James Barnett, the definitive chronicler of the history of the American celebration of Christmas,[51] explicitly links the invention of the secular Christmas and Protestant acceptance of its celebration. While Catholic immigrants brought Christmas traditions with them from Europe as part of their Catholicism, many Protestant churches became willing to celebrate Christmas and to display crèches *only after* and *because* it became a secular holiday and the crèche had become secularized:

By about 1870 Christmas was an accepted lesson topic in the publications of the Sunday School Union. This demonstrates a widespread change in the attitude of most denominations toward Christmas between 1830 and 1870. An interesting confirmation of this is found in the fact that many of the popular Christmas songs of a religious character were composed between the years 1850 and 1868.[52]

Protestant attitudes toward the celebration of Christmas are correspondingly less religious.[53] The crèche originated for them as a part of the department store Christmas and is less vulnerable to desecration.

It is not that Protestants do not believe in the Incarnation but that that belief is not located in the image of the nativity scene in the way it is for Catholics. In many Catholic homes, for example, when the crèche is put up, the crib is left empty until Christmas Eve and the Magi are reserved for adding to the scene at Epiphany. There is a sense of participation in the materialism of the Incarnation, and, perhaps, also, of the wonder and awe, of which Justice Brennan speaks.

Justice Brennan, like Judge Pettine, seems unable, however, to see beyond this devotional attitude toward the crèche. While Burger cannot see the religiousness of the crèche, Brennan and Pettine cannot see its secularity, the radical disjunction between God and the world that is

---

[51] James Barnett, *The American Christmas: A Study in National Culture* (New York: Macmillan, 1954).

[52] Barnett, *The American Christmas*, 7.

[53] The books of Laura Ingalls Wilder describing life on the American frontier in the 1880s confirm Barnett's conclusion. Whereas the Ingalls girls are pictured as well-instructed in their faith even in the roughest of circumstances, dressing up every Sunday, memorizing Psalms, and attending church when possible, Christmas for them is about Santa Claus, not about Christ. Laura Ingalls Wilder, *Little House on the Prairie* (New York: Harper & Row, 1935).

characteristic of a Protestant sensibility. None of them sees the historically relative location of his own cultural reading.

A JEFFERSONIAN FIRST AMENDMENT

Combined with an intensely Catholic reading of the symbolism of the crèche, in the cases of both Pettine and Brennan, is a fierce commitment to a Jeffersonian reading of the First Amendment—a reading that has been the dominant one in the last fifty years. In formulating its test of constitutionality under the establishment clause, the *Lemon* Court, in a majority opinion ironically written by Chief Justice Burger, had announced this uncompromising goal:

The objective is to prevent, as far as possible, the intrusion of either [the state or religious institutions] into the precincts of the other.[54]

Both Judge Pettine and Justice Brennan, after reaffirming their commitment to the test set forth in the *Lemon* decision, quote Justice Frankfurter, an avid separationist, on the establishment clause. Pettine quotes Frankfurter's concurring opinion in *McCollum*:

We have staked the very existence of our country on the faith that complete separation between the state and religion is best for the state and best for religion.[55]

Brennan quotes from Frankfurter's concurring opinion in the *McGowan* decision:

[The establishment clause] withdr[aws] from the sphere of legitimate legislative concern and competence a specific, but comprehensive, area of human conduct: man's belief or disbelief in the verity of some transcendental idea and man's expression in action of that belief or disbelief.[56]

All three of these statements by the Court, in *Lemon*, *McCollum*, and *McGowan*, attempt to sum up the meaning of the establishment clause as being fulfilled only in a complete separation of religion and the state.

The *Lynch* majority represents a major break with past cases in this respect. Brennan's dissenting opinion is the first of the opinions in

---

[54] Lemon v. Kurtzman 403 U.S. 602, 614 (1971).

[55] McCollum v. Board of Education, 333 U.S. 203, 213 (1948) (Frankfurter, J., concurring).

[56] McGowan v. Maryland, 366 U.S. 420, 465–66 (1961) (Frankfurter, J., concurring).

Lynch to express a commitment to the ideal of separation. Neither Burger's nor O'Connor's opinions see *separation* as the goal. Earlier First Amendment decisions of the Court, beginning with *Everson*, had explicitly traced the establishment clause directly to its supposed progenitors, James Madison and Thomas Jefferson, as proponents of a strict separation of church and state. Madison's "Memorial and Remonstrance" and Jefferson's letters had frequently been looked to by both majorities and dissents on the Court as *the* relevant legislative history explaining the meaning of separation, a legislative history succinctly summarized for many by Jefferson's metaphor of a wall of separation.[57]

On 1 January 1802, during his first term in office, Thomas Jefferson had written to "Messrs. Nehemiah Dodge and Others, a Committee of the Danbury Baptist Association in the State of Connecticut," thanking them for their support and expressing his own understanding of the meaning of the religion clauses of the First Amendment:

Believing with you that religion is a matter which lies solely between man and his God, that he owes account to none other for his faith or his worship, that the legitimate powers of government reach actions only, and not opinions, I contemplate with sovereign reverence that act of the whole American people which declared that their legislature should "make no law respecting an establishment of religion, or prohibiting the free exercise thereof," thus building *a wall of separation between church and State*. Adhering to this expression of the supreme will of the nation in behalf of the rights of conscience, I shall see with sincere satisfaction the progress of those sentiments which tend to restore to man all his natural rights, convinced he has no natural right in opposition to his social duties. . . .

I reciprocate your kind prayers for the protection and blessing of the common Father and Creator of man, and tender you for yourselves and your religious association, assurances of my high respect and esteem. (emphasis added)[58]

Jefferson's words, "a wall of separation between church and State," were quoted by the Supreme Court in its first free exercise case, *Reynolds v. U.S.*,[59] and again in *Everson*, and thereafter enshrined as

---

[57] Madison's "Memorial and Remonstrance," for example, is appended in its entirety to the dissenting opinions in *Everson*.

[58] *Writings of Thomas Jefferson* (New York: Library of America, 1984), 510.

[59] 98 U.S. 145 (1878).

the defining metaphor in its interpretation of the First Amendment. Many Americans are surprised that the words of Jefferson's letter do not appear in the Constitution. Jefferson and Madison, for both political and theological reasons, considered religion "a private matter." It could and should be kept separate.

Notwithstanding its virtual absence from the opinions of the Supreme Court before 1940, it is difficult to overstate the formative role of the underlying philosophy of the First Amendment in the development of the idiosyncratic shape of American religion. As Sidney Mead forcefully argues, the flourishing of religion in America and the particular defining characteristics of American religion—denominationalism, voluntarism and an anti-intellectual piety—were all direct results of the disestablishment of the church and the multiplicity of sects in America.[60] While Mead also argues that disestablishment was itself originally the result more of the force of circumstances than of theological commitment, there were Americans, including James Madison and Roger Williams, for whom separation was also a matter of faith and, in time, it became part of the creed of American religion—Protestant, Catholic, and Jewish.

The final and fourth part of Brennan's opinion affirms his commitment to a strict separation of church and state and to a privatist understanding of religion:

Because the Framers of the Establishment Clause understood that "religion is too personal, too sacred, too holy, to permit its 'unhallowed perversion' by civil [authorities]," the clause demands that government play no role in this effort. (citations omitted)[61]

Both components of Brennan's viewpoint, the private nature of religion and the need for separation, ironically find their origin in an American Protestantism that was fiercely hostile to Roman Catholicism.

---

[60] Sidney E. Mead, *The Lively Experiment: The Shaping of Christianity in America* (New York: Harper & Row, 1963). See, also, Will Herberg, *Protestant, Catholic, Jew: An Essay in American Religious Sociology* (Garden City: Anchor Books, 1960).

Michael Tenzer has argued, in an interesting parallel case, that the flourishing of the arts in the villages of Bali is the direct result of the "disestablishment" of art when the royal courts of Bali were deposed by the Dutch. Michael Tenzer, *Balinese Music* (Berkeley: Periplus Editions, 1991).

[61] 465 U.S. at 725.

A JEFFERSONIAN CATHOLIC

There is a necessary and intimate interdependence between one's reading of the First Amendment and one's theology and philosophy of religion. One's ecclesiology cannot help but be part of one's understanding of the relationship of religion and government. John Courtney Murray, who is often regarded as *the* Catholic spokesman on the First Amendment, and who so represented himself, attempted to separate the two. He regarded the religion clauses, he said, as articles of peace, not articles of faith, because, as he said in 1960 in *We Hold These Truths*, "[r]eligious pluralism is against the will of God."[62] While Murray agreed with Sidney Mead that circumstances, rather than ideology, dictated the need for the First Amendment, he saw that pragmatic political judgment as in opposition to the unifying ideal expressed in his theology. The universal church as it was understood in the 1950s formed a piece with the other unifying cultural impulses of that time, Catholic and non-Catholic. Although Murray is still widely quoted for the Catholic view of religious freedom, both the Roman Catholic Church and American society have changed.

If Murray still represents, however, the orthodox Catholic view on the First Amendment,[63] how is it that Brennan, a Roman Catholic of Murray's time, is on the wrong side of the debate? How is it that for Brennan, as for Jefferson and many other Americans, the First Amendment religion clauses seem to be articles of faith, not simply articles of peace? How is it that Brennan agrees with Jefferson that pluralism *is* the will of God? There are several answers. Brennan is writing in the 1980s, not the 1950s. What Murray accomplished at Vatican II in the Declaration on Religious Freedom has perhaps gone beyond his own expectations in this respect, and his biographers suggest that toward the end of his life Murray was more open to the grace of pluralism.[64]

---

[62] John Courtney Murray, *We Hold These Truths: Catholic Reflections on the American Proposition* (New York: Sheed & Ward, 1960), 23.

[63] He struggled to convince his own church that these articles of peace were compatible with Catholic theology, and was vindicated by the adoption of his views by the Second Vatican Council in its Declaration on Religious Freedom. Walter M. Abbott, ed., *The Documents of Vatican II* (New York: Herder & Herder, 1966), 675–96.

[64] J. Leon Hooper, *The Ethics of Discourse: The Social Philosophy of John Courtney Murray* (Washington: Georgetown University Press, 1986), 212.

Notwithstanding Murray, however, and the pretences of much of the American Catholic community in the 1950s, there is a long tradition within American Catholicism that has eagerly embraced a Jeffersonian reading of the religion clauses of the First Amendment as articles of faith. The materialism of Catholic universalism, which, after Vatican II, has produced a remarkably diverse expression in the vernacular liturgies of the world's Catholics, has also produced a distinctively American Catholic response to American religious pluralism.

John Carroll, the first American Catholic bishop, and friend to Benjamin Franklin and Thomas Jefferson, argued strenuously in his early career for the conscious creation of a distinctly American Catholicism, emerging out of the American experience. This American Catholicism would have a distinctive institutional shape consistent with that experience. It would be, in Jay Dolan's words:

[A] national, American church which would be independent of all foreign jurisdiction and would endorse pluralism and toleration in religion; a church in which religion was grounded in intelligibility and where a vernacular liturgy was normative; and finally a church in which the spirit of democracy permeated the government of local communities.[65]

Carroll's Catholicism was grounded in the colonial experience, seen in the light of a deeply humanistic Catholic analogical imagination (in David Tracy's sense),[66] an imagination that had revealed a profound truth about human religion. Alexis de Tocqueville remarked on the enthusiasm of American Catholic priests for disestablishment.[67]

Carroll lost his nerve at the end of his life, looking more to Rome for leadership, pressured apparently by an increasingly diverse immigrant population. Indeed, the greater part of American Catholicism, by the time of Vatican I, had, with the rest of the church, moved away from Carroll's vision in its preoccupation with the needs of ministering to a flood of immigrants. Nevertheless, a thread of Jeffersonian Catholicism can be seen continuing in the work and writings of Bishops

---

[65] Jay P. Dolan, *The American Catholic Experience* (Garden City: Doubleday, 1985), 111.

[66] See David Tracy, *The Analogical Imagination* (New York: Crossroad, 1981), and p. 147 above.

[67] Alexis de Tocqueville, *De la démocratie en Amérique: Les grand thèmes* (Paris, 1835, 1840; reprint, Paris: Gallimard, 1968), 220–32.

John England, John Ireland, and James Gibbons and of the Americanists of the turn of the century, among others.[68] Justice Brennan arguably belongs in this company.

The influence of their Catholicism on their role as justices has been considered in numerous articles about the Catholic justices.[69] These articles have focused principally on the question, asked also of other Catholics in politics, as to whether the pope will tell them how to decide cases, in other words, whether they are bound by the magisterium as to a foreign power. Catholicism, on this reading, is about doctrinal authority. Paul Giles cites this view of Catholics as based on a common American misconception about Catholicisms in America. On the contrary, he argues, "the universalist temper of American Catholicism has gone hand in hand with a destabilizing tone of all-embracing scepticism."[70] For many Catholics, too, who have often internalized the common perception, the issue has been seen as one of doctrine and authority. Brennan has been widely criticized within the Catholic community for betraying the faith in the contraception and abortion decisions, for being a "bad" Catholic.

This criticism trivializes and misunderstands the Catholicism of Brennan's opinions. It is not Catholic dogma that influences his decisions, but the texture of his piety. Brennan's opinion in *Lynch* is not Catholic in the sense that he espouses orthodox Catholic teaching; possibly he tends to the unorthodox, at times. He is Catholic in his response to the crèche, even a cheap, tawdry crèche,[71] as an occasion of grace and in his sacralizing of the material pluralism of the human

[68] Dolan, *The American Catholic Experience*, 304–18.

[69] See, for example, John T. Noonan, "The Catholic Justices of the United States Supreme Court," *Catholic Historical Review* 67 (July 1981): 369–85; George Kannar, "The Constitutional Catechism of Antonin Scalia," *Yale Law Journal* 99 (April 1990): 1297–357; Sanford Levinson, "The Confrontation of Religious Faith and Civil Religion: Catholics Becoming Justices," *DePaul Law Review* 39 (summer 1990): 1047–81; Thomas Shaffer, "On Checking the Artifacts of Canaan: A Comment on Levinson's 'Confrontation'," *DePaul Law Review* 39 (summer 1990): 1133–42; Howard J. Vogel, "The Judicial Oath and the American Creed: Comments on Sanford Levinson's 'The Confrontation of Religious Faith and Civil Religion: Catholics Becoming Justices'," *DePaul Law Review* 39 (summer 1990): 1107–31.

[70] Giles, *American Catholic Arts and Fictions*, 507.

[71] Perhaps it is especially the case with a "cheap, tawdry" crèche. See Giles, *American Catholic Arts and Fictions*, 512, on good taste as a Protestant phenomenon.

condition.[72] Ironically, perhaps, then, he is also "Catholic" in his enthusiasm for a Jeffersonian reading of the First Amendment.

Marc Galanter has considered a parallel enthusiasm for the First Amendment in the Jewish community, a community which, historically, in Europe, like the Catholic community, might have had little within its own tradition to support such an idea. Galanter concludes that the First Amendment has allowed Jewish immigrants to shed the oppression of religious establishment and has allowed Jews and Judaism to flourish, albeit strongly altered by the First Amendment and the circumstances of American religion.[73] Similarly, I would argue, Catholicism flourishes in the United States, and is understood by many Catholics to flourish because of the separation of church and state.[74]

The opinions in the *Lynch* case seem to reveal a curious reversal, one in which the dissenting separatist sects of Europe have become the *de facto* establishment of American cultural Protestantism while the cultural religions of Europe have become separatist dissenting sects.[75] Burger, a Protestant, defends the cultural domination of Protestantism while Brennan, a Catholic, lines up with Jefferson and the eighteenth-century Baptists in support of religion being a private matter and in support of the separation of church and state. Perhaps it is Brennan who is the latter-day Roger Williams—passionate about the difference religion makes and yet confident of our capacity for civil society, even though we are mostly heathens. For Brennan law and religion are different kinds of social facts. They must be kept distinct. But, for Brennan, as for Jefferson and Williams, the location for this distinction is in the individual. Religion, whether of the austere Puritan, the Enlightenment deist, or the Catholic sacramentalist, is located in the individual person. It is not about culture or society or political power.

[72] See David Tracy, *The Analogical Imagination* and *Inter-religious Dialogue.*

[73] Marc Galanter, "Separation Anxiety: Church, State and the Jews in the 1990s or the Jewish Stake in the First Amendment's Religion Clauses," paper presented at the Jonathan Newman Memorial Conference on Law and Religion, Northwestern School of Law at Lewis and Clark College, Portland, Oregon, 23 October 1992.

[74] This is not, of course, the only Catholic view. It may be the dominant one today in terms of numbers. The American Catholic community in the 1990s, like other American religious communities, is sharply divided on social issues.

[75] See Ernst Troeltsch. *The Social Teaching of the Christian Church*, trans. Olive Wyon (New York: Macmillan, 1931).

Chapter 6

A New Discourse and Practice

For Thoreau, it is natural for a person to be alone, but for Mary McCarthy it is natural for a person to be in a group.
—Giles, *American Catholic Arts and Fictions*[1]

Human culture is an ingredient not supplementary to human thought.
—Geertz, *The Interpretation of Cultures*[2]

Just those elements in Catholicism which most shocked protestants and rationalists—the miraculous cures and visions, the cults of saints and relics, the adoration of the Virgin—make it most meaningful for readers of *The Golden Bough* and *Totem and Taboo.*
—Davis in "Religion and the Intellectuals"[3]

Is the logical result of the criticisms of the *Lynch* opinions found in these chapters that the First Amendment has become unworkable? Is religion too unreliable a category? Especially in a postmodern world? Like truth in *Rashomon*? If anything *can* be religion and if nothing is *exclusively* so, how then can the Supreme Court decide when the government is establishing it?

Disestablishment, the separation of church and state, is a modern Western notion, as Stephen Toulmin defines modernity.[4] It is a product

---

[1] Giles, *American Catholic Arts and Fictions*, 526.
[2] Clifford Geertz, *The Interpretation of Cultures* (New York: Basic Books, 1973), 77.
[3] Robert Gorham Davis, "Religion and the Intellectuals III," *Partisan Review* 17 (April 1950).
[4] Stephen Toulmin, *Cosmopolis: The Hidden Agenda of Modernity* (Chicago: University of Chicago Press, 1990).

of the Reformation and of the Thirty Years' War, what Toulmin calls
the Counter-Renaissance. Its historical articulation must be seen in the
context of the rationalist dogmatism of the seventeenth and eighteenth
centuries, the emergence of the sovereign and secular nation-state, and
the distinctively modern piety of the individual.

Toulmin reminds us that the invention of rationalism—the quest for
certainty—was a response to a particular historical situation in the West.
The philosophers of modernity were reacting, he says, to the grim
realities of seventeenth-century Europe. Thus, modernity was, beginning with Descartes, a retreat from the broad and tolerant humanism
of sixteenth-century Europe, the Europe of Montaigne and Shakespeare,
a retreat whose beginning is marked by the assassination of Henry IV
of France and the revocation of the Edict of Nantes. According to
Toulmin, economic depression, disease, and war taught theorists to
distrust the practical philosophy of Renaissance humanism and caused
them to seek, in its place, timeless universal dogmas that would
transcend the violence and messiness of particular cultural situations.

Toulmin further argues that the harsh realities of the first half of
the twentieth century and the accompanying breakdown of the nation-
state are now teaching Europe, and perhaps all of Western culture, to
mistrust, in turn, the rational cosmopolis. The conditions of postmodern
Europe are challenging it to remember its early modern past and to
seek a more tolerant, more Renaissance, view of the finitude of human
beings and of their capacities. Toulmin is remarkably, maybe naïvely,
hopeful for this new humanism and its promise of tolerance. He also
reminds us that humanism in its first, its Renaissance, incarnation, was
not secular. Erasmus and Montaigne, although always skeptical of
human religious creations, assumed a religious worldview. Toulmin
seems to assume that the new twentieth-, or twenty-first-, century
humanism will also be, in some sense, religious.

Whereas Toulmin speaks of all Western culture as a unity, the United
States is perhaps more of a different case than he acknowledges. Its
sovereign existence has been defined exclusively within and by
modernity, as Toulmin understands it, but, while rationalism plagues
its institutions and culture in analogous ways, it has no Renaissance to
remember or to which it might return. It may make more sense in the
American context to see the needed correction to modernity—a tolerant
humanist impulse—as coming from and sympathetic to the subversive

and insistent voices of the suppressed communities of America, of Native Americans, of African Americans, of Catholics, of women, of Jews, of fundamentalists and evangelicals, which are challenging the rationalism and individualism of mainstream American Protestant culture.

The present crisis in the interpretation of the First Amendment provides a neat test of Toulmin's thesis. In one sense the religion clauses were a very modern solution to a very modern problem. The hardening of doctrinal differences and the resulting intersectarian violence in the Reformation led to the need for disestablishment. Whereas religious persecution was not a modern invention, the idea that the solution was a secular public space and private religious practice is peculiarly modern and is most fully realized in the American context. The First Amendment, as understood by Jefferson and Madison, proposes a theoretically clean and apparently practical solution to the discord of the seventeenth century.

And it has worked remarkably well. Religious freedom and disestablishment are hallmarks of a country in which religion seems to flourish. Yet the stifling effect of modernity's quest for certainty, marvelously evoked by Toulmin, is also present. An increasingly heavy price of the First Amendment, of modern disestablishment and of its underlying philosophy, has been the "establishment" of an excessively narrow understanding of religion and a sometimes strained ghettoization of religion from the rest of life.

Postmodernism—Toulmin's humanistic postmodernism—can be seen in religion as well as in architecture, his privileged example. Religion, like architectural decoration, seems to be bursting out all over—and all across the United States—in complicated and ornate ways: fundamentalisms, new age, neo-pagans, Muslims, voodoo, millennialists, and more. Like the baroque decorative flourishes of post-Miesian architecture, these religious phenomena are hard to explain within modern rational theories and institutions. (Unfortunately, they and their critics may also be resistant to the tolerant humanism of Stephen Toulmin.) American religion is changing and we are changing the way we understand our own religious history. These realities demand that we change our understanding of the First Amendment.

This is not an easy project. In a bibliographical note, Toulmin cites with approval, as an example of a tolerant humanist impulse, the modern Indian custom of visiting the homes of friends of other religious traditions on *their* religious holidays to congratulate them.[5] Religious violence in India, a country which has, for many, exemplified the possibility of the peaceful coexistence of diverse religious traditions, today belies the success of such polite cultural solutions. Furthermore, few Jews would wish to return to Renaissance Europe, even to the France of Henry IV.

In response to the changing climate of postmodern religion, the academic legal community has gone into high gear in the last five or ten years in an effort to solve the problem of the First Amendment.[6] A great deal of serious thought has been given to reconstructing the history of the First Amendment and to attempting to propose rules of constitutional interpretation that will provide a more consistent basis for the Court's decisions in this area.[7] Underlying and undercutting most of these proposals, however, is a religious anthropology that is rarely acknowledged and is by no means universal. The dominant discourse about religion represented in the opinions of the Court and in the academic legal literature is, even in its variety, narrowly and culturally bound and needs to be expanded and made more self-critical if it is humanistically to represent American religion.[8]

INTERPRETING THE FIRST AMENDMENT

Academic commentators would almost all agree with the following statement by Michael McConnell that the current state of First Amendment jurisprudence is chaotic:

[5] Toulmin, *Cosmopolis*, 219.

[6] Law reviews have devoted numerous special issues to the subject. See, for example, "Symposium on Politics, Religion and the Relationship Between Church and State," *DePaul Law Review* 39 (summer 1990); "Symposium: Confronting the Wall of Separation: A New Dialogue Between Law and Religion on the Meaning of the First Amendment," *DePaul Law Review* 42 (fall 1992). Numerous conferences have been held. New journals devoted to law and religion have been started—for example, *The Journal of Law and Religion* and *First Things*. Courses on law and religion have been newly added to law school curricula.

[7] See, for example, Levy, *The Establishment Clause*; Cord, *Separation of Church and State*; Laycock, "Substantive Neutrality"; and McConnell, "Religious Freedom at a Crossroads."

[8] See my review of Stephen Carter, *The Culture of Disbelief* (New York, 1993), in *Journal of Religion* 75 (January 1995), forthcoming.

Thus, as of today, it is constitutional for a state to hire a Presbyterian minister to lead the legislature in daily prayers, but unconstitutional for a state to set aside a moment of silence in the schools for children to pray if they want to. It is unconstitutional for a state to require employers to accommodate their employees' work schedules to their sabbath observances, but constitutionally mandatory for a state to require employers to pay workers compensation when the resulting inconsistency between work and sabbath leads to discharge. It is constitutional for the government to give money to religiously-affiliated organizations to teach adolescents about proper sexual behavior, but not to teach them science or history. It is constitutional for the government to provide religious school pupils with books, but not with maps; with bus rides to religious schools, but not from school to a museum on a field trip; with cash to pay for state-mandated tests, but not to pay for safety-related maintenance. It is a mess.[9]

How should the Court decide these cases? How can government officials know how to conduct themselves? How do we, the public, know what is constitutional? The culture about law and religion created by the Supreme Court is largely one of confusion and is often an object of derision.

One difficulty with the present interpretation of the First Amendment is that the two clauses, the free exercise and the establishment clauses, get in each other's way. While all religion cases raise both issues, the outcome of a case and the way in which religion is understood in that case can depend on whether it is framed as a free exercise or an establishment clause case. For example, while *Lynch* is framed as an establishment clause case, there are free exercise issues raised both by banning religious symbols from public spaces and by limiting such displays to only one religious tradition. Similarly, while *Employment Division v. Smith*—the peyote case—was framed as a free exercise case, selective exemptions to state law for members of particular religious groups raise serious establishment clause issues.[10]

One strategy for avoiding the problem of the independence of the two clauses creating conflicting precedents is to read them together into

---

[9] McConnell, "Religious Freedom at a Crossroads," 119–20.

[10] See Board of Education v. Grumet, in which the Court considered a constitutional challenge to the creation of a public school district to accommodate Hasidic children needing special education.

one principle and then to enforce that principle. On the whole, the principle which has been said to unite the two clauses, and which is said to be the central goal of the First Amendment, is neutrality— neutrality of government as among religions and neutrality of government as between religion and non-religion. A number of serious efforts have been made to fix the meaning of neutrality and to develop methods of testing neutrality on the part of the government.[11]

Michael McConnell and Richard Posner have proposed that economic cost-benefit analysis is the best way of maximizing religious free choice and of testing the neutrality of government regulation of religion.[12] As an example, a religious exemption from prohibition laws would be economically rational based on a balance between the destructive impact on the religious group of no exemption and the marginal impact on the government of an exemption. But, McConnell and Posner disclaim any intention to articulate the "meaning" of the First Amendment. Economic analysis, they suggest, cannot decide what the First Amendment means; it can only help sort out the hidden costs and benefits of regulating religion. Among general conclusions they reach about the economic effect of the Court's First Amendment decisions are that "[t]he courts may. . .have played a role in the precipitous decline of the mainline Protestant churches in recent decades," and that "the courts may well have increased the demand for religion by increasing the amount of religious 'product variety'."[13]

McConnell and Posner explicitly assume that the goal of the First Amendment is a free market in religion—the deregulation of religion so as to maximize free choice. This approach risks reducing religion to an economic good and implies that economic analysis is independent

---

[11] See, for example, Kurland, *Religion and the Law*; and Laycock, "Formal, Substantive, and Disaggregated Neutrality."

[12] Michael W. McConnell and Richard A. Posner, "An Economic Approach to Issues of Religious Freedom," *University of Chicago Law Review* 56 (winter 1989): 1–60. Elsewhere, however, McConnell has suggested that his one principle would be religious freedom, that is, neutrality with a bias in favor of religious freedom. Michael W. McConnell, "Free Exercise Revisionism and the *Smith* Decision," *University of Chicago Law Review* 57 (fall 1990): 1109–53.

[13] McConnell and Posner, "An Economic Approach to Issues of Religious Freedom," 59.

of value-laden questions about the anthropology of the human person.[14] The model for human religion they use is one in which religion is defined as a matter of individual free choice and is worth protecting only insofar as it has utilitarian value. Although there is strong historical support for this reading of the First Amendment and for this under-standing of religion as being a common one in this country from the late eighteenth century to the present, it is a reading with a seriously inadequate religious anthropology for twentieth-century Americans.

The apparent rationality and neutrality of the economic approach is, in McConnell's case as well as in that of others, often used to disguise an impulse to promote religion as a public good. The mechanical and antiseptic nature of its discourse conceals a particular understanding of what religion is and can be. An economic approach assumes that the language that is used to talk about religion is unimportant. All that need be done is to decide on the regulatory goal, and the application of economic analysis will determine, in a clean, analytical way, the results in particular cases.

The argument made in the discussion in this book is that the language does matter and that its effect is inescapable. How the courts talk about religion is critical, because the texture of the public discourse about religion creates a culture about religion. People's lives are given meaning in the spaces created by words. If the courts distort American religion when they talk about it, they both do violence to peoples' experiences and undermine their own authority. Necessary to a successful First Amendment discourse about human religion is the recognition that religion—in a general sense—cannot be evaluated as good or bad. Human beings create religion. That should be acknowledged. Religion is both a constructive and a destructive force. It is not the role of the government to reify or endorse any particular version.

In an article summarizing his own view of the First Amendment for a bicentennial symposium on the Bill of Rights at the University of

---

[14] McConnell and Posner explicitly deny any implicit normative agenda, although both are clearly concerned that religion may not always yield readily to their model.

Similar criticisms have been made of Posner's theories with respect to economics and to sex. See White, "The Language and Culture of Economics," and Martha Nussbaum, "'Only Grey Matter'?: Richard Posner's Cost-Benefit Analysis of Sex," *University of Chicago Law Review* (fall 1992): 1689–734.

Chicago Law School, McConnell acknowledges that neutrality only makes sense if it is known what one is being neutral about, if one knows the base line against which one is measuring neutrality. For McConnell, that base line is also a battle line. McConnell sees the current debate about the First Amendment as boiling down to those who are for and those (the secular humanists) who are against religion, between those who, like him, believe that the Constitution mandates what he calls a pluralist approach and those who believe the Constitution mandates a secular common culture. McConnell sees "a gulf between a largely secularized professional and academic elite and most ordinary citizens, for whom religion commonly remains a central aspect of life."[15] McConnell is concerned that *"authentic* religion must be shoved to the margins of public life"(emphasis added).[16]

Whether or not such a polarization in fact exists between a secular elite and the religious masses in this country, the perception that it exists can be blamed, at least partially, on the failure of the Supreme Court's discourse on religion in general and on the majority opinions in *Lynch* and *Smith* in particular. As a result of these decisions, the issue has now been framed in those terms: either the First Amendment gives religion a privileged status or it does not. Either religion is recognized as a public good or it is condemned as a public evil.

The argument is strong that religion was viewed as a privileged public good by *all* of the founders. The pro-religionists argue, then, that the only constitutional issue is the equal treatment of religions and of believers. McConnell summarizes his views as follows:

The religious freedom cases under the First Amendment have been distorted by the false choice between secularism and majoritarianism, neither of which faithfully reflects the pluralistic philosophy of the Religion Clauses. Instead, the Free Exercise and Establishment Clauses should protect against government-induced uniformity in matters of religion. In the modern welfare-regulatory state, this means that the state must not favor religion over nonreligion, nonreligion over religion, or one religion over another in distributing financial resources; that the state must create exceptions to laws

---

[15] McConnell, "Religious Freedom at a Crossroads," 126.

[16] McConnell, "Religious Freedom at a Crossroads," 127. See also Carter, *The Culture of Disbelief*, for a lengthy and impassioned argument of this position.

of general applicability when these laws threaten the religious convictions or practices of religious institutions or individuals; that the state should eschew both religious favoritism and secular bias in its own participation in the formation of public culture. This interpretation will tolerate a more prominent place for religion in the public sphere, but will simultaneously guarantee religious freedom for faiths both large and small.[17]

McConnell's statement represents what might be called a sophisticated pro-religion stance, complete with a coopting of multiculturalism and a reading back of that contemporary political agenda into the eighteenth century.

If religion does not have a constitutionally privileged status, a position strongly represented by Justice Black, Philip Kurland, Justice O'Connor, and others, religion will have to take its chances in the legislatures. We will have more martyrs, and sacraments will have to campaign for legislative exemption. Some sacraments may, in fact, fare better in the legislature than in the courts. The religious use of peyote, for example, is specifically exempt under the federal narcotics laws and under most state narcotics laws, as was the sacramental use of wine during Prohibition from regulations controlling the sale and con-sumption of alcohol.[18] The Supreme Court, meanwhile, has found no constitutional protection for the religious consumption of peyote and would, presumably, after *Smith*, find no such protection for the sacramental consumption of alcohol.

If, from a statist political perspective, a certain kind of religion is useful to provide ceremony, to perform charitable works, and to provide Sunday schools where citizens learn to be good citizens, then, the argument runs, religion should be privileged. It is doing something for the state that would take a tremendous, perhaps impossible, effort for the state to reproduce. From a larger political perspective the argument is made that religion provides a location of autonomy for public-spirited criticism of the government and religion should therefore be privileged. If, on the other hand, as many theorists would have it, religion is now seen as a free-floating and always changing cultural resource mobilized

---

[17] McConnell, "Religious Freedom at a Crossroads," 194.
[18] 21 C.F.R. sec. 130.31 (1989), National Prohibition Act, Title II, sec. 3, 41 Stat. 308.

by fragmented alliances of politically like-minded individuals to express ethnic and political solidarity, perhaps it should not.[19]

Should religion be privileged? Is religion threatened? That is what is currently seen as being at stake in considering the interpretation of the First Amendment.[20] Let us take one step back from that question.

I am inclined to agree with McConnell that the First Amendment was not intended to—nor should it—be read as establishing a Deweyan secular faith.[21] A Madisonian pluralism is probably closer to what was intended and to what is presently appropriate. More is still needed, though. Secularization is not the problem, or even the situation, as a growing number of sociologists acknowledge. It is not true that the country is divided between a secular elite and a religious proletariat, although there may be a range of different contemporary discourses about religion founded on different underlying assumptions. Michael McConnell and other academic lawyers[22] are indulging in inflated rhetoric on this issue by, in effect, pointing fingers at the unregenerate on the Court and in the universities, by setting up this conversation as one between those who are for and those who are against religion—a classic Calvinist division between the saved and the damned.[23]

It is not that McConnell and the others who advocate a pro-religion stand are intentionally exclusive. On the contrary, they are sincerely committed to pluralism. They want to include all "authentic"[24] religious impulses. But, like the Buddhism discovered by avid Romantic

---

[19] N. J. Demerath, III, and Rhys Williams, "Secularization in a Community Context: Tensions of Religion and Politics in a New England City," *Journal for the Scientific Study of Religion* 31 (December 1992): 189–206.

[20] See Carter, *The Culture of Disbelief*.

[21] See, for the view that the Constitution established a Deweyan common faith, Kathleen M. Sullivan, "Religion and Liberal Democracy," *University of Chicago Law Review* 59 (winter 1992): 195–223. Sullivan's obviously reluctant acknowledgment of the continued importance of sectarian religion is a paragraph about the political power of Cardinal Law of Boston, Cardinal O'Connor of New York, and Jerry Falwell. She sets up secularism as a necessary faith to protect us from religion in the shape of these right-wing authoritarian religious figures.

[22] Stephen Carter, for example, in his *The Culture of Disbelief*.

[23] While I here accuse McConnell of a covert theological agenda, I am not sure that avoiding theologizing on this subject is possible. All we can do is to do our best to be aware of the ways in which our language about religion, albeit unintentional, makes theological assumptions.

[24] McConnell, "Religious Freedom at a Crossroads," 127.

researchers, the diverse American religions they celebrate all look very much like Protestantism. A radical reorientation is necessary in order to see other peoples' religion as they themselves see it and not to make of it what one will—particularly when one is offering to share public space with it. Virtually everyone in this debate is working with a model of religion that is historically and culturally bound in ways that are rarely fully acknowledged.

Each of the opinions in *Lynch* represents a tough strand in American culture. Together they affirm values we hold in common: the continued importance of religious culture in American life, the primacy of political equality, and a respect for privacy and for the value of religious diversity and particularity. Together these opinions also reify a certain kind of American religion.

The First Amendment is central to American identity. It is a critical element of our public creed. We understand ourselves to be a people committed to the separation of church and state and to the free exercise of religion. We take pride in it. Our religious identity and our religious institutions—our faith, both civic and denominational—are formed by these words. We may squabble over particular cases, but we hold firmly to the words. It causes scandal that the Supreme Court is perceived as betraying them. We need to find a language in which to articulate our common concern about religion. I would venture to say that none of the justices and few Americans wish to live in a country without religion, or believe that such a state would be possible, were it even desirable.

The Supreme Court is an important location in the United States for the creation and expression of American identity. One might say that, after *Marbury v. Madison*,[25] it is expressly licensed by the Constitution to play such a role. With respect to religion its role is unique within the government because of constitutional limitations on the other two branches. How then should the Court talk about religion? Can it find a way to articulate the rich complexity of American religious experience, mind and body, within the framework of the words of the First Amendment? The frustration of the *Lynch* decision, as Brennan observed, is that it manages to offend everyone who cares at all,

---

[25] Marbury v. Madison, 1 Cranch 137 (1803). The Court held in *Marbury* that the Supreme Court had jurisdiction to review the constitutionality of actions by the other branches of government, that it was the final arbiter of the constitutionality of government action.

"believers and non-believers alike."[26] To the "believer" religion seems by these opinions to be trivialized, marginalized, or privatized. To the "non-believer" the opinions appear to belabor a dead issue. The opinions in the peyote case have similar problems. The Court needs to begin to talk and act about religion in a way in which the values of the First Amendment can be creatively expressed while justice to religion can be seen to be done by everyone.

TALKING AND ACTING ABOUT RELIGION

These chapters have attempted, through a history of religions reading of the Court's opinions in *Lynch*, to illustrate both the diversity within the Court's own discourse about religion and the limitations of that discourse. The Court's discourse and practice about religion is deconstructed from within while also being examined within the context of the cross-cultural comparative study of law and religion, rather than only from within the context of American religious and political history.

The three Supreme Court opinions in *Lynch* offer three typical American alternatives of ways to talk about religion. These are by no means the only ones. The judges in the lower courts and the witnesses at the trial offered others. Chief Justice Burger's opinion for the majority represents one American way of talking about religion—religion as celebratory, irenic, and passive, religion with no difference, no power. It is a religion that has made its peace with law and with modern culture. Justice O'Connor's opinion represents another: Law has superseded particular religious traditions as the unifying, motivating, and explanatory force for Americans. The Constitution is our creed. Explicitly religious voices are muffled. Finally, Justice Brennan speaks from within a "dissenting" American religious tradition, seeking to hold on to the intensity of its grace while insisting on the possibility of a common public life, a secular common life. There are overlaps in these discourses. Taken together, they subvert and nuance each other, like the witnesses in *Rashomon*.

Paul Giles, in his study of American Catholic art and literature,[27] portrays the culture of the American Catholic community as a kind of

---

[26] There is indeed a sizable group who consider the matter trivial.

[27] Giles, *American Catholic Arts and Fictions*.

subversive in-house critic of the dominant Protestant culture. Whereas the Protestant culture stresses individualism, a pastoral ideal, and an active pioneer quest, Catholic culture is skeptical about the autonomy of the individual, is largely urban, and tends toward a passive impotence. In an explicitly religious context, Protestantism stresses individual belief, free choice, and freedom of conscience, while Catholicism stresses a tradition that incorporates the individual and downplays the individual's attitude towards his faith. Giles concludes:

[O]ne of the contributions of Catholicism within American culture may be to problematize the idea of what is considered natural. . . . The culture of Catholicism deconstructs the more celebrated American ideologies (Protestant, pastoral, and so on) to reveal them as provisional systems.[28]

The existence of other American religious cultures, including an American Catholic culture, thus calls into question the meaning of religion. For the First Amendment this means that religion in its "natural" state, the religion we are to be neutral about, cannot be limited to any one voice or way of being. It cannot be seen as only private, individual, voluntary, and a matter of conscience.

Ironically, I think, for many Protestants and for some Catholics, another contribution Giles sees Catholicism as making is a faith in pluralism:

[W]ithin the American Catholic idiom skepticism is the antithesis of dogmatism, not the antithesis of belief. . . . This illumination of heterogeneity subverts all rigid linear conceptions of rationality and hierarchy; instead, the variety of "Grace" is positioned as a challenge to the institution of human reason.[29]

The ancestors of American Catholicism, Giles argues, in this "onto-logical burlesque" are Erasmus and Montaigne, not the neo-scholastics. This Catholic sensibility suggests a different kind of neutrality and a different kind of pluralism. Rather than leaving everyone alone out of a restrained Protestant respect for individual autonomy, this pluralism and this neutrality is attempted in the Joycean spirit of "Here comes everybody."[30]

---

[28] Giles, *American Catholic Arts and Fictions*, 526, 531.

[29] Giles, *American Catholic Arts and Fictions*, 508.

[30] Giles, *American Catholic Arts and Fictions*, 506.

The in-house critique of American religion by American Catholicisms suggested by Giles could be done from the viewpoint of the many dissenting traditions.[31] All such critiques can be seen as history of religions in practice and as subversive of mainstream American cultural assumptions about religion.[32] Daniel Gold, a historian of religions who studies the religions of India, argues that the purpose of history of religions is to make sense of the worlds conceived by human beings struggling to comprehend their existence in this world.[33] He further argues that while historians of religion are somewhat distanced from the existential truths revealed to religious subjects, the multiple constructs of history of religions derive much of their power from the diversity and depth of the traditions they attempt to describe. Thus, Gold sees the fragmentation in history of religions as inevitable and as reflecting the fragmentation in religion itself.

Seeing the values of the First Amendment played out in the Japanese context and interpreted by the Japanese Court challenges Americans to reconsider the construction they have put on American religion, to reconsider what is considered "natural." Perhaps it would be more helpful, and more accurate, to see many Americans, as many Japanese see themselves, as commonly participating in more than one religious tradition—both sectarian and civil—during their lifetimes, rather than as making exclusive and lifelong "monogamous" choices.

What would a history of religions opinion in *Lynch* look like? It would begin by acknowledging the crèche and its accompaniment as a complex, ambiguous, and multivalent location for Pawtucket piety, a location combining shifting sacred and secular elements. The genius of the American Christmas, and of its symbolism, Theodore Caplow and his co-authors argue in *All Faithful People*, lies in its ability to

---

[31] See, for example, Long, *Significations*, on African-American religion.

[32] Another related strategy is the widespread effort in American church history in the last twenty years to retrieve the other traditions that make up American religion, to problematize the canon of American religious history. See, for example, Albanese, *America: Religions and Religion*; Albert Raboteau, *Slave Religion: The "Invisible Institution" in the Antebellum South* (Oxford: Oxford University Press, 1980); and the myriad efforts to make a space for the others of American religion, including Native American and Asian religious traditions.

[33] Gold, *Comprehending the Guru*, 6–7.

draw together religious and secular themes that reinforce each other, particularly within the institution of the family.[34] Such a reading would acknowledge the diversity both within the Christian community and among religious traditions. And it would acknowledge the inherent ambivalence of religious symbols, challenging the positive utilitarian reading given by the majority in *Lynch* and by many others. Even Christmas has its menacing aspect. It is not accidental that the crèche occupies the central position in the display. It is intended to dominate. Historians of religion have spent much time analyzing the ideological significance of the center in terms of the religious symbolism of power.[35] We should not therefore be surprised that plaintiff Donnelly said that his reaction to the display was one of "fear."

Such a reading would not need to be an academic monograph. It *would* need to give attention to and allow the articulation of strong voices in the American legal and religious traditions, voices that understand religion to be a social as well as an individual matter, to be historically and culturally situated, to be material and embodied, and to be potentially dangerous and destructive.

In his charming book-length essay on the First Amendment,[36] William Lee Miller, after a biting satirical reduction of the Court's establishment clause cases, concludes, as does Mark DeWolfe Howe, that the Court's difficulty arises out of its equation of religion and race as discriminatory categories. He says:

"Creed" and "religion" are not unchangeable givens of a human being's biological makeup or accident of birth, or unalterable past ("previous condition of servitude"), but entail—however theoretically in demographic fact—mind, and will, and choice. Religious belief is not part of the ineluctable externals of a human being's existence, but part of the substance to which he or she has an inner, changing, substantive relationship, and which, individually and communally, provides the frame to guide and shape conduct and define the great issues of living. A human being can become a heretic, a convert, or a

---

[34] Caplow, *All Faithful People*, 192. See, also, Adam Kuper, "The English Christmas and the Family: Time Out and Alternative Realities," in Miller, *Unwrapping Christmas.*

[35] See, for example, Smith, *Map is not Territory.*

[36] William Lee Miller, *The First Liberty: Religion and the American Republic* (New York: Paragon House, 1985).

backslider, even though in fact most do not. A believer can become an unbeliever; those who come to scoff can stay to pray; Saul of Tarsus and Martin Luther and Roger Williams and Ignatius Loyola and John Henry Newman can alter their beliefs. The young Edmund Wilson—if we may reverse and perhaps descend a little—reading a sentence of Shaw's while riding on the train back to school from Philadelphia, can feel the whole weight of his ancestral Presbyterianism lifted from his shoulders before he reaches Norristown. Religion is culture not nature; belief not biology; mind and spirit not ethnicity.[37]

It is not the Court's business, Miller argues, to get involved in "cultural politics." The Court should stay out of the competition "to articulate truth and win men's souls."

But people do not so easily divide into nature and culture.[38] And culture is not as much a matter of "mind, and will, and choice" as Miller would like. The examples he gives, looked at from an historical perspective, seem much less dramatic to us, than they did to those particular individuals or to their communities. In many important ways Saul of Tarsus was still a Romanized Jew and Martin Luther a Catholic monk. Roger Williams is part of the Puritan story as well as the Baptist. Newman is a towering figure in the Anglican as well as in the Roman Church. Even Edmund Wilson remained a Presbyterian in important ways. It does not diminish the importance of the critiques they made to say that religion is not simply a matter of individual conscience and of free choice.

The intractability of the Court's discourse on religion does not arise from its failure to stay out of cultural politics. In that it has no choice. It arises from its anthropology. Religion is a given to a greater extent than Miller acknowledges. Brennan's attitude toward the crèche is not merely a decorative flourish to his freely chosen religious belief. The crèche and other material embodiments of the sacred constitute an inescapable cultural location for his religion. Miller's understanding of religion, like that of many Americans, is profoundly affected and limited by American evangelical piety, a piety that locates religion in

[37] Miller, *The First Liberty*, 320.
[38] See, for a discussion of the relationship of biology and culture, Clifford Geertz, "The Growth of Culture and the Evolution of Mind," in his *The Interpretation of Cultures*.

the individual mind and heart and that sees conversion, rather than Christian nurture, as the model for making new Christians.[39]

The religious traditions that history of religions has struggled to understand have challenged it to come to grips with a more material and varied spirituality. These traditions challenge Americans to move from religion viewed as a matter of mind and will and free choice to a view of individuals and of human culture inescapably and creatively various in a religiousness that, like other human cultural productions, involves both cultural givens and creative reinterpretation.

Looking at the ways in which the categories of history of religions play themselves out in the American political discourse can also highlight the political nature of academic discourse, the contradictions between the ideologies of academic and political discourses, and the problematic relationship between history of religions and Christianity.

LAW AND RELIGION

Understanding the relationship of law and religion is central to understanding American religion. As many have observed, legal structures, institutional and linguistic, have played a key role in shaping American religion. Religious structures, in turn, have played a foundational role in shaping American law and identity. This close interconnection, sometimes harmonious, often in tension, between religion and law is revealed by events throughout American history and across religious traditions. A high level of self-consciousness about the need to reconcile the two is also present in many of these contexts, although there are also locations in which the mutually constitutive roles of law and religion require critical retrieval.

At the same time, however, while acknowledgment should be made of the tremendous influence each has had in shaping the other in this country and in the Western tradition generally, it is also clear that the two are caught in opposition. It is an opposition that might be traced, in the Western conversation, from Paul's preoccupation with the opposition of faith and law through the reformers' concerns with faith and works. Perhaps one of the reasons it is difficult to achieve a felicitous reading of the First Amendment is that the tension is merely preserved, not transcended, by it. The problem is not solved. It is

[39] Mead, *The Lively Experiment*, 125.

acknowledged. In a sense the First Amendment embodies a tension that cannot be resolved. Religion has a special relationship to law.

The public celebration of Christmas in the United States presents a nice problem for interpreters of the First Amendment. As an event, as a cultural location for meaning, it displays a tantalizing blend of sacred and secular, public and private, religion and politics, while revealing a kaleidoscope of glimpses of the history of religion and law in the West. Any one reading seems to dissolve before one's eyes. Christmas is many things to many people. The history of the public celebration of Christmas also shows how our sensibilities have changed. Our increased uneasiness regarding the messages that public symbols and public events convey further destabilizes the meaning.

At the risk of being presumptuous, I submit the following introduction to a proposed opinion in the *Lynch* case—as a trial balloon. Let us start to forge a new language about religion that honors both the commitment of the First Amendment and the lived experience of American religious history. Let us, through that effort, "pay the words extra."

PROPOSED OPINION IN *LYNCH V. DONNELLY*

I

The parties to this action ask this Court to draw a bright line between the religious and the secular in order to determine the constitutionality of a part of a city's Christmas display. The city of Pawtucket, Rhode Island, erected, among other symbols of the season, a "crèche"—a diorama with life-sized figures depicting a scene immediately following the birth of Jesus Christ, the founder of Christianity—in a public park, as a part of a civic holiday celebration. It is the constitutional appropriateness of this crèche as a public symbol that is at issue in this case.

This Court has always been extremely reluctant to draw such lines, believing that the First Amendment religion clauses prohibit government from entering into theological discussions or trying to define the permissible contours of religious belief and practice. The First Amendment, however, of course, also can only make sense if the word "religion," as it appears in it, has some comprehensible referent. Whatever our reluctance, it is inescapably the difficult task of this Court to define the meaning of that word. That task is not one that can be done in a few words or in a single case. It is a task that requires the careful building up of understanding, and it is one that must acknowledge that such definitions—definitions of whole categories of human culture—are social products that change over time. Religion has a history that extends over the length and breadth of human history. Its definition has challenged scholars for centuries. With its consideration of this case, the Court can only make a contribution to that task. But it does so conscious of a host of witnesses from a rich human history.

Petitioners—the mayor and other officials of the city of Pawtucket—argue in their brief that Christmas in the United States has become a national folk festival, that Christmas as a religious holiday has been superseded by a celebration of secular humanism:

> Government celebration of Christmas is a secular activity. The American Christmas is a national folk festival which derives from the Christian celebration of the nativity. Although the nativity theme has not disappeared from the contemporary observance, it has been heavily overshadowed by the secular components of the national festival. Most of the modern secularity in Christmas is traceable, one way or another, to religious roots. But the contemporary festival is a vast conglomeration of folk customs and symbols, feasting and fraternizing, music, literature and art. The religious origins in the holiday have evolved into a secular humanism and the nativity scene has evolved into a major element of the artistic component of the national festival.
>
> The City's Christmas observance in this case is completely typical of the American folk festival. It is heavily secular in tone and content. The crèche is one symbol among the Santas and reindeer, Old English figurines, snowmen, cartoon character cut-outs, trees, lights, bells, candles and stars. There are Christmas carols, parties, free candy and carousel rides. The entire observance is a mélange of the familiar trappings of the American Christmas season.[40]

---

[40] Petitioners' Brief at 8.

The crèche, petitioners argue, has become secularized along with the rest of Christmas and is, therefore, a perfectly proper part of a secular city celebration. Any religious meaning it has is part of its past.

In its Amicus Brief supporting the petitioners' brief, the solicitor general, on behalf of the United States government, argues the opposite. The solicitor general argues that Christmas and the crèche are indeed religious, but that the First Amendment permits government sponsorship of such religious symbols:

The United States, like the City of Pawtucket and countless other state and local governments, has long participated in the celebration of the Christmas season. Congress has declared Christmas to be a national holiday, and the United States has in past years sponsored Christmas pageants that included nativity scenes. Since the days of the Pilgrims, we have devoted, as a Nation, one day every year to giving thanks to God. More broadly, the federal government has, from the earliest days of the Republic to the present, felt free to acknowledge and recognize that religion is a part of our heritage and should continue to be an element in our public life and public occasions. The United States has a deep and abiding interest in maintaining this long-standing tradition.[41]

The solicitor general seems eager to affirm the country's faith and eager not to cede what the government sees as the ancient and, to its mind, constitutional, right of the state to engage in its priestly function.

Respondents offer a third view of Pawtucket's Christmas display. They argue that, of the many objects displayed, only the crèche is religious and that it is only the presence of the crèche that gives a religious taint to what is otherwise a secular display:

Pawtucket's crèche depicts the miraculous birth of Jesus to Joseph and the Virgin Mary in a manger in Bethlehem. It symbolically re-enacts a central event in Christian religious belief. . . . Pawtucket has placed the imprimatur of the government on a "plainly religious" belief in flat disregard of the Establishment Clause.[42]

[41] Brief for the United States at 1–2.
[42] Respondents' Brief at 21–22.

If the crèche is removed, they argue, Pawtucket's display will be cleansed and secular—and therefore constitutional.

The district court and the majority opinion in the Court of Appeals for the First Circuit agree with respondents. The crèche is religious, but the Christmas holiday, as a government-sponsored public celebration, is secular. Judge Bownes of the first circuit, sums up this position:

Today's American Christmas is a result of the mixing of diverse folk customs and religious beliefs in the melting pot of the new World. Christmas has roots that are embedded in the Christian religion; its roots also extend to folk customs and pagan rites that predate the birth of Christ.

The crèche, however, is tied firmly to the Christian religion; it tells the story of the birth of Christ, the Son of God. Unlike today's Christmas holiday, the crèche is not the result of the combination of folk culture and tradition. The crèche is purely a Christian religious symbol.[43]

Judge Campbell, in dissent, disagrees. Christmas cannot be divided up into sacred and secular:

[E]ither Christmas itself, because of its inextricably intertwined religious roots, cannot constitutionally be a national holiday, in which case displays of this type here in issue would also be unconstitutional; or else Christmas is constitutional, in which case all its relevant symbols, including those depicting the nativity, are likewise constitutional, *so long as displayed for the purpose of announcing the holiday. . . .*

The fact is, Christmas, with its clear religious as well as its secular roots, has become an ingrained part of our culture. Were one today to seek to make a national holiday out of such a church festival, constitutional objections might well prevail. But Christmas is water over the dam. And so, I would argue, are *all* its established symbols, including carols and crèches. To retain the holiday but outlawing these ancient symbols seems to me an empty even boorish gesture. If crèches are to be outlawed, so too should stars and carols. And, surely, the name itself—Christmas, deriving from "Christ" and "mass"—should be the first to go if the Constitution requires the

---

[43] 691 F. 2d at 1037.

eradication of any and all religious connotations! (emphasis in original)[44]

This Court is asked to choose between these different versions of the crèche and of Christmas.

Is Christmas a religious holiday? Is a crèche always or only sometimes a religious symbol? Does the presence of a crèche make Christmas more religious? What does the First Amendment have to say about Christmas? The answers to these questions cannot be found in a reconstruction of eighteenth-century Christmas celebrations. Both Christmas and government have changed too much since then. Deciding this case demands that the Court pay attention to the role of religion and of government in America today. The question in this case is: Is the public display of a crèche at Christmas by an American city government at the end of the twentieth century the establishment of religion, religion as it is meant by the religion clauses of the First Amendment?

Religion is not a natural category.[45] It has no universal meaning. Indeed, in many languages there is no word for "religion." Religion is a socially and historically constructed category. This has at least two consequences. On the one hand, the historical meaning of "religion" in the First Amendment must be seen to be a changing and culturally specific one. On the other, constructing a meaning for American religion under the First Amendment must be seen as a civic task for all Americans at the end of the twentieth century. We have a responsibility to take account of the depth and diversity of American religiousness, a diversity that is only symbolized on a very small scale by the diversity among the parties to the Court and the judges below. We must take account and invest ourselves in it so that the concern for American religion that the Constitution demands is focused on American religion as it exists, rich and varied as it is, and as it is constantly changing and being recreated. It must also be a concern that takes its

---

[44] 691 F. 2d at 1038.

[45] See Smith, *The Meaning and End of Religion*, and Smith, *Divine Drudgery*.

cue from the Fourteenth Amendment mandate that government treat all Americans equally.[46]

Americans face this task of attending to the meaning of religion in public life at a time when the assumptions underlying the secular state are coming into question all over the world. In India, citizenship is being remolded as Indians, concerned to preserve an ancient cultural identity, insist that to be Indian is, in some sense, also to be Hindu—to be part of the tradition of the Vedas. In Eastern Europe communities formerly part of communist countries are searching for ways to assert their precious historical location through a self-definition in religious terms. In Africa socialist ideologies, indigenous religious traditions, and various Islams and Christianities compete to define what it is to be African. In each case the assumption that the law can and should be secular and that religion can and should be private is being questioned.

The historical study of religion teaches us that religion is of many types. Religion can be priestly or prophetic. It can celebrate the center or remain on the periphery. It can be about God or gods, or not. It can be coextensive with culture or set itself up as separate or as in opposition. It can be about saving the individual soul or about preserving the community. It can be more about what you do or more about what you believe. It includes myth, ritual, prayer, philosophy, sacrifice, etc. American religion is all of these.

II

While honoring the significance of religion to Americans, both today and in the past, the First Amendment, as applied to the states through the Fourteenth Amendment, requires that the government not "establish" religion. Has the city of Pawtucket done so in erecting a crèche as a part of a civic holiday display? Has it established either religion in general or a particular religious faith?

---

[46] Addressing the legal meaning of religion is not the same thing as advocating increased religiosity. That is a task for religion, not for government.

Like most vital symbols, the Pawtucket crèche means different things to different people at different times. Understanding must begin with acknowledging that the crèche cannot be permanently labeled either religious or secular. It is clearly both, as is Christmas. It is also important to acknowledge that to be a folk festival or a folk symbol is not necessarily to be non-religious. The opposition of religion to folk traditions is an inheritance of the Reformation and smacks of anti-Catholicism.[47]

The three solutions offered by the briefs seem to the court to be inadequate. Petitioners argue for the permissibility of Pawtucket's activities by eliminating the distinctions between religion and non-religion. The First Amendment will not permit such a solution. The First Amendment insists that religion is different.

The United States argues that it is the government's role to thank God and to participate in religious celebrations. This is an ancient role of the state. The recitation by the government of the many historical examples of government endorsement of religious expression seems to us an example of government's failure to withstand public pressure to give a privileged place to a certain kind of dominant Protestant Christianity rather than evidence of the constitutionality of such activity.

Respondents' insistence, like that of the district court, on the unique religiousness of the crèche also seems myopic. It leaves little room for multiple religious and secular responses to what is a very common cultural symbol in the context of a multifaceted cultural and religious event.

When the government undertakes to represent the community, and to celebrate for it, when it fulfills its priestly role, it must be scrupulously careful not to do so in a way that defines persons out of the community because of their religion. The crèche is not more or less religious than the reindeer or the star. But, for more of the observers of the display, display of the crèche is seen as the establishment of an exclusive version of the human story. The set of cultural meanings it evokes is

[47] See Brown, *The Cult of Saints.*

located in the tradition of a very specific community. The religious meaning of the rest of the display, as well as of the holiday as a whole, is arguably more diffuse and open to a range of interpretations.

Disestablishment means that government must strive to remain secular. To be secular within the meaning of the First Amendment necessitates the resistance of all efforts to narrow or to confine the meaning of religion to the interpretation of a particular tradition. It also means that secular ideologies, such as law, may not be established either. Put positively, disestablishment means that the courts, and all government, must see religion as powerful, universal, and varied—a human cultural creation that cannot be confined to a particular religious philosophy or practice. It is the obligation of government to resist any religious expression that reifies a particular interpretation of what religion is. . . .

The First Amendment requires the Supreme Court to talk about religion. It also mandates disestablishment. It has been the argument of this book that disestablishment requires the deconstruction of religion, of any particular religion, while it also requires the acknowledgment of religion as a universal, diverse, and powerful human creation. The First Amendment asks of all of us that we constantly reimagine the relationship of religion and law in this country.

A new discourse about the relationship of religion and government must begin with a law that is secular because religion is disestablished. A public conversation about religion requires attention to the variety and complexity of human religiousness. The solution here identified with Justices Black and O'Connor is unconstitutional to the extent that it establishes law as religion. Further, no particular construction of what religion is may be established, as Justice Brennan does in *Lynch*. And, finally, the power and distinctiveness of human religiousness must be acknowledged and honored, as the majority opinion in *Lynch* fails to do. Somehow, by giving our attention to what we mean by religion, we must acknowledge the religiousness of Americans without establishing religion.

Attention has been called in a number of different contexts to the problematic nature of writing—of texts—of reducing life to words.

Claude Lévi-Strauss, in *Tristes Tropiques*, cautioning against the powerful lies made possible through writing, asserts that "the primary function of written communication is to facilitate slavery."[48] Johannes Fabian has carefully shown the ways in which anthropologists, through various stylistic habits of their writing, distance themselves from the lives of the people of whom they write.[49] Michel Foucault has made us all painfully conscious of the insidious combination of power and limitation in our language.[50]

Religion and law, although largely concerned, particularly in the Western context, with the production and study of texts, share an inescapable materialism. Each has real effects on the material circumstances of peoples' lives. For Christians, the Incarnation is more than an idea expressed in words. It transformed the world and continues to transform peoples' lives. It holds, for many, implications upon which we act and it colors our perception of the material world. A crèche displayed is not simply the illustration of a text. Law, too, is embodied not just in statute books and case reports but in the people whose lives it shapes and distorts. The violence and the power of religion and of law are evident in the physical shape of our existence. The possibilities for peace and understanding also are there embodied.

Johannes Fabian, Charles Long, and Lawrence Sullivan have all called for a form of praxis as a way of overcoming the distances and distortions caused by the texts of cultural studies—texts interpreting other peoples' lives.[51] Fabian calls for the dialectic of "communicative praxis."[52] Long calls for "exchange."[53] Sullivan calls for "the end of the text."[54] Each seeks in different ways to turn attention from the words

---

[48] Claude Lévi-Strauss, *Tristes Tropiques*, trans. John and Doreen Weightman (New York: Atheneum, 1984), 299.

[49] Fabian, *Time and the Other*. See, also, Clifford Geertz, *Works and Lives: The Anthropologist as Author* (Stanford: Stanford University Press, 1988).

[50] Foucault, *The Order of Things*.

[51] Fabian, *Time and the Other*; Charles H. Long, "The University, the Liberal Arts, and the Teaching and Study of Religion," and Lawrence E. Sullivan, "'Seeking an End to the Primary Text' or 'Putting an End to the Text as Primary'," in *Beyond the Classics?: Essays in Religious Studies and Liberal Education*, eds. Frank E. Reynolds and Sheryl L. Burkhalter (Atlanta: Scholars Press, 1990), 19–40 and 41–59.

[52] Fabian, *Time and the Other*, 71.

[53] Long, "The University, the Liberal Arts and the Teaching and Study of Religion," 37.

[54] Sullivan, "'Seeking an End to the Primary Text'," 44.

to the ways words are used to enslave,[55] but each also seeks to transcend the enslaving power of words in a shared community.

In interpreting the words of the Constitution respecting religion, the United States Supreme Court has an opportunity to acknowledge the material circumstances and embodiedness of religion and of law. It has an opportunity to act about religion in a way that embraces religious actors—to create a practical discourse about human religiousness.

I conceive my suggestion to be part of a larger project to seek out ways to talk and act about our diversity and our unity. For, as Geertz says, "nobody is leaving anyone else alone and isn't ever again going to."[56] We need to find ways to live with the fact that the crèche is holy in different ways and that it is both holy and not holy. The Court, as a cultural location for a discourse and practice about the role of religion in American public life, needs to talk and act about American religion in a way that acknowledges the varied and changing religiousness of Americans without establishing religion.

[55] In a footnote, Milner Ball quotes the poet Coleman Barks, commenting on his (Ball's) view of law as language: "One possible weakness, or unfairness of law as medium—fluid argument—shifting consensus—might be: that those with the best language come out with more power—those with the most command of the most sensitive instrument (English) might plead their biases and blindnesses more than they should. I worry about the Belizians, and the Hopi, who might take a huge grand symbol into a room where slosh and counterslosh is having its way." *Lying Down Together*, 160, n. 158. So it is with poets and nonverbal types of all cultures, not just non-literate ones.

[56] Geertz, *Local Knowledge*, 234.

Selected Bibliography

LEGAL SOURCES

AMERICAN CONSTITUTIONAL AND STATUTORY SOURCES

Constitution of the United States, art. 6, amends. 1, 5, 14, 18.

National Prohibition Act, Title 2, sec. 3, 41 Stat. 308.

Religious Freedom Restoration Act. Pub. L. 103–41 (16 November 1993).

21 CFR sec. 130.31 (1989).

Constitution of Rhode Island, art. 1, sec. 3.

AMERICAN CASES

Abington School District v. Schempp, 374 U.S. 203 (1963).

Allegheny v. ACLU, 492 U.S. 573 (1989).

Board of Education v. Grumet, 1994 WL 279673 (U.S.N.Y.).

Bob Jones University v. U.S, 461 U.S. 574 (1983).

Brown v. Board of Education, 347 U.S. 483 (1954).

Church of the Lukumi Babalu Aye v. City of Hialeah, No. 91–948 (11 June 1993).

Donnelly v. Lynch, 525 F. Supp. 1150 (1981).

Donnelly v. Lynch, 691 F. 2d 1029 (1982)

Employment Division v. Smith, 494 U.S. 872 (1991).

Engel v. Vitale, 370 U.S. 421 (1962).

Epperson v. Arkansas, 393 U.S. 107 (1968).

Everson v. Board of Education, 330 U.S. 1 (1947).

Gitlow v. N.Y., 268 U.S. 652 (1925).

Larson v. Valente, 456 U.S. 228 (1982).

Lee v. Weisman, 112 S.Ct. 2649 (1992).

Lemon v. Kurtzman, 403 U.S. 602 (1971).

Lynch v. Donnelly, 691 F. 2d 1029 (1981).

Lynch v. Donnelly, 465 U.S. 668 (1983).

McCollum v. Board of Education, 333 U.S. 203 (1948).

McGowan v. Maryland, 366 U.S. 420 (1961).

Marbury v. Madison, 1 Cranch 137 (1803).

Marsh v. Chambers, 463 U.S. 783 (1983).

Murphy v. Derwinski, 990 F.2d 540 (1993).

Palsgraf v. Long Island Railroad Co., 248 N.Y. 339 (Court of Appeals, 1928).

Plessy v. Ferguson, 163 U.S. 537 (1896).

Reynolds v. U.S., 98 U.S. 145 (1879).

Stone v. Graham, 449 U.S. 39 (1980).

Texas v. Johnson, 491 U.S. 397 (1989).

Texas Monthly v. Bullock, 489 U.S. 1 (1989).

Torcaso v. Watkins, 367 U.S. 488 (1961).

Walz v. Tax Commission, 397 U.S. 664 (1970).

Watson v. Jones, 80 U.S. 679 (1871).

West Virginia State Board of Education v. Barnette, 319 U.S. 624 (1943).

Wisconsin v. Yoder, 406 U.S. 205 (1972).

Zorach v. Clauson, 343 U.S. 306 (1952)

JAPANESE LEGAL SOURCES

Kenpō [Constitution], arts. 1, 20, 24, 32, 89.

Tsu, Showa 52 [1977] July 13.

Nakaya, Showa 63 [1988] June 1.

BOOKS AND ARTICLES

Abraham, Henry. *Freedom and the Court: Civil Rights and Liberties in the United States.* 5th ed. Oxford: Oxford University Press, 1988.

———. *Justices and Presidents: A Political History of Appointments to the Supreme Court.* 3d ed. Oxford: Oxford University Press, 1992.

Abu-Lughod, Lila. *Veiled Sentiments: Honor and Poetry in a Bedouin Society.* Berkeley: University of California Press, 1986.

Albanese, Catherine L. *America: Religion and Religions.* Belmont: Wadsworth, 1981.

————. *Nature Religion in America: From the Algonkian Indians to the New Age.* Chicago: University of Chicago Press, 1990.

————. *Sons of the Fathers: The Civil Religion of the American Revolution.* Philadelphia: Temple University Press, 1976.

Alles, Gregory. "Wach, Eliade and the Critique from Totality." *Numen* 35 (July 1988): 108–38.

Anchor Bible Dictionary. s.v. "Infancy Narratives in the NT Gospels."

Arjomand, Said Amir. "Constitutions and the Struggle for Political Order: A Study in the Modernization of Political Traditions," *Archives européenes de sociologie. European Journal of Sociology* 33 (1992): 39–82.

Ball, Milner. *Lying Down Together: Law, Metaphor and Theology.* Madison: University of Wisconsin Press, 1985.

Barnett, James. *The American Christmas: A Study in National Culture.* New York: Macmillan, 1954.

Barth, Karl. *Church Dogmatics: The Doctrine of the Word of God, Pt II.* Translated by G. T. Thomson and Harold Knight. Edinburgh: T. & T. Clark, 1956.

Bartlett, John Russell, ed., *Records of the Colony of Rhode Island and Providence Plantations.* Providence: A. Crawford Greene and Brother, 1856.

Bastien, Joseph W. *Mountain of the Condor: Metaphor and Ritual in an Andean Ayllu.* Prospect Heights: Waveland Press, 1978.

Becker, Mary. "The Politics of Women's Wrongs and the Bill of 'Rights:' A Bicentennial Perspective." *University of Chicago Law Review* 59 (winter 1992): 453–517.

Beckford, James. *Religion and Advanced Industrial Society.* London: Unwin Hyman, 1989.

Beeman, Richard, Stephen Botein, and Edward C. Carter, II, eds. *Beyond Confederation: Origins of the Constitution and American National Identity.* Chapel Hill: University of North Carolina Press, 1987.

Bellah, Robert N. *Tokugawa Religion: The Cultural Roots of Modern Japan.* Rev. ed. New York: The Free Press, 1985.

Bellah, Robert N., Richard Madsen, William M. Sullivan, Ann Swidler, and Steven M. Tipton. *Habits of the Heart: Individualism and Commitment in American Life*. Berkeley: University of California Press, 1985.

Benda-Beckmann, Keebet, and Fons Strijbosch, eds. *Anthropology of Law in the Netherlands: Essays on Legal Pluralism*. Dordrecht: Foris Publications, 1986.

Berger, Peter. *The Sacred Canopy: Elements of a Sociological Theory of Religion*. Garden City: Doubleday, 1967.

Berman, Harold. *Law and Revolution: The Formation of the Western Legal Tradition*. Cambridge: Harvard University Press, 1983.

Beschle, Donald L. "The Conservative as Liberal: The Religion Clauses, Liberal Neutrality and the Approach of Justice O'Connor." *Notre Dame Law Review* 62 (spring 1987): 151–91.

Black, Hugo L. *A Constitutional Faith*. New York: Alfred A. Knopf, 1968.

Botein, Stephen. "Religious Dimensions of the Early American State." In *Beyond Confederation: Origins of the Constitution and American National Identity*, edited by Richard Beeman, Stephen Botein, and Edward C. Carter, II. Chapel Hill: University of North Carolina Press, 1987.

Brown, Peter. *The Cult of Saints: Its Rise and Function in Latin Christianity*. Chicago: University of Chicago Press, 1981.

Bynum, Caroline Walker. *Fragmentation and Redemption: Essays on Gender and the Human Body in Medieval Religion*. New York: Zone Books, 1991.

———. *Holy Feast and Holy Fast: The Religious Significance of Food to Medieval Women*. Berkeley: University of California Press, 1987.

Candland, Christopher. *The Spirit of Violence: An Interdisciplinary Bibliography of Religion and Violence*. New York: The Harry Frank Guggenheim Foundation, 1992.

Caplow, Theodore, Howard N. Bahr, Bruce A. Chadwick, Dwight W. Hoover, Laurence A. Martin, Joseph B. Tamney, and Margaret Holmes Williamson. *All Faithful People: Change and Continuity in Middletown's Religion*. Minneapolis: University of Minnesota Press, 1983.

Cardozo, Benjamin. *The Nature of the Judicial Process*. New Haven: Yale University Press, 1931; reprint, 1960.

Carlin, David R., Jr. "Pawtucket and Its Nativity Scene." *Commonweal*, 16 December 1983, 682–84.

Carrasco, David. *Quetzacoatl and the Irony of Empire: Myths and Prophecies in the Aztec Tradition.* Chicago: University of Chicago Press, 1992.

Carter, Stephen. *The Culture of Disbelief: How American Law and Politics Trivialize Religious Devotion.* New York: Basic Books, 1993.

Cashman, Sean Dennis. *Prohibition: The Lie of the Land.* New York: The Free Press, 1981.

Catholicisme hier aujourd'hui et demain: Encyclopédie publiée sous la direction du Centre Interdisciplinaire des Facultés Catholiques de Lille. s.v. "Noël."

Clifford, James. *The Predicament of Culture.* Cambridge: Harvard University Press, 1988.

Cobb, Sanford. *The Rise of Religious Liberty in America: A History.* New York: Macmillan, 1902. Reprint, New York: Burt Franklin, 1970.

Cocks, R. C. J. *Sir Henry Maine: A Study in Victorian Jurisprudence.* Cambridge: Cambridge University Press, 1988.

Colson, Elizabeth. *Tradition and Contract: The Problem of Order.* Chicago: Aldine, 1974.

Comaroff, Jean. *Body of Power, Spirit of Resistance: The Culture and History of a South Africa People.* Chicago: University of Chicago Press, 1985.

Comaroff, Jean, and John Comaroff. *Ethnography and the Historical Imagination.* Boulder: Westview Press, 1992.

————. *Of Revelation and Revolution: Christianity, Colonialism, and Consciousness in South Africa.* Chicago: University of Chicago Press, 1991.

Comaroff, John L., and Simon Roberts. *Rules and Processes: The Cultural Logic of Disputes in an African Context.* Chicago: University of Chicago Press, 1981.

Cord, Robert L. *Separation of Church and State: Historical Fact and Current Fiction.* New York: Lambeth Press, 1982.

Cover, Robert M. "Foreword: *Nomos* and Narrative." *Harvard Law Review* 97 (November 1983): 4–68.

Culianu, Ioan P. *Eros and Magic in the Renaissance.* Translated by Margaret Cook. Chicago: University of Chicago Press, 1987.

Davis, David Brion. *The Problem of Slavery in the Age of Revolution: 1770–1823.* Ithaca: Cornell University Press, 1975.

Delaney, Carol. *The Seed and the Soil: Gender and Cosmology in Turkish Village Society.* Berkeley: University of California Press, 1991.

Demerath, N. J., III, and Rhys Williams. *A Bridging of Faiths: Religion and Politics in a New England City.* Princeton: Princeton University Press, 1992.

————. "Secularization in a Community Context: Tensions of Religion and Politics in a New England City." *Journal for the Scientific Study of Religion* 31 (December 1992): 189–206.

Diamond, Allen, ed. *The Victorian Achievement of Sir Henry Maine: A Centennial Reappraisal.* Cambridge: Cambridge University Press, 1991.

Dickens, Charles. *A Christmas Carol.* London, 1843. Reprint, Boston: The Atlantic Monthly Press, 1920.

Dolan, Jay P. *The American Catholic Experience.* Garden City: Doubleday, 1985.

Dubois, W. E. B. *The Souls of Black Folk.* Chicago: A. C. McClurg, 1903. Reprint, New York: Bantam Books, 1989.

Dumont, Louis. *Homo Hierarchicus: The Caste System and Its Implications.* Translated by Mark Sainsbury, Louis Dumont, and Basia Gulati. Rev. ed. Chicago: University of Chicago Press, 1980.

Durkheim, Emile. *The Elementary Forms of the Religious Life.* Translated by Joseph Ward Swain. New York: The Free Press, 1918.

Earhart, Byron. *Religions of Japan: Many Traditions Within One Sacred Way.* San Francisco: Harper & Row, 1984.

Eliade, Mircea. *Patterns in Comparative Religion.* Translated by Rosemary Sheed. New York: Sheed & Ward, 1958. Reprint, New York: New American Library, 1963.

Encyclopedia Britannica, 15th ed. s.v. "Crèche" and "Rhode Island."

Encyclopedia of Religion. s.v. "Apotheosis."

Encyclopedia of Religion and Ethics. s.v. "Christmas."

Epstein, Richard. *Forbidden Grounds: The Case Against Employment Discrimination Laws.* Cambridge: Harvard University Press, 1992.

Fabian, Johannes. *Time and the Other: How Anthropology Makes Its Object.* New York: Columbia University Press, 1983.

Fallers, Lloyd A. *Law Without Precedent: Legal Ideas in Action in the Courts of Colonial Busoga.* Chicago: University of Chicago Press, 1969.

Field, Norma. *In the Realm of the Dying Emperor.* New York: Pantheon Books, 1991.

Foucault, Michel. *The Order of Things: An Archeology of the Human Sciences.* New York: Vintage Books, 1970.

Freund, Paul A. "The First Amendment: Freedom of Religion." In *Hugo Black and the Bill of Rights: Proceedings of the First Hugo Black Symposium in American History on "The Bill of Rights and American Democracy."* Edited by Virginia Van der Veer Hamilton. University: University of Alabama Press, 1978.

Fuller, Lon. *The Morality of Law.* Rev. ed. New Haven: Yale University Press 1969.

Galanter, Marc. *Law and Society in Modern India.* Delhi: Oxford University Press, 1989.

———. "Separation Anxiety: Church, State and the Jews in the 1990s or the Jewish Stake in the First Amendment's Religion Clauses," unpublished paper presented at the Jonathan Newman Memorial Conference on Law and Religion, Northwestern School of Law at Lewis and Clark College, Portland, Oregon, 23 October 1992.

Gamwell, Franklin I. *The Divine Good: Modern Moral Theory and the Necessity of God.* San Francisco: Harper, 1990.

Geertz, Clifford. *The Interpretation of Cultures.* New York: Basic Books, 1973.

———. *Local Knowledge: Further Essays in Interpretive Anthropology.* New York: Basic Books, 1983.

———. *Works and Lives: The Anthropologist as Author.* Stanford: Stanford University Press, 1988.

Gellner, Ernst. *Postmodernism, Reason and Religion.* London: Routledge, 1992.

Giles, Paul. *American Catholic Arts and Fictions.* Cambridge: Cambridge University Press, 1992.

Gilpin, Clark. *The Millenarian Piety of Roger Williams.* Chicago: University of Chicago Press, 1979.

Girard, Rene. *Violence and the Sacred.* Translated by Patrick Gregory. Baltimore: Johns Hopkins University Press, 1972.

Glendon, Mary Ann. *Abortion and Divorce in Western Law.* Cambridge: Harvard University Press, 1987.

————. *Rights Talk: The Impoverishment of Political Discourse.* New York: The Free Press, 1991.

Gluck, Carol. *Japan's Modern Myths.* Princeton: Princeton University Press, 1991.

Gluckman, Max. *The Judicial Process among the Barotse of Northern Rhodesia (Zambia).* 2d ed. Manchester: Manchester University Press, 1967.

Godlove, Terry, Jr. "Interpretation, Reductionism, and Belief in God." *Journal of Religion* 69 (April 1989): 184–98.

Golby, J. M., and A. W. Purdue. *The Making of Modern Christmas.* Athens: University of Georgia Press, 1986.

Gold, Ann Grodzins. *Fruitful Journeys: The Ways of Rajasthani Pilgrims.* Berkeley: University of California Press, 1987.

Gold, Daniel. *Comprehending the Guru: Toward a Grammar of Religious Perception.* Atlanta: Scholars Press, 1988.

Greenawalt, Kent. *Religious Convictions and Political Choice.* New York: Oxford University Press, 1988.

Greenhouse, Carol. *Praying for Justice: Faith, Order and Community in an American Town.* Ithaca: Cornell University Press, 1986.

Griffiths, Paul J. *An Apology for Apologetics: A Study on the Logic of Interreligious Dialogue.* Maryknoll: Orbis Books, 1991.

Hammerton-Kelly, Robert, ed. *Violent Origins: Walter Burkert, Rene Girard and Jonathan Z. Smith on Ritual Killing and Cultural Formation.* Stanford: Stanford University Press, 1987.

Hammond, Phillip E. "Religious Pluralism and Durkheim's Integration Thesis." In *Changing Perspectives in the Scientific Study of Religion,* edited by Allen W. Eister. New York: John Wiley & Sons, 1974.

Hardacre, Helen. *Shinto and the State, 1868–1945.* Princeton: Princeton University Press, 1989.

Henderson, Dan Fenno. "Law and Political Modernization in Japan." In *Political Development in Modern Japan,* edited by Robert E. Ward. Princeton: Princeton University Press, 1968.

Herberg, Will. *Protestant, Catholic, Jew: An Essay in American Religious Sociology.* Garden City: Anchor Books, 1960.

Hobsbawm, Eric, and Terence Ranger. *The Invention of Tradition.* Cambridge: Cambridge University Press, 1983.

Holleman, J. F., ed. *Van Vollenhoven on Indonesian Adat Law.* The Hague: M. Nijhoff, 1981.

Holtom, D. C. *Modern Japan and Shinto Nationalism: A Study of Present-Day Trends in Japanese Religion.* Rev. ed. New York: Paragon Book Reprint Co., 1963.

Hooper, J. Leon. *The Ethics of Discourse: The Social Philosophy of John Courtney Murray.* Washington: Georgetown University Press, 1986.

Horwitz, Morton J. *The Transformation of American Law 1870–1960: The Crisis of Legal Orthodoxy.* New York: Oxford University Press, 1992.

Howe, Mark DeWolfe. *The Garden and the Wilderness: Religion and Government in American Constitutional History.* Chicago: University of Chicago Press, 1965.

Huber, Peter W. *Galileo's Revenge: Junk Science in the Courtroom.* New York: Basic Books, 1991.

Inoue, Kyoko. *MacArthur's Japanese Constitution: A Linguistic and Cultural Study of Its Making.* Chicago: University of Chicago Press, 1991.

Jacobs, Joseph, ed. *Celtic Fairy Tales.* London: D. Nutt, 1892.

James, William. *The Varieties of Religious Experience.* New York: Longmans, Green & Co., 1902. Reprint, Middlesex: Penguin Books, 1982.

———. *The Will to Believe and Other Essays in Popular Philosophy.* New York: Longmans, Green & Co., 1897. Reprint, New York: Dover, 1956.

Jasanoff, Sheila. "Acceptable Evidence in a Pluralistic Society." In *Acceptable Evidence: Science and Values in Risk Management,* edited by Deborah G. Mayo and Rachelle D. Hollander. New York: Oxford University Press, 1991.

Jay, Nancy. *Throughout Your Generations Forever: Religion, Sacrifice and Paternity.* Chicago: University of Chicago Press, 1992.

Kalven, Harry, Jr. *A Worthy Tradition: Freedom of Speech in America.* New York: Harper & Row, 1988.

Kannar, George. "The Constitutional Catechism of Antonin Scalia." *Yale Law Journal* 99 (April 1990): 1297–357.

Kellner, Menachem. Review of *Judaism, Human Values, and the Jewish State,* by Yeshayahu Leibowitz. In *The New York Times Book Review,* 19 July 1992, 7.

Kipling, Rudyard. *Kim.* London: Macmillan, 1901; reprint, 1958.

Kitagawa, Joseph. *History of Religions: Retrospect and Prospect: A Collection of Essays.* New York: Macmillan, 1985.

———. *On Understanding Japanese Religion.* Princeton: Princeton University Press, 1987.

———. *Religion in Japanese History.* New York: Columbia University Press, 1966.

———. "Some Reflections on Japanese Religion and Its Relationship to the Imperial System." *Japanese Journal of Religious Studies* 17 (December 1990): 169–74.

Kurland, Philip B. "Of Church and State and the Supreme Court." *University of Chicago Law Review* 29 (autumn 1961): 1–96.

———. *Religion and the Law: Of Church and State and the Supreme Court.* Chicago: Aldine, 1961.

———. "The Religion Clauses and the Burger Court." *Catholic University Law Review* 34 (fall 1984): 1–18.

Kurland, Philip, and Gerhard Casper, eds. *Landmark Briefs and Arguments of the Supreme Court of the United States.* Washington: University Publications of America, 1975–.

Kyvig, David E. *Repealing National Prohibition.* Chicago: University of Chicago Press, 1979.

Laycock, Douglas. "Formal, Substantive and Disaggregated Neutrality towards Religion." *De Paul Law Review* 39 (summer 1990): 993–1018.

Leibowits, Yeshayahu. *Judaism, Human Values, and the Jewish State.* Cambridge: Harvard University Press, 1992.

Levi, Edward. *An Introduction to Legal Reasoning.* Chicago: University of Chicago Press, 1948.

Levin, Stephenie Seto. "The Overthrow of the *Kapu* System in Hawaii." *Journal of the Polynesian Society* 77 (December 1968): 402–30.

Levinson, Sanford. "The Confrontation of Religious Faith and Civil Religion: Catholics Becoming Justices." *DePaul Law Review* 39 (summer 1990): 1047–81.

———. *Constitutional Faith.* Princeton: Princeton University Press, 1988.

Lévi-Strauss, Claude. *The Raw and the Cooked.* Translated by John and Doreen Weightman. *Introduction to a Science of Mythology,* vol. 1. New York: Harper & Row, 1969.

———. *Tristes Tropiques*. Translated by John and Doreen Weightman. New York: Atheneum, 1984.

Levy, Leonard. *The Establishment Clause: Religion and the First Amendment*. New York: Macmillan, 1986.

Lietzau, William K. "Rediscovering the Establishment Clause: Federalism and the Rollback of Incorporation." *DePaul Law Review* 39 (summer 1990): 1191–234.

Lincoln, Bruce. *Discourse and the Construction of Society*. Oxford: Oxford University Press, 1985.

Llewellyn, Karl N., and E. Adamson Hoebel. *The Cheyenne Way: Conflict and Case Law in Primitive Jurisprudence*. Norman: University of Oklahoma Press, 1941.

Lokowandt, Ernst. *Die Rechtliche Entwicklung des Staats-Shintô in der Ersten Hälfte der Meiji-Zeit (1868–1890)*. Wiesbaden: Otto Harrassowitz, 1978.

Long, Charles H. *Significations: Signs, Symbols, and Images in the Interpretation of Religion*. Philadelphia: Fortress Press, 1986.

———. "The University, the Liberal Arts, and the Teaching and Study of Religion." In *Beyond the Classics?: Essays in Religious Studies and Liberal Education*, edited by Frank E. Reynolds and Sheryl L. Burkhalter. Atlanta: Scholars Press, 1990.

McConnell, Michael. "Free Exercise Revisionism and the *Smith* Decision." *University of Chicago Law Review* 57 (fall 1990): 1109–53.

———. "The Origins and Historical Understanding of Free Exercise of Religion." *Harvard Law Review* 103 (May 1990): 1409–517.

———. "Religious Freedom at a Crossroads." *University of Chicago Law Review* 59 (winter 1992): 115–94.

McConnell, Michael, and Richard Posner. "An Economic Approach to Issues of Religious Freedom." *University of Chicago Law Review* 56 (winter 1989): 1–60.

McLeod, Hugh. *Religion and the People of Western Europe: 1789–1970*. Oxford: Oxford University Press, 1981.

McManners, John. *The French Revolution and the Church*. New York: Harper & Row, 1969.

Maffly-Kipp, Laurie. *Religion and Society in Frontier California*. New Haven: Yale University Press, 1994.

Maine, Henry Sumner. *Ancient Law: Its Connection with the Early History of Society, and Its Relation to Modern Ideas.* New York: Holt, 1864. Reprint, Tucson: University of Arizona Press, 1986.

Maki, John, ed. *Japan's Commission on the Constitution: The Final Report.* Seattle: University of Washington, 1980.

Malinowski, Bronislaw. *Crime and Custom in Savage Society.* London: Kegan Paul, Trench, Trubner, 1926.

Marty, Martin. *Religion and Republic: The American Circumstance.* Boston: Beacon Press, 1987.

May, Henry. *The Enlightenment in America.* New York: Oxford University Press, 1976.

Mead, Sidney E. *The Lively Experiment: The Shaping of Christianity in America.* New York: Harper & Row, 1963.

Merryman, John Henry. *The Civil Law Tradition: An Introduction to the Legal Systems of Western Europe and Latin America.* 2d ed. Palo Alto: Stanford University Press, 1985.

Miles, Clement A. *Christmas in Ritual and Tradition: Christian and Pagan.* London: T. Fisher Unwin, 1912.

Miller, Daniel, ed. *Unwrapping Christmas.* Oxford: Clarendon Press, 1993.

Miller, William Lee. *The First Liberty: Religion and the American Republic.* New York: Paragon House, 1985.

Moore, Sally Falk. *Law as Process: An Anthropological Approach.* London: Routledge & K. Paul, 1978.

―――. *Social Facts and Fabrications: "Customary" Law on Kilimanjaro, 1880–1980.* Cambridge: Cambridge University Press, 1986.

Murray, John Courtney. *We Hold These Truths: Catholic Reflections on the American Proposition.* New York: Sheed & Ward, 1960.

Myers, Robert J. *Celebrations: The Complete Book of American Holidays.* Garden City: Doubleday & Co., 1972.

Neuhaus, Richard. *The Naked Public Square: Religion and Democracy in America.* New York: W. B. Eerdmans, 1984.

New Catholic Encyclopedia. s.v. "Christmas."

Noonan, John T. *The Believer and the Powers That Are: Cases, History, and Other Data Bearing on the Relation of Religion and Government.* New York: Macmillan, 1987.

————. "The Catholic Justices of the United States Supreme Court." *Catholic Historical Review* 67 (July 1981): 369–85.

————. *Persons and Masks of the Law: Cardozo, Holmes, Jefferson, and Whythe as Makers of the Masks.* New York: Farrar, Straus and Giroux, 1976.

Nussbaum, Martha. " 'Only Grey Matter'?: Richard Posner's Cost-Benefit Analysis of Sex." *University of Chicago Law Review* (fall 1992): 1689–734.

Otto, Rudolf. *The Idea of the Holy.* 2d ed. Translated by John W. Harvey. Oxford: Oxford University Press, 1950.

Pals, Daniel. "Is Religion a *Sui Generis* Phenomenon?" *Journal of the American Academy of Religion* 55 (summer 1987): 259–82.

————. "Reductionism and Belief: An Appraisal of Recent Attacks on the Doctrine of Irreducible Religion." *Journal of Religion* 66 (January 1986): 18–36.

Pelikan, Jaroslav. *Christian Doctrine and Modern Culture (Since 1700).* Chicago: University of Chicago Press, 1989.

Penner, Hans H. *Impasse and Resolution: A Critique of the Study of Religion.* New York: Peter Lang, 1989.

Perry, Michael. *Morality, Politics and Law: A Bicentennial Essay.* Oxford: Oxford University Press, 1988.

Pole, J. R. *The Pursuit of Equality in American History.* Berkeley: University of California Press, 1978.

Pope, Dudley. *Life in Nelson's Navy.* Annapolis: Naval Institute Press, 1981.

Posner, Richard A. *Cardozo: A Study in Reputation.* Chicago: University of Chicago Press, 1990.

Raboteau, Albert. *Slave Religion: The "Invisible Institution" in the Antebellum South.* Oxford: Oxford University Press, 1980.

Raheja, Gloria Goodwin. "India: Caste, Kingship, and Dominance Reconsidered." *Annual Review of Anthropology* 17 (1988): 497–522.

"Religion and the Intellectuals: A Symposium." *Partisan Review* 17 (February 1950): 103–42.

"Religion and the Intellectuals II." *Partisan Review* 17 (March 1950): 215–56.

"Religion and the Intellectuals III." *Partisan Review* 17 (April 1950): 313–39.

"Religion and the Intellectuals IV." *Partisan Review* 17 (May–June 1950): 456–83.

Reynolds, Frank E., and Sheryl L. Burkhalter, eds. *Beyond the Classics? Essays in Religious Studies and Liberal Education.* Atlanta: Scholars Press, 1990.

Richie, Donald. *Rashomon.* New Brunswick: Rutgers University Press, 1987.

Rosen, Lawrence. *The Anthropology of Justice: Law as Culture in Islamic Society.* Cambridge: Cambridge University Press, 1989.

———. *Bargaining for Reality: The Construction of Social Relations in a Muslim Community.* Chicago: University of Chicago Press, 1984.

Sahlins, Marshall. *Islands of History.* Chicago: University of Chicago Press, 1985.

Said, Edward. *Orientalism.* New York: Vintage Books, 1978.

Sanson, William. *A Book of Christmas.* New York: McGraw Hill, 1968.

Segal, Robert A. "In Defense of Reductionism." *Journal of the American Academy of Religion* 51 (March 1983): 97–124.

Shaffer, Thomas. "On Checking the Artifacts of Canaan: A Comment on Levinson's 'Confrontation'." *DePaul Law Review* 39 (summer 1990): 1133–42.

Shils, Edward. *The Center and the Periphery: Essays in Macrosociology.* Chicago: University of Chicago Press, 1975.

———. "Henry Sumner Maine in the Tradition of the Analysis of Society." In *The Victorian Achievement of Sir Henry Maine: A Centennial Reappraisal,* edited by Allen Diamond. Cambridge: Cambridge University Press, 1991.

Shrader-Frechette, Kristin. "Reductionist Approaches to Risk." In *Acceptable Evidence: Science and Values in Risk Management,* edited by Deborah G. Mayo and Rachelle D. Hollander. New York: Oxford University Press, 1991.

Smart, Ninian, "The History of Religions and Its Conversation Partners." In *History of Religions: Retrospect and Prospect: A Collection of Essays,* edited by Joseph M. Kitagawa. New York: Macmillan, 1985.

Smith, Jonathan Z. "Adde Parvum Parvo Magnus Acervus Erit." *History of Religions* 11 (August 1971): 67–90.

———. *Drudgery Divine: On the Comparison of Early Christianities and on Religions of Late Antiquity.* Chicago: University of Chicago Press, 1990.

————. *Imagining Religion: From Babylon to Jonestown.* Chicago: University of Chicago Press, 1982.

————. *Map is Not Territory: Studies in the History of Religions.* Leiden: E. J. Brill, 1978.

Smith, Wilfred Cantwell. *The Meaning and End of Religion.* New York: Harper & Row, 1978.

Stone, Suzanne Last. "In Pursuit of the Counter-Text: The Turn to the Jewish Legal Model in Contemporary Legal Theory." *Harvard Law Review* 106 (February 1993): 813–94.

Story, Joseph. *Commentaries on the Constitution of the United States.* Boston: Hilliard, Gray & Co., 1833. Reprint, Durham: Carolina Academic Press, 1987.

Sullivan, Barry. "Historical Reconstruction, Reconstruction History and the Proper Scope of Section 1981." *Yale Law Journal* 98 (January 1989): 541–64.

Sullivan, Kathleen M. "Religion and Liberal Democracy." *University of Chicago Law Review* 59 (winter 1992): 195–223.

Sullivan, Lawrence E. *Icanchu's Drum: An Orientation to Meaning in South American Religion.* New York: Macmillan, 1988.

————. "Recommendations to the U.S. Departments of Justice and the Treasury concerning Incidents Such as the Branch Davidian Standoff in Waco, Texas, September 12, 1993." Cambridge: Harvard University Center for the Study of World Religions.

————. "'Seeking an End to the Primary Text' or 'Putting an End to the Text as Primary'." In *Beyond the Classics?: Essays in Religious Studies and Liberal Education*, edited by Frank E. Reynolds and Sheryl L. Burkhalter. Atlanta: Scholars Press, 1990.

Sullivan, Winnifred F. "Religion and Law in the United States: 1870 to the Present." In *Church and State in America: A Bibliographical Guide: The Civil War to the Present Day*, edited by John F. Wilson. New York: Greenwood Press, 1987.

————. Review article of *The Culture of Disbelief: How American Law and Politics Trivialize Religious Devotion*, by Stephen L. Carter. In *Journal of Religion* 75 (January 1995).

"The Supreme Court, 1983 Term." *Harvard Law Review* 98 (November 1984): 1–314.

Swanson, Wayne. *The Christ Child Goes to Court.* Philadelphia: Temple University Press, 1990.

"Symposium: Confronting the Wall of Separation: A New Dialogue between Law and Religion on the Meaning of the First Amendment." *DePaul Law Review* 42 (fall 1992).

"Symposium on Politics, Religion and the Relationship between Church and State." *DePaul Law Review* 39 (summer 1990).

Takeshi, Sakai. "A Matter of Faith." *Japan Quarterly* (October–December 1988): 357–64.

Teitel, Ruti. "Original Intent, History and Levy's *Establishment Clause.*" *Law and Social Inquiry* 5 (December 1992): 591–609.

Tenzer, Michael. *Balinese Music.* Berkeley: Periplus Editions, 1991.

Tocqueville, Alexis de. *De la démocratie en Amérique: Les grands thèmes.* Paris, 1835, 1840. Reprint, Paris: Gallimard, 1968.

Toulmin, Stephen. *Cosmopolis: The Hidden Agenda of Modernity.* Chicago: University of Chicago Press, 1990.

Tracy, David. *The Analogical Imagination.* New York: Crossroad, 1981.

———. *Dialogue with the Other: The Inter-religious Dialogue.* Louvain: Peeters Press, 1990.

Troeltsch, Ernst. *The Social Teaching of the Christian Church.* Translated by Olive Wyon. New York: Macmillan, 1931.

Trollope, Anthony. *Phineas Redux.* London, 1873. Reprint, London: Oxford University Press, 1973.

U.S. Bureau of the Census. *1980 Census of Population and Housing: Congressional Districts of the 98th Congress.* Pt. 41 Rhode Island. 1983.

Vining, Joseph. *The Authoritative and the Authoritarian.* Chicago: University of Chicago Press, 1986.

Vogel, Howard J. "The Judicial Oath and the American Creed: Comments on Sanford Levinson's 'The Confrontation of Religious Faith and Civil Religion: Catholics Becoming Justices'." *DePaul Law Review* 39 (summer 1990): 1107–31.

Wach, Joachim. *Sociology of Religion.* London: Kegan Paul, Trench, Trubner, 1947.

Weber, Max. *The Protestant Ethic and the Spirit of Capitalism.* Translated by Talcott Parsons. New York: Scribner, 1976.

White, James Boyd. *Justice as Translation: An Essay in Cultural and Legal Criticism.* Chicago: University of Chicago Press, 1990.

————. *The Legal Imagination: Studies in the Nature of Legal Thought and Expression.* Boston: Little, Brown, 1973.

White, Morton. *Philosophy, The Federalist and the Constitution.* New York: Oxford University Press, 1987.

Wilder, Laura Ingalls. *Little House on the Prairie.* New York: Harper & Row, 1935.

Williams, Roger. *Christenings make not Christians, or A Briefe Discourse concerning that name Heathen, commonly given to the Indians. As also concerning that great point of their conversion* (London, 1645). In *The Complete Writings of Roger Williams*, edited by Perry Miller. Vol. 7. New York: Russell & Russell, 1963.

Woodward, William P. *The Allied Occupation of Japan 1945–1952 and Japanese Religions.* Leiden: E. J. Brill, 1972.

Writings of Thomas Jefferson. New York: Library of America, 1984.

Wuthnow, Robert. *The Restructuring of American Religion: Society and Faith since World War II.* Princeton: Princeton University Press, 1988.

Yoichi, Higuchi. "When Society Is Itself the Tyrant." *Japan Quarterly* (October–December 1988): 350–56.

Index

Abington School District v. Schempp, 82

Abraham, Henry, 64n, 115, 117n, 118

accommodation of religion, xx, 60, 72, 81–82, 84, 87, 89, 90, 111, 122, 125, 126, 130, 131–39

accommodationist, 49n, 59, 74, 75n, 77–78, 94

ACLU, 50, 51, 56

adat, 12

Albanese, Catherine, 91n, 94n, 170n

Alice (in *Through the Looking Glass*), xix, xx

Allegheny v. ACLU, 60n, 66n, 130, 131

Americanists, 155

analogical imagination, 147, 154

anthropology of law, 7n, 10, 12, 15, 21, 40

anti-Catholicism, 63n, 82n, 145, 180

apotheosis, xx, 103, 104, 105, 107, 108, 110

Aquinas, Thomas, 6, 147

Aristotle, 6n

Arjomand, Said, 95n

Arlington National Cemetery, 107

Augustine, 6n, 18, 141

Austin, John, 6n

Ball, Milner, 6n, 16n, 21, 22, 129, 183n

Barth, Karl, 125n

Barnett, James, 149

Bastien, Joseph, 28

Becker, Mary, 6n, 127n

Beckford, James, 26, 29n

Bellah, Robert, xxiiin, 4n, 99n

Benda-Beckmann, Keebet von, 7n

Berger, Peter, 147

Berman, Harold, 36n, 45n

Beschle, Donald, 128

Bill of Rights, 62n, 67, 83, 115, 116, 118, 163

Black, Hugo, 78, 121, 125, 128, 165, 181

constitutional faith, 114–18, 131

Everson opinion, 63–64, 115, 116, 119, 124

Blackmun, Harry, 130

Lynch dissent, 71, 72–73, 77, 87, 88, 134, 135, 138, 144

Blackstone, William, 17

Board of Education v. Grumet, 49n, 63n, 161n

Bob Jones University v. U.S., 41, 126, 127

Bonhoeffer, Dietrich, 22

Botein, Stephen, 42, 90, 91, 92, 94n

Bownes, Judge, 68, 69, 141, 177

Brennan, William, 82, 92, 130, 133

Catholicism of, 78, 135, 136–50, 153–56, 172

interpretation of First Amendment, 150–52

Lynch dissent, 71, 72, 77, 78, 86, 87, 88, 133–56, 167–68, 181

Brennan, William (*continued*)
  view of crèche, 138, 139–41,
    144–46, 147, 149
Bronson, Orestes, 147
Brown, Peter, 29, 143n, 180n
Brown v. Board of Education, 120
Burger, Warren, xix, 65, 127, 150
  accommodation theory of, 76,
    81–84, 87, 94, 110–11
  discourse about religion, 75, 80–
    94, 147–48, 156, 168
  interpretation of First Amend-
    ment, 89–93, 140, 145, 151
  Lynch majority opinion, 71–72,
    77, 78, 79–12
  view of crèche, 81, 86, 94, 109,
    123, 134, 138, 149
Bynum, Caroline Walker, 31n, 47n

Campbell, Judge, 69, 177
canon law. *See* law: canon
Caplow, Theodore, 145, 170, 171n
Cardozo, Benjamin, 11, 17, 18
Carlin, David, 51, 66n
Carroll, John, 154
Carroll, Lewis, xix, 111
Carter, Stephen, 22n, 94n, 164n,
  166n
Catholicism, Roman, 18, 38, 43,
    111, 140, 144
  American, 43, 125, 152, 153–56,
    168–70
  of Justice Brennan, 78, 135, 136–
    50, 153–56, 172
  materialism of, 147, 154
  of Pawtucket, 50–51, 93n, 135
  sacramental theology, 145–50
Channukah, 135n
Christ, 133, 137, 143, 144, 146,
    147–48, 174, 177
Christendom, 75
Christianity, 36, 74–75, 84, 122,
    173, 174, 177

Christmas, 79, 86, 92, 135, 144,
    145, 146, 148, 171
  American, 80, 81, 84, 92–93,
    139–41, 146, 148–49, 170–
    71, 174–78
  constitutionality of holiday, 66,
    69, 90, 93, 138, 140
  and family, 143, 170–71
  as global festival, 141–43
  and materialism, 89, 143
  Pawtucket display. *See* Paw-
    tucket, city of: Christmas
    display; crèche: Pawtucket
  sacred or secular, 56, 66, 70, 94,
    131, 149, 174–78, 180
Christmas tree, 130, 131
christology, 147, 148
church and state. *See also* religion
    and law
  separation of
    in Japan, 101, 102, 107, 108
    in United States, xx, xxiii, 36,
      37, 40, 54, 63, 67, 72, 73,
      81, 82, 119n, 136, 140,
      150–52, 156, 157, 167
*Church of the Lukumi Babalu Aye
    v. City of Hialeah*, 127n
civil religion
  American, 91n
  Japanese, 101
Clifford, James, xxi
Cobb, Sanford, 139n
Cocks, R. C. J., 9, 10n
Comaroff, Jean, 14n, 29n, 30n, 31n
Comaroff, John, 7n, 14n, 29n, 30n
comparison, 78, 79, 95
  of Japanese and American cases,
    109–12
constitution. *See* India: Constitution;
    Japan: Constitution (1946);
    Rhode Island: Constitution;
    United States: Constitution
Coppola, Francis Ford, 147

Cord, Robert, 60n, 61n, 83n, 160n
Cover, Robert, 6n, 8n, 16, 18, 19, 21
creationism, 63
crèche, 63, 70, 83, 86, 109, 130–31, 135, 182
  Catholic reading of, 136–50, 155, 172
  origin of, 47n
  Pawtucket, xix, 47, 50, 68, 78, 80, 81, 170, 174
  description of, 52
  sacred or secular symbol, xx, 53–56, 57–59, 66–68, 71–73, 84–86, 87–89, 94, 105, 122–23, 134–36, 174–81, 183
Culianu, Ioan, 27n

Davis, David Brion, 18n
Declaration on Religious Freedom, 153
deification. *See* apotheosis
Demerath, N. J., III, 26n, 51n, 166n
Descartes, René, 158
Dewey, John, 129
dharma 12, 35
Dickens, Charles, 79, 93
disestablishment, xxiii, 41, 111n, 117, 122, 124, 152, 157, 159, 181
Dolan, Jay, 154
Donnelly, Daniel, 50, 54, 58, 66n, 171
Donnelly v. Lynch, 50–68
Douglas, William O., 67, 82, 83
Du Bois, W. E. B., 33
Dumont, Louis, 38
Durkheim, Emil, 9n, 11, 29n, 81, 89, 94, 110
Durkheimian, 25, 44, 57, 77, 78, 80

Earhart, H. Byron, 99n
Easter, 141
ecclesiology, 153

Edict of Nantes, 158
Eliade, Mircea, 25, 27, 53n
Employment Division v. Smith, 21n, 124–25, 127, 161, 164, 165
Engel v. Vitale, 63n, 67n, 139
England, John, 155
Enlightenment, xxiiin, xxiv, 22, 24, 31n, 33, 34, 36, 40, 41, 44, 78, 156
Epperson v. Arkansas, 63n
Epstein, Richard, 113
equality, xxiv, 43–44, 77–78, 120–21, 122, 125–26, 128, 131, 134
  of believers, 60, 64, 120
  gender, 41, 127n
  racial, 41, 127
Erasmus, 158, 169
establishment of religion. *See also* United States: Constitution; 59, 60, 65, 74–75, 84, 111, 117, 183
  de facto, xx, 59, 76, 84, 156
Everson v. Board of Education, 60n, 63–64, 115, 116, 119–20, 124
expert witnesses, 56

Fabian, Johannes, 30, 53n, 182
Fairchild, Judge, 68, 69
Fallers, Lloyd, 13n, 19n
feminist theory, 38
Field, Norma, 95n, 108, 109n
folk traditions, 53, 141, 143, 144, 180
Foucault, Michel, 19n, 182
Francis of Assisi, 47, 143
Frankfurter, Felix, 3, 150
Franklin, Benjamin, 154
Freeman, David, 55, 57, 58
Freund, Paul, 79
Fuller, Lon, 3, 6n, 15, 129

Galanter, Marc, 39n, 41, 156
Gamwell, Franklin, 22n

Geertz, Clifford, xxi, xxiin, 5n, 12–13, 19, 24, 109, 157, 183n
Gellner, Ernst, 22n, 33n
Gibbons, James, 155
Giles, Paul, 147, 148n, 155, 157, 168, 170
Gilpin, Clark, 73
Girard, René, 32, 38n, 40n
Gitlow v. N.Y., 119n
Glendon, Mary Ann, 4n, 19
Gluck, Carol, 95n, 100n
Gluckman, Max, 10, 11, 12, 40, 41
Godlove, Terry, 26n
Gold, Daniel, 29n, 39n, 170
Greenawalt, Kent, 22n
Greenfield, Meg, 49
Greenhouse, Carol, 13n
Griffiths, Paul, 27n

Hammond, Phillip, 126, 129
Hardacre, Helen, 95n, 101, 104n
haqq, 12
Herberg, Will, 152n
hierarchy, 38
hierophany, 25
history of religions, xxiii, 24–35, 168, 170, 171, 173
Hobbes, Thomas, 6n
Hoebel, E. Adamson, 10, 11, 12
Holmes, Oliver Wendell, 18
Howe, Mark deWolfe, 4n, 43, 47, 59, 62n, 64n, 120, 121n, 127, 128n, 171
human rights, 108
humanism, 158
Humpty Dumpty, xix, xx, xxiv

idolatry, 146, 148
incarnation, 135, 137, 141, 147, 149, 182
Incorporation Doctrine. *See* United States: Constitution: Incorporation Doctrine

India, 160, 179
Constitution, 41
Hindu Nation Movement, 111
Supreme Court, 41
infancy narratives, 92, 142
Inouye, Kyoko, 95n, 96, 97n, 98, 101n, 102n, 103n, 110n
invention of tradition, 93
Ireland, John, 155
Irving, Washington, 93
Ito, Justice, 102n, 108

James, William, 29n, 87–88
Japan, 80, 95, 100
church and state. *See* church and state: separation of: in Japan
Constitution (1946), 80, 108
drafting of, 95–103
language of, 96–99, 106n
and religion, 99–103, 110
emperor of, 97, 104
Meiji constitution, 95, 96, 97, 100, 101
Meiji government, 99, 101, 110
military in, 100, 109n
religion in. *See* religion: Japanese
Religious Organizations Law of 1939, 101
rights consciousness in, 98, 106n
Special Defense Forces, 103, 104, 105, 106, 107, 109
Supreme Court of, xx, 80, 94–95, 99, 103, 105, 106n, 111, 134, 170
discourse about religion, 78, 103, 108
emphasis on harmony, 106, 108
Taiyukai, 103
Jay, Nancy, 25n, 32n, 38, 53
Jefferson, Thomas, xxii, 17, 61, 73, 75, 78, 93, 117, 135, 151–52, 153, 154, 156

Jeffersonian, xxii, 49n, 77, 121, 136, 150, 156
Jehovah's Witnesses, 41
Jesus, 133, 144, 147, 148, 174
Jichinsai, xx
Jonestown, 30
Judaism, 156

Kalven, Harry, 115
Kennedy, Anthony, 130
Kipling, Rudyard, 47
Kitigawa, Joseph, 29, 99n, 100n, 101n
Kung, Hans, 148
Kurland, Philip, 36, 48n, 60n, 70n, 71n, 128, 128n, 162n, 165
Kurosawa, Akira, 133, 135

Larson v. Valente, 68
law
    American, 42, 43, 45
        critique of, 5, 8, 18, 20, 21
    anthropology of. *See* anthropology of law
    canon, 35
    Cheyenne, 10, 11, 40
    of church and state, xxii, 120, 121
    colonial, 14
    comparative study of, 19, 36
    as conversation, 15
    as cultural discourse, 6–8, 10, 15, 23, 45
    and culture, 10, 12, 13, 15, 16, 20
    culture of, 9
    customary, 10, 11, 12, 13n
    ethics of, 16, 23
    and fact, 4–5
    instrumental view of, 5, 12
    Jewish, 16
    judicial reasoning, 11
    and language, 10, 19, 21n, 23
    as local, 13

as love, 18
Lozi, 10, 11, 40–41
materialism of, 182
Moroccan, 13
on Mt. Kilimanjaro, 14
nature of, 6
pluralism of, 12, 45
and power, 15, 23, 182
practice of, xxi, 10
of property, 17
as rational, 20
read narrowly, 45
and religion. *See* religion: and law
as religion, 39n, 77, 124, 126, 128–31, 134
religious, 38
as secular, 36, 39, 40, 41
separate from culture, 4
of slavery, 17
and social change, 8, 9
Soga, 13n
success or failure of, 12, 14, 20
as text, 32
and theology, 21–23
as translation, 12, 16
of Trobriand Islands, 10–11, 40
utilitarian view of, 8, 12, 23
and violence, 182
law and literature movement, 7n, 8, 15, 21, 23
law school. *See* legal education
lawyers, xxiii, 4, 5, 10, 15, 21n, 36, 45
Laycock, Douglas, 128, 160n, 162n
Lee v. Weisman, 60n, 63n, 106n
legal education, 4, 4n, 10, 15
legal realism, 20n, 22
Lemon test. *See* United States: Constitution: First Amendment: Establishment Clause: *Lemon* test
Lemon v. Kurtzman, 64–65, 67, 68, 71, 122, 136, 138, 150

Levi, Edward, 15
Levinson, Sanford, 21, 23n, 155n
Lévi-Strauss, Claude, 57n, 182
Levy, Leonard, 60n, 61n, 62n, 117n, 160n
Lincoln, Abraham, 43, 92
Lincoln, Bruce, 25n, 40n, 110n
Llewellyn, Karl, 10, 11, 12, 40
Lokowandt, Ernst, 95n
Long, Charles, 30, 33–34, 87–88, 170n, 182
Luther, Martin, 172
Lynch, Dennis, 50, 54, 56, 58, 73, 80–81, 89, 107, 122
Lynch v. Donnelly (Ct. of App.), 68
Lynch v. Donnelly (Sup. Ct.), xxiii–xxiv, 6, 23, 45, 47–49, 70–73, 77–78, 105, 107, 151, 156, 157, 161, 167–68, 170, 174–81
  dissents, 135–51, 152
  majority, xix–xx, 80–94, 109–12, 150, 164, 171
  O'Connor, Sandra Day, 113–14, 121–31

MacArthur, Douglas, 95–96, 99–100, 100n
McCollum v. Board of Education, 82, 150
McConnell, Michael, 65, 83n, 160, 162–66
McGowan v. Maryland, 63n, 139n, 150
McManners, John, 43
Madison, James, xxii, 62n, 78, 93, 117, 135, 136, 151, 152
Maine, Henry, 8–10, 11, 14, 40
Malinowski, Bronislaw, 10–11, 11n, 12, 40
Marbury v. Madison, 167
Marsh v. Chambers, 63n, 89–90, 92, 126, 140

Marshall, Thurgood, 88, 130, 135
Marx, Karl, 36
Massachusetts, 117n
Massachusetts Bay Colony, 50, 73–74, 93, 139
Mead, Sidney, 152, 153, 173n
menorah, 66n, 130, 131
Miller, Daniel, 141n, 142n, 143n, 171n
Miller, William Lee, 75, 171–72
modernity, 33, 157
Montaigne, Michel de, 158, 169
Montesquieu, 6n
Moore, Sally Falk, 7n, 12n, 13–14
Mormon Church, 119, 127n
Murphy v. Derwinski, 127n
Murray, John Courtney, 153–54

Nagashima, Justice, 107
Nakaya, Takafumi, 103, 105, 107
Nakaya, Yasuko, 103–6, 107–8, 109n
Nakaya case, 80, 94, 102n, 103–9, 109–12
  majority opinion, 94–109, 106n, 110, 111
Napoleon, 111
Narrangansett, 50, 74
natural law, 129
Native American Church, 124
nativity scene. *See* crèche
Neuhaus, Richard, 4n, 128n
neutrality, 42, 60, 77, 78, 107, 121, 128, 130, 131, 134, 162, 169
Newman, John Henry, 148, 172
Noonan, John T., 4n, 16–19, 21, 31n, 53n, 112, 127, 129, 155n
norms and narratives, 16

O'Connor, Sandra Day, 128–29, 165, 181
  Allegheny opinion, 66n, 130–31
  concurrence in *Smith*, 125

concurrences, 126, 129–30
endorsement test, 71, 121–23,
    126, 130, 131
Lynch opinion, 71, 77, 78, 86,
    107, 121–31, 134, 151, 168
view of religion, 123, 124
Okuno, Justice, 107
otherness, 30, 34, 88, 89
Otto, Rudolph, 135

*Palsgraf v. Long Island Railroad
    Co.*, 17–18, 18n
Paul. *See* Saul of Tarsus
Pawtucket, city of, 50–51, 54, 58,
    68, 71, 73–74, 80, 92, 107,
    109
    Christmas display, xix–xx, 47–
        48, 51–56, 67–68, 81, 84–
        85, 89, 122–23, 135, 138,
        144, 174, 176, 179–81
Penner, Hans, 25n
Perry, Michael, 22
Pettine, Raymond
    Catholicism of, 51, 135, 148,
        149–50
    interpretation of First Amend-
        ment, 59, 65–66
    Lynch trial, 50–68, 72, 84, 122
    reading of crèche, 52–54, 57–59,
        66–68, 69, 135, 148, 149–
        50
peyote case. *See Employment Divi-
    sion v. Smith*
pietism, 44
Pledge of Allegiance, 93
Plessy v. Ferguson, 120
pluralism, 45, 86, 129, 131, 153,
    154, 169
Pole, J. R., 75, 113, 121n
politics as religion, 116
Posner, Richard, 6n, 18n, 162
Pound, Roscoe, 6n

Prohibition, 165
Protestantism, xxiv, xxivn, 43, 145,
    147–50, 152, 159, 169
Puritans, 50, 74, 76, 93, 139, 146,
    148, 156

qadi, 13

Raboteau, Albert, 170n
Raheja, Gloria, 38n
Ramsbey, Thomas, 54, 55, 57, 58
Rashomon, 133–34, 135, 157
Rawls, John, 6n
Reagan, Ronald, 77
reductionism, 23n, 26n, 28, 29
Reformation, 39, 129, 158, 159, 180
Rehnquist, William, 130
religion
    African-American, 34, 88
    American, xxii, xxiv, 35, 42–43,
        45, 62, 71, 72, 76–77, 80,
        86, 87, 89, 94, 110, 144,
        152, 156, 159, 167, 170,
        173, 179, 183
    belief or action, 124–25
    and change, 26, 28, 29
    comparative study of, 30, 36
    as compromised, 32
    as conscience, 31, 115
    and culture, 24, 26
    discourse about, xx, xxiii, 24–35,
        49, 76–77, 112, 181–83
        accommodationist, 77–78, 80,
            86
        by lawyers, 6, 36–37, 41, 44–
            45, 110, 163, 167
        inadequacy of, xxiv, 78, 160,
            164, 172
        law as religion, 77–78, 113–
            14
        separationist, 77–78
    in eighteenth century, 43

religion (*continued*)
  as embodied, 31
  flattened view of, 28
  and gender, 32
  as good, 164
  and government. *See also* church
      and state; 88, 99, 178
  as human creation, 25
  Japanese, 99, 99n, 100, 103, 108,
      110
  and law, xxi, xxiii, 23, 35–45, 49,
      59
    comparative study of, 39, 79
    distinctness of, 39–42, 156
    historical study of church and
        state, 35–36, 141
    in opposition, 37–42, 44
    in United States, xxiv, 3, 21–
        23, 161, 173–83
  materialism of, 30, 31, 182
  meaning of religious events, 53,
      157
  meaning of word, xx, 23, 24, 25,
      31, 60, 76, 175, 178–79
  men's, 38
  in nineteenth century, 43
  phenomenology, 25, 31
  pluralism of, 22, 37, 45
  and politics, 29, 48n, 58, 116, 126
  and postmodernity, 159
  and power, 182
  read broadly, 45
  as real, 27
  replaced by law, 36
  revolutionary, 43, 91
  Roman, 141, 143
  sociology of, 26
  structural study of, 31
  study of, 24, 34, 53, 78
  as text, 32
  and theology, 29, 33
  in twentieth century, 43, 49

  as universal 25
  and violence, 32, 40n, 182
  women's, 38
religious anthropology, 44, 80, 160,
    163, 172
religious freedom, 59, 73, 75, 117,
    126, 128, 134, 167
  in Japan, 101–2
  private cause of action, 105
Religious Freedom Act, 124
religious right, xxin, 48, 112
religiousness, human, 24, 29, 31, 181
revolution
  American, 43
  French, 43, 111
Reynolds v. U. S., 119n, 124, 151
Rheinstein, Max, 19
Rhode Island, 47, 50n, 51, 58, 65,
    73–76
  Constitution, 50, 117
Roman Catholic Church. *See* Ca-
    tholicism, Roman
Rosen, Lawrence, 9n, 10, 12–13,
    19n

sacramental theology, 145, 146
sacred, 25, 29, 53
sacred and secular, distinguishing,
    68, 89, 109
sacredness of central authority, 109
sacrifice, 38, 39
Sahlins, Marshall, 14n, 29n
Said, Edward, 30
Sakagami, Justice, 107
Sanson, William, 53n, 133, 142
Sato, Justice, 107
Sato Gisen, 110
Saul of Tarsus, 172, 173
Scalia, Antonin, 21n, 106, 124,
    125n, 126n, 130, 155n
schools
    parochial, 63, 64, 65

prayer in, 63, 67n, 139
public, 63n, 82n, 161n
secularism, 44, 49n, 111n, 181
secularization, 26, 36, 38, 110, 144, 166
separation of church and state. *See* church and state: separation of
Shaffer, Thomas, 155
Shakespeare, William, 3, 158
shar'ia, 35
Shils, Edward, 9n, 29n, 110
Shimatani, Justice, 107
Shinto. *See also* religion: Japanese; xx, 99n, 100, 101, 103, 104, 110
signification, 88
slavery. *See* law: of slavery
Smart, Ninian, 33n
Smith, Jonathan Z., 27, 30, 32, 33n, 44n, 79n, 89, 143n, 171n
Smith, Wilfred Cantwell, 25n, 76
sovereignty, theories of, 97
spiritual, 31
state
   priestly function of, 176, 180
   as secular, 179
Stevens, John Paul, 88, 130, 135
Stone v. Graham, 63n
Story, Joseph, 84
"strict scrutiny" test, 68
Sullivan, Kathleen, 166n
Sullivan, Lawrence E., xxiii, 28, 30, 182
Sunday Closing Laws, 63, 138
Supreme Court. *See* India: Supreme Court; Japan: Supreme Court; United States: Supreme Court
Swanson, Tod, 28
Swanson, Wayne, 48n, 50n, 51n, 55n
symbols
   theories of, 55–58, 66n, 69, 71, 80, 138, 171, 176
   use by state, 94, 110, 123
syncretism, 138, 141

Takashima, Justice, 107
tax exemption for religious institutions, 62, 64, 90, 127
Tenzer, Michael, 152n
Texas v. Johnson, 69
Texas Monthly v. Bullock, 126n
Thanksgiving, 83, 123, 138
theology
   pluralism of 22
Tocqueville, Alexis de, 154
Torcaso v. Watkins, 67n
Toulmin, Stephen, 157–59
Tracy, David, 27n, 147, 154, 156n
Trobriand Islands. *See* law: of Trobriand Islands
Troeltsch, Ernst, 156n
Trollope, Anthony, 79
Tsu case, 105, 105n, 108
Tsu City, 109

ultramontanism, 111
United States
   armed services, 107
   congress, 60, 111, 117, 118
   chaplaincy, 63, 83, 89–90, 92, 123, 126
   First Congress, 83, 89–90, 92
   Constitution, 80, 95, 97, 98, 114–15, 140, 167
   First Amendment, 44, 86, 90, 119, 129, 153, 156, 171, 174
      establishment clause, 50, 60n, 70 116, 119, 120–21, 130, 150–52, 161, 171, 179; accommodation doctrine, 81–83; endorsement test, 71, 122–23, 126, 130–31; establishment, meaning of, 62–65, 69; *Lemon* test, 84–86, 122, 136–38; quoted, 47n, 59

United States (*continued*)
  Constitution (*continued*)
    First Amendment (*continued*)
      free exercise clause, 79, 91,
        115, 116, 119, 127,
        151, 161
      freedom of the press, 115
      free speech, 115, 116
      how to interpret, 23, 45,
        60–62, 76, 94, 160–
        68, 173–74, 180–81
      meaning of, 36, 42, 62, 63,
        66, 74, 82, 84, 89–90,
        105, 113–14, 121–22,
        124n, 150, 169–70
      quoted, xxiin
      and religion, 42, 82, 121,
        124, 125, 183
      religion clauses of, 60, 65,
        71, 117, 121, 153, 154,
        159, 164, 174, 176
    Fifth Amendment, 118
    Fourteenth Amendment, 60n,
      117, 119, 122, 128–29,
      179
      due process, 118
      equal protection, 118
      how to interpret, 59–62, 70,
        71, 76, 81, 92, 93
      Incorporation Doctrine, 44,
        60n, 77, 116–19
      secularity of, 91
  federal government, 35, 70–71,
    84, 91, 117, 121, 176, 180
  Supreme Court
    amicus briefs, 49, 70–71, 72,
      176
    language of, 6, 35, 126

  on religion, xix–xxi, 6, 35, 42–
    44, 48, 59, 62, 76–78, 111,
    113, 119–20, 152, 161,
    167–68, 175, 181, 183
  role of, xxiii, 45, 95, 172
  White House, 71, 111
Utah, 119n

Vatican I, 154
Vatican II, 153, 154
Vietnam Memorial, 107
Vining, Joseph, 14n, 21

Wach, Joachim, 27, 29n
Waco, Branch Davidian Standoff in,
  30n
Walz v. Tax Commission, 63n, 65,
  90, 160
Washington, D.C., 91
Watson v. Jones, 119n
Weber, Max, 5n, 9n, 29, 36
Werle, Michael, 54–55, 56–57, 58
West Virginia State Board of Edu-
  cation v. Barnette, 3, 69
White, Byron, 130
White, James Boyd, 6n, 8n, 11n, 12n,
  15–16, 18–19, 20n, 21, 62, 129
Wilder, Laura Ingalls, 149
Williams, Rhys, 26n, 51n, 166n
Williams, Roger, xxiii, 73–75, 152,
  156, 172
Wilson, Edmund, 172
Wisconsin v. Yoder, 63n
Woodward, William P., 100
writing, 182
Wuthnow, Robert, 26n, 35
Wythe, George, 17

Yasukuni Shrine, 104, 106, 107, 109n
Yatsuya, Justice, 107

Zorach v. Clauson, 82, 83–84, 138